Great Mystics
and Social Justice

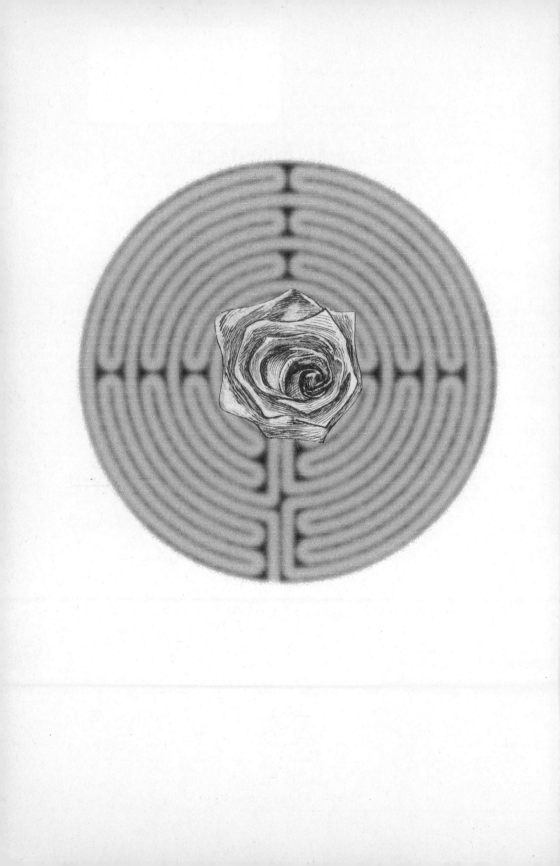

Great Mystics and Social Justice

Walking on the Two Feet of Love

SUSAN RAKOCZY, IHM

Paulist Press
New York/Mahwah, N.J.

Cover photograph of strikers' soup kitchen, 1934 truck strike, Minneapolis, © The Minnesota Historical Society. Used by permission of the Minnesota Historical Society.

Original artwork by Nancy Rakoczy
Cover design by Cynthia Dunne

Library of Congress Cataloging-in-Publication Data

Rakoczy, Susan.
    Great mystics and social justice : walking on the two feet of love / Susan Rakoczy.
        p. cm.
    Includes bibliographical references.
    ISBN 0-8091-4307-0 (alk. paper)
    1. Christianity and justice.   2. Social justice—Religious aspects—Christianity.
3. Christian life.   4. Mysticism.   5. Mystics—Biography.   I. Title.
    BR115.J8R315 2005
    261.8—dc22

                                                                    2005006078

Published by Paulist Press
997 Macarthur Boulevard
Mahwah, New Jersey 07430

www.paulistpress.com

Printed and bound in the
United States of America

CONTENTS

ACKNOWLEDGMENTS

The Scripture quotations contained herein are from the New Revised Standard Version: Catholic Edition, copyright © 1989 and 1993, by the Division of Christian Education of the National Council of the Churches of Christ in the United States of America. Used by permission. All rights reserved.

The chapter "Martha and Mary: Sorting Out the Dilemmas" was first published in *Studies in Spirituality* 8 (1998), pp. 58–80. Reprinted with permission.

Some of the material in the chapters on Evelyn Underhill and Thomas Merton was first published in "Mysticism and Social Commitment: Underhill and Merton on Peace," in *Magistra* 2/2 (1996), pp. 124–46. Reprinted with permission.

Extracts from the documents of the Second Vatican Council are either the author's translation or are from Walter Abbot's edition of *The Documents of Vatican II,* © 1966 by America Press. Used by kind permission of America Press. Visit www.americamagazine.org.

Permission to use the icon of St. Ignatius Loyola, © 1989 by Robert Lentz, OFM. Seraphic Icons. Color reproductions available at www.BridgeBuilding.com.

"St. Catherine of Siena" by Joseph Trepiccione after the portrait of St. Catherine by Andrea Vanni in the Church of St. Dominic in Siena. Originally appeared on the cover of Paulist Press's title *Classics of Western Spirituality: Catherine of Siena*.

Photograph of Dorothy Day used by permission of Raynor Memorial Libraries, Department of Special Collections and Archives, Marquette University.

Photograph of Thomas Merton by John Howard Griffin. Used with permission of the Merton Legacy Trust and the Griffin Estate.

Photograph of Evelyn Underhill appears courtesy of the Evelyn Underhill Association.

Photograph of Archbishop Denis Hurley appears courtesy of Paddy Kearney and Costa Criticos of the Denis Hurley Fund. Used by permission.

TO MARY JO MAHER, IHM,
with love and gratitude

ABBREVIATIONS

GS	*Gaudium et spes*
JW	*Justice in the World*
LG	*Lumen gentium*
PT	*Pacem in terris*
SpEx	*Spiritual Exercises*
ST	*Summa Theologica*

1

Prayer or Action?
The Tension Explored

What is our future as committed Christians as the third millennium begins? How shall we live the Christian life—how *do* we live the gospel now—as we seek to create a new, just, peaceful world? What resources of the Spirit of God are available to us in the quest to transform our cultures and societies?

Two temptations are enticing. One is to plunge into activism without a spiritual grounding. The other, especially insidious, is to take a deep breath, close the doors of the churches on the problems of society, and focus on a private experience of religion. For some, a "Jesus and me" religiosity is very satisfying since it allows them to seek personal holiness without attention to those outside their religious circle. This, however, is a corruption of the gospel, whose basic principle is love of God *and* love of neighbor.

Many persons of faith find themselves spiritually undernourished and weak as they struggle to live their lives with integrity. The problems of the world—whether in the countries of the South or the North—are so intricate and intertwined that just to attempt to understand their complexity is daunting. And understanding is only the first to step to a praxis of transforming love and justice. Where will we find the nourishment that will provide the strength and conviction that we so obviously need?

It is clear mere good will and technical skills will not create the ethos of the new society we desire. Human beings in the twenty-first century, as before, remain weak, selfish, suffering from the effects of personal and social sin. Women and men of all cultures and societies do strive to transform their part of the world, but a vision of a new society is not sufficient of itself to sustain persons and communities over the long haul. Something more is needed.

Prayer or Working for Justice?

People like simplicity. It is much easier to choose one thing and focus all of one's efforts on it. Thus dichotomies are born, two-headed creatures that seem to speak two languages. Today Christians are often confronted with the dichotomy between being a person of prayer and living a private type of Christian life and being committed to the struggle for justice and peace.

At first glance it seems incredible that such a monster should be among us, for certainly there cannot be a choice between these two dimensions of Christian life. Yet if we reflect on our experience, most people will have heard at least some of the following statements:

"I need a lot of time for prayer and time for myself; I simply don't have
    time to get involved in social justice things."
"Prayer is wasting time that can be better spent at a meeting working for
    justice in a real way."
"Look at all those people at prayer meetings: they don't know anything
    about what the struggle for justice is really about."
"Activists never pray; they just follow the latest party line."

But we cannot simply choose one and ignore the other. Our God is a God of justice and peace[1] and we come to know God both in prayer and in concrete action toward justice, peace, and the care of creation. Jesus the Christ to whom Christians commit their entire selves is revealed in the Gospels as one who sought deserted places in which to pray early in the morning (Mark 1:35–36), who prayed all night (Luke 6:12), and who announced his mission as bringing liberty to the poor (Luke 4:18). In the life of Jesus as given to us in the Gospel witness we see no choice between prayer or his mission of liberation. Rather, we see the integration of these two dimensions of life.

It is not hard to convince most Christians that at least "some" prayer is a good thing in life. Persons may struggle to find time to pray, wonder if they are praying well, and desire a deeper life of prayer. Seldom is prayer rejected out of hand by a sincere Christian believer.

But commitment to the social mission of the gospel is much more problematic. Within the Catholic tradition, we have seen a dramatic change in attitudes toward the world in the last one hundred years, but especially since Vatican II (1962–65). No longer is the posture of the Catholic Church one of constructing ever-higher walls between the Church and the world. The poetic statement of the opening lines of "The Pastoral Constitution on the Church in the Modern World" (*Gaudium et spes*) describes this new perspective: "The joys and the hopes, the griefs and the anxieties of the [people] of this age, especially those who are poor or in any way afflicted, these too are the joys and hopes, the griefs and anxieties of the followers of Christ" (*GS* 1).[2]

In addition, the statement of the Synod of Bishops of 1971, "Justice in the World," made a very bold departure from past understandings of prayer and action. The call now is to understand that action for justice and peace is at the heart of the gospel:

> Action on behalf of justice and participation in the transformation of the world fully appear to us as a constitutive dimension of the preaching of the Gospel, or, in other words, of the Church's mission for the redemption of the human race and its liberation from every oppressive situation. (*JW* 6)[3]

This is a call not only to the work of personal charity, but also to efforts to transform social structures so that people are no longer poor, hungry, illiterate, homeless, unemployed—and that nations and continents have a fair share of the world economic pie. This is especially crucial in Africa, the poorest continent, one sometimes described as "hopeless" by transnational business leaders and other bodies with its wars, famines, unemployment, the ravages of HIV/AIDS, and immense global debt.

The challenge before us is to be persons of deep prayer and authentic commitment to the works of justice and peace. It does not matter which conversion happens first: to a deeper faith commitment in Jesus the Christ or an awakening to the imperative to labor for a just and peaceful society. Growth in both must continue apace. Peter Henriot writes:

> But as important as it may be to see this commitment to act for social justice as being a consequence of growth in true spirituality, it is even more important to understand—and to practice—this commitment as being *simultaneous* to the growth process itself. This emphasis upon simultaneity is a more difficult conclusion to demonstrate. It rests upon an appreciation of the reality of the "public dimension" of personal human experience. Such an appreciation comes with an understanding of social structures and of our own existential relationship with those structures.[4]

The call to contemporary Christians throughout the world is to learn how to do this: to grow *simultaneously* in the life of prayer and in commitment to social transformation, to walk on the two feet of love of God and love of neighbor.

Food for the Journey to Justice

In Matthew 13:52 we read of the householder who is able to bring both old and new things out of the storeroom. If we investigate some of the treasures in the Christian storeroom, we shall find plentiful resources for our commitment in prayer, love, and action to help build a world in which the tears will be wiped from humanity's eyes (Rev 21:4), or at least more realistically, to work so that at least some tears will no longer be shed!

The great Catholic theologian Karl Rahner stated, "In the future we shall be mystics . . . or we shall be nothing."[5] It is in the teachings of some of the great teachers of prayer in the Christian tradition, those adventurers of the Spirit we have termed *mystics*, that good and plentiful food for the journey to wholeness in personal and communal life will be found.

St. Augustine's description of the human heart remains true as we stand at the beginning of this new century: "You have made us for yourself, and our heart is restless until it rests in you."[6] The life stories of the great women and men of the Christian tradition whose lives of prayer were focused on union with the One they loved do not demonstrate a lack of care and concern for the world in which they lived. Rather, since they lived the basic dynamic of the Christian life in a growing fullness—union of the love of God and love of neighbor—their teachings contain important resources for us in our journey today.

In an ecumenical interpretation of the history of Christian spirituality, it is important to realize that the wisdom of the great teachers of prayer belongs to all Christians. Some lived and wrote before the Reformation in the sixteenth century; their legacy is part of the whole Christian heritage. Since the sixteenth century, Christians in the West have experienced a radical institutional brokenness of the body of Christ. Here the mystics can help to heal the divisions since their message cuts across denominational lines and ecclesial fences to speak of the essential themes of Christian life: faith, hope, love, experience of God in prayer, mission.

Mystical experience is not one of separation, of real or artificial dichotomies, but one of wholeness. The life of a person of intense prayer may be lived in solitude, in community, or in public—but his or her experience is never individual and unrelated to the concerns of the times. Thus it is to the mystics that we turn in our search for resources for our journey in prayer and transformation of our society.

A Map for the Journey

We will begin with a short discussion of the meaning and dynamics of mystical experience in order to demonstrate how important these resources are for Christians today. Then our journey will take us to Italy, Spain, England, the United States, and South Africa, where we will meet Catherine of Siena, Ignatius Loyola, Evelyn Underhill, Thomas Merton, Dorothy Day, and four South Africans: Denis Hurley, Nelson Mandela, Beyers Naudé, and Desmond Tutu, who bear witness to the gospel's call to reconciliation. We will also examine the various interpretations of the Martha-Mary text (Luke 10:38–42), which has often been used to rank prayer above service.

Catherine will help us to plumb the depths of the scriptural injunction to love God and neighbor equally and intensely, to "walk on the two feet of love." Ignatius's special gift is the call to seek and find God in all things. The theme of "Martha and Mary" was considered by many Christian writers, including Meister Eckhart and Teresa of Avila. They overturned the traditional dichotomy of prayer and action supposedly upheld by the story in told in Luke's Gospel. In Underhill and Merton we meet two twentieth-century mystics who both have important things to say about peace and nonviolence, subjects that are never out of fashion. Dorothy Day, a pacifist, lived a seamless witness of poverty, prayer, and love. The South African voices speak of human dignity, unity, love, reconciliation, and forgiveness.

And so it is to the nature of mystical experience that we now turn.

Notes

1. Cf. Exod 22:21–23; Isa 11:3–4; 58:1–10; 61:1–2; Amos 2:6–8, 5:10–13, 21–24; Matt 5:44, 23:23, 25:31–46; Luke 4:18–19; Jas 2:1–9; 1 John 3:17–18, among a multitude of texts.

2. All quotations from the documents of Vatican II are from *The Documents of Vatican II*, ed. Walter M. Abbott, SJ (New York: Guild, America, Association, 1966).

3. See *The Gospel of Peace and Justice*, ed. Joseph Gremillion (Maryknoll, NY: Orbis, 1976), pp. 513–29, for the text of this document.

4. Quoted in John T. Pawlikowski, "Spirituality and the Quest for Justice," in *Liturgical Foundations of Social Policy in the Catholic and Jewish Traditions*, ed. Daniel F. Polish and Eugene J. Fisher (Notre Dame, IN: University of Notre Dame Press, 1983), pp. 80–81.

5. Karl Rahner, "The Spirituality of the Future," in *Theological Investigations*, vol. 20, trans. Edward Quinn (London: Darton, Longman & Todd, 1981), p. 149.

6. *Confessions* I.1.

2

Mystical Experience:
The Common Call

A survey of a few persons leaving church on Sunday who are asked, "What is mysticism? Do you know any mystics?" would probably yield mostly blank stares of nonrecognition. Possibly several might say something like, "You mean really holy persons in a monastery?" or "Those are saints, I think."

Most Christians have placed mystics on high pedestals of holiness whose tops are lost in the clouds. Their experience of the Gospel life is thought to be so rarefied and unique that there cannot be any connection between themselves and ordinary people of whatever era or culture.

What a tragedy! The rich teachings of these women and men of intense prayer, who fortunately wrote of their experiences, present to us not impossibly high mountain peaks that only a few may attempt to scale, but paths leading upward from the bottom of the mountain to which all are invited. How far one travels up the path is shaped by many factors, the most important of which is desire. How far does one want to go?

A central insight of Vatican II on the meaning of the Christian life is the insistence that *all* the baptized are called to the fullness of holiness and the perfection of charity (*LG* 40). This statement abolished the hierarchy of vocations in the Catholic Church that had seen priesthood and religious life, which demand celibacy, as "higher" than marriage or a single state.[1] It recalls believers back to the gospel call to the fullness of life promised by Christ Jesus: "I have come that they may have life, and have it abundantly" (John 10:10).

Fullness of life in Christ in the power of the Spirit is mystical experience. It is the development of the grace of baptism, lived intensely and deeply. Gospel holiness is not marked by the extraordinary phenomena we usually think of when we consider mysticism, such as levitation, trances, and visions, but the fullness of love—for God and for others. Karl Rahner writes: "Mysticism . . . occurs within the framework of normal graces and within the experience of faith. To this extent, those who insist that mystical experience is not specifically different from the ordinary life of grace (as such) are certainly right."[2]

Following William Johnston, the perspective of this book is that "mysticism is the core of religious experience and that it is for everyone."[3] It is important to stress that mysticism is a process, a way of life. The whole journey is significant, and the twists and turns of the road are as essential as the places where we can rest and enjoy the scenery.

Some Definitions and Descriptions of Mysticism

How is mysticism defined or described? If mystical experience is "for all," why do we continue to differentiate ordinary faith experience and "mystical" experience?

The word *mysticism* finds its origin in the mystery religions of the Greco-Roman world in the early centuries of the Christian era. The mystic (Greek *mustes*) took an oath of secrecy about the beliefs and rituals of these religions. Thus the first meaning of mysticism was linked to mystery and secrecy.

The term later became associated with Neoplatonic philosophy. Here it took on a slightly different connotation, that of excluding the outer world in order to be "alone with the alone." Plotinus and Proclus used the word *muo* to describe a person whose eyes were closed to the world "while the inner eye was open and searching for wisdom."[4] The word *mysticism* entered into the Christian vocabulary in the late fifth or early sixth century through the writings of an anonymous Syrian monk whom we now know as Pseudo-Dionysius. In his work *Mystica Theologia* Dionysius insists that one leave behind the senses and operations of the intellect in order to be united with God.

> Do thou, then, in the intent practice of mystic contemplation, leave behind the senses and the operations of the intellect, and all things that the senses or the intellect can perceive, and all things which are not and things which are, and strain upwards in unknowing, as far as may be, towards the union with Him Who is above all things and knowledge. For by unceasing and absolute withdrawal from thyself and all things in purity, abandoning all and set free from all, thou shalt be borne up to the ray of divine darkness that surpasseth all being.[5]

The teaching of Dionysius is supremely important in the history of mysticism because of his insistence that concepts and images of God are *not* the way to union with God.[6] We come to union with God not by thinking about God and having the correct "ideas" about God because God is beyond all concepts and theological statements. As Augustine has said: "For if you have fully grasped what you want to say, it isn't God. If you have been able to comprehend it, you have comprehended something else instead of God."[7]

Students of mysticism distinguish two types of mystical experience. One is a mysticism of knowledge and understanding that issues forth from the desire within the person to grasp the inner nature of reality, that is, to attempt to grasp the divine essence. It is the desire to *know* God as God is in Godself. As John's Gospel states, "I tell you, anyone who hears my word and believes him who sent me has eternal life" (5:24). Meister Eckhart (1260–1328) is a prime example of this way of wisdom as the path to union with God.

The second type is a mysticism of love and union, whose dynamic is the ultimate escape from the existential sense of separation that is the core of human loneliness. It is the desire for participation in Nature or in God that will bring supreme peace to the person. This type of mystical experience is often expressed in bridal or marital imagery and its supreme model is the Spanish mystic, Teresa of Avila (1515–82).

The stress on love as the way to experience God is shown in some of the classic definitions of mysticism:

Jean Gerson (1363–1429), chancellor of the University of Paris: "Mystical theology is experimental knowledge of God through the embrace of unitive love."[8]

St. Bonaventure (1217–74), Franciscan theologian: "Mystical theology is the raising of the mind to God through the desire of love."[8]

St. John of the Cross (1542–91), Carmelite reformer (with St. Teresa of Avila) and mystic, speaks of mysticism in the language of both wisdom and love. Describing prayer he says that "contemplation is the mystical theology which theologians call secret wisdom and which St. Thomas says is communicated and infused into the soul through love."[9] Love and knowledge are united in the mystical experience: "The sweet and living knowledge she says He taught her is mystical theology, that secret knowledge of God which spiritual persons call contemplation. This knowledge is very delightful because it is a knowledge through love."[10]

All these definitions recall the scriptural teaching that God is love (1 John 4:7–14) and that to know love is to know God. To love others is also to know God. The "knowing" that mystical experience describes is that of the heart: a knowledge not "about God," because conceptual knowledge is surpassed by the experience of love. Yet the mystics insist that there is a *real* knowledge of God that is experienced, one that is known in love.

This very brief exploration into the nature of mystical experience demonstrates that it is the experience hinted at many times in the Scriptures. In John's Gospel Jesus speaks of union with God using the images of the vine and the branches, inviting the believer "to abide in me as I abide in you" (15:4) and to "abide in my love" (15:9). Paul prays that the Ephesians will have "the eyes of your heart enlightened (so that) you may know what is the hope to which he has called you, what are riches of his glorious inheritance among the saints, and what is the immeasurable greatness of his power for us who believe" (3:18–19). What is described here is not the domain of a few select mystics but the call to all believers.

Some Characteristics of Mystical Experience

The literature relating to mysticism both philosophically and theologically is vast.[11] The purpose of this chapter is not to explore and settle all the arguments about the nature of mystical experience but to provide some background that will make understandable the thesis of this book: that the writings of the mystics have important things to say to contemporary Christians as they seek to integrate prayer and commitment to justice and peace.

Evelyn Underhill's classic study, *Mysticism* (first published in 1911 and continuously in print), describes four important characteristics of mystical experience. Mysticism is "active and practical; its aims are wholly transcendental and spiritual; this One is for the mystic . . . a living and personal object of Love; living union with this One . . . is a definite state or form of enhanced life".[12] She placed herself in opposition to William James's description of the four "marks" of the mystic state: ineffability, noetic quality, transciency, and passivity.[13]

Underhill states that "true mysticism is active and practical, not passive and theoretical. It is an organic life process, a something which the whole self does; not something as to which its intellect holds an opinion."[14] The entire person is engaged in the life of prayer which leads to union with God and that experience affects the totality of their life experience. As one believes, so one acts.

Of her four elements of mystical experience, three remain valid today. It is the second that is problematic. Underhill's assertion that the aims of mysticism "are wholly transcendental and spiritual. It is no way concerned with adding to, exploring, re-arranging, or imposing anything in the visible universe"[15] is not congruent with the perspective we are establishing: that the teachings of the mystics can and do have important things to say about "re-remaking things in the universe." Underhill wrote *Mysticism* early in her career as a writer and it is possible to trace the evolution of her thought on the relationship of prayer and action.[16] Her later writings do not reflect this "other-worldly" perspective. "This One is for the mystic, not merely the Reality of all that is, but also a living and personal Object of Love; never an object of exploration. It draws his whole being homeward, but always under the guidance of the heart."[17]

Underhill's statement echoes that of John of the Cross and other mystics we have already noted.

Living union with this One—which is the term of his adventure—
is a definite state or form of enhanced life. . . . It is arrived at by an
arduous psychological and spiritual process—the so-called Mystic
Way—entailing the complete remaking of character and the liberation of a new, or rather latent, form of consciousness . . . named the
Unitive State.[18]

The journey to union with God is not a matter of few good resolutions or
a plan of life; it is a process of lifelong and intense conversion and transformation of the whole person. This is the call to all believers, the call to
holiness as a life of full-hearted love of God and others.

Underhill's descriptions help us to situate mystical experience—
union with the One we call the Triune God—as real experience of God
in love that transforms the person in every dimension of her or his being.
Nothing is excluded from the power of this "sweet and loving knowledge," including how one views the social and political problems of one's
culture and society.

Rahner's Contribution

Karl Rahner, SJ (1904–84), the preeminent Catholic theologian of the
twentieth century, has been called the "Doctor mysticus" of our time.[19]
Rahner's theology and thus his approach to mysticism is founded on the
orientation of the person to the mystery of God. Standing within the
apophatic tradition, the tradition of "unknowing," Rahner consistently
speaks of God as Holy Mystery.

Rahner distinguishes between transcendental experience, that is, the
openness of the person to mystery, and experience of Holy Mystery in
which the divine closeness is communicated in love and intimacy. This is
seen directly in the person of Jesus the Christ. For Rahner, God is both
the "question," the "whither" of the longings of the human heart, and
the "answer" given in the experience of revelation.

He describes the unity (but not *identity*) of the self and God. This
unity means that "the personal history of the experience of God signifies,
over and above itself, the personal history of the experience of the self . . .
[and] the experience of self is the condition which makes it possible to

experience God."[20] Thus not only are the experiences of God and the self one, but the experiences of self and one's neighbor are also one, constituting "a single reality with three aspects mutually conditioning one another."[21] This unity is the basis for the biblical assertion of the unity between the love of God and the love of neighbor, a theme that Rahner developed in a significant essay.[22]

For Rahner, mystical experience "is present as [the] innermost sustaining ground (even though unnoticed) in the simple act itself of Christian living in faith, hope and love."[23] Such experience has a paradigmatic character in which God's self-communication is given to the person in grace and accepted in freedom. Mystical experience is thus not a "higher state" in the life of grace.

Rahner speaks of mystical experience in two ways. There is "the mysticism of everyday life, the discovery of God in all things,"[24] the experience of the Spirit of God in human experience. There are also distinct "mystical" experiences that are known in both Christianity and other religions. These can be described as intensifications of the experience of God open to all, "peak religious experiences."

Unfortunately, Rahner does not offer an extended discussion of these special experiences in his writings. Sometimes he equates these types of religious experience with the classical states described by other Christian mystics and "at other times, he speaks of two dimensions of mystical experience conceived analogously according to the models of the traditional *via negativa* and *via eminentia* and capable of being encountered in everyday life."[25]

Bernard McGinn evaluates Rahner's interpretation of mystical experience as "ordinary" or extraordinary by stating that "on the issue of whether mystical experience represents a higher level beyond the ordinary life of faith (the root of many Protestant objections to mysticism), Rahner's answer is 'no' theologically and 'maybe' psychologically."[26]

Rahner's contribution to the discussion is significant because of his starting point: the human person's a priori transcendental orientation to God, named as Holy Mystery. This is not a matter of choice: that I will to be orientated to Holy Mystery. Rather, because we have been created by God, we are drawn to God in the depths of our being. It is the theological equivalent of the law of gravity. Such experience is thematized in specific religious language and concepts, like revelation and prayer.

But the fact that it is primordial experience helps us to grasp the link between the experience of the mystics and ourselves. Everyone is drawn to Holy Mystery. Some people realize this; some people act on it. Some speak of it (and write of it). The distinct experiences persons such as Teresa of Avila or Thomas Merton describe are not separated from the primordial experience of all persons, but are experiences on the continuum toward full union with God.

Lonergan's Voice

The voice of Bernard Lonergan, SJ (1904–84), Canadian philosopher and theologian, now enters the discussion. Lonergan's insights on conversion are central to his corpus of work as he describes intellectual, moral, and religious conversion.[27] He states that "religious conversion is being grasped by ultimate concern. It is other-worldly falling in love . . . total and permanent self-surrender," "being in love in an unrestricted fashion."[28] This experience is interpreted differently in the various world religions. Lonergan describes it for Christians as "God's love flooding our hearts through the Holy Spirit given to us,"[29] echoing Romans 5:5, the gift of grace.

There are two moments in this experience: the gift of God's love and being in love with God, the human response to this gift. Lonergan distinguishes between religious consciousness, which is a feeling of "being in love with God," and mystical consciousness, which is the gift of God's love itself.[30] The distinction is described by James Robertson Price III: "That is to say, whereas religious consciousness intends an object, mystical consciousness does not. It is a consciousness of vital, intersubjective union quite different from the intentional subject-subject or subject-object relation of religious consciousness."[31]

Mystical consciousness is an absorption into the gift of God's love. This experience is available to all. Lonergan compares the gift of God's love to ever-present music. One can be aware of it or not since "it is the subject's attention, not God's love, that is intermittent, and the goal of a mystical life that is available to everyone is to become progressively more attentive to what has in fact been going on all along."[32]

Lonergan aids us in understanding that the experiences of the mystics, even if described in language that stretches the limits of expression, are not strangers in our garden. Rather, they are part of the family of religious experience whose goal is union with God in love.

Mysticism and Integration

Most people probably regard mystical experience as akin to visits of creatures from other planets: totally outside the realm of ordinary experience. And thus the effects of mystical experience might be thought to be equally strange, producing a tribe of eccentrics. Certainly there are extremes in behavior in the life of certain mystics, such as radical penances (done out of love for the Beloved), but the actual fruits are quite different: wholeness, integration of life, and fruitfulness of love and compassion for others.

Louis Dupré asserts that mystical experience has a "remarkable ability to integrate life, to achieve unity within the diversity complexity of opposite tendencies."[33] The experience of God's overwhelming love must be shared; it cannot be hidden away in a private treasure box. He maintains that "mystical marriage invariably leads to spiritual parenthood,"[34] an experience of loving fruitfulness.

Integration of the person, wholeness in God, is not reached by denying reality outside of oneself. Rather, as one approaches more closely to the Center who is God, one comes also into closer union with others. Dorotheus of Gaza (seventh century) wrote: "This is the nature of love: to the extent that we distance ourselves from the center (of the circle) and do not love God, we distance ourselves from our neighbor; but if we love God, then the nearer we draw to him in love, the more we are united with our neighbor in love."[35]

This unity can have many dimensions. The first is compassion, feeling with, the ability to be united with others in their sufferings and joys as God is lovingly present to all creation. Isaac of Nineveh (seventh century) recommends, "Let the weight of compassion in you weigh you down until you feel in your heart the same compassion that God has for the world."[36] He stresses that union in compassion is expressed primarily through intercessory prayer, which is the central act of compassionate love of those who live a cloistered or solitary life but who are not separate from the concerns of the world. One is able to enter into the suffering of the world because the solitary has met the pain and suffering of her or his own life, which is a microcosm of all suffering. For the deeper that one experiences the reality of God, the more profoundly one finds everything and everyone else: good and bad, poor and rich, peace and violence, love and hate.

The compassion that is the fruit of mystical union (and of the whole path to union) is seen in a transformed life of active love. Underhill describes this: "Fresh life is imparted, by which our lives are made complete; new creative powers are conferred."[37] Teresa of Avila reminds her sisters that the whole purpose of the journey to God in prayer is active love: "This is the true sign of a thing, or favor, being from God."[38]

The lives of the mystics bear witness to this fruitfulness: Francis of Assisi's active love for the poor shown in being poor, Catherine of Siena's care for the sick and poor, Teresa of Avila and John of the Cross's reforming the Carmelite life, Ignatius of Loyola's pastoral zeal, and many more. In our own day, in which we have learned that personal charity is one part of the gospel mandate and that efforts to change social and economic structures are equally urgent, we would hope for a new type of mystic, one whose prayer and union with God are evident in social and political commitment for the sake of freedom and liberation. The distinctive character of mystical union is thus the active love that Paul has described in 1 Corinthians: a love that "bears all things, believes all things, hopes all things, endures all things" (13:7).

The specific activities of those traveling on the way to union in God vary according to the circumstances and gifts of the person. Each path is different since each person is unique. But the authentic fruits are always the same: "love, joy, peace, patience, kindness, generosity, faithfulness, gentleness, and self-control" (Gal 5:22).

The Way Forward

In this brief exploration of the nature and dynamics of mystical experience, we have seen that it is a caricature to describe the mystic as out of touch with reality. Rather, it is the mystic who knows Reality since she or he is deeply in love with God who is Reality. This experience has its own internal energy that urges the person forward in compassion and love.

Thus the writings and teachings of those who have traveled this path are of supreme importance to us today. It is true that culture and context are different. But the desires of the human person and the human community have not changed. People still yearn for love, for acceptance, for a better world, for peace within themselves and within their families and communities. The voices of the mystics speak to us today in words and images that can both focus our desires and give us the energy to do the active works of love and compassion so needed in our world.

Notes

1. This insight had been reached much earlier in Christian history, at the time of the Reformation, when marriage was accepted as a true way to holiness. In his *Commentary on 1 Corinthians 7* Martin Luther repudiated the traditional understanding that consecrated virginity is inherently superior to marriage. See Martin Luther, *Luther's Works,* vol. 28, ed. H. C. Oswald, trans. Edward Sittler (St. Louis: Concordia Publishing House, 1973), pp. 16, 48–49.

2. Karl Rahner, "Mysticism: Theological Interpretation," in *The Encyclopedia of Theology,* ed. Karl Rahner (London: Burns & Oates, 1975), pp. 1010–11.

3. William Johnston, *The Inner Eye of Love: Mysticism and Religion* (San Francisco: Harper & Row, 1978), p. 31.

4. Ibid., p. 16.

5. *Mystica Theologia* I, I, quoted in ibid., pp. 17–18.

6. This is also the teaching of the fourteenth-century English author of *The Cloud of Unknowing,* who, following Pseudo-Dionysius, insists that God may be known by love but never by thought.

7. Augustine of Hippo, "Sermon 52," in *Sermons III/Vol. III (51–94) on the New Testament,* trans. Edmund Hill, OP, ed. John E. Rotelle, OSA (Brooklyn, NY: New City, 1991), no. 16, p. 57.

8. Both the Jean Gerson and St. Bonaventure quotes are cited from Johnston, *The Inner Eye of Love,* p. 19.

9. John of the Cross, "The Dark Night of the Soul," in *The Collected Works of St. John of the Cross,* trans. Kieran Kavanaugh, OCD, and Otilio Rodriguez, OCD (Washington, DC: Institute of Carmelite Studies, 1979), II.17.2, p. 368.

10. John of the Cross, "The Spiritual Canticle," in *The Collected Works of St. John of the Cross,* trans. Kieran Kavanaugh, OCD, and Otilio Rodriguez, OCD (Washington, DC: Institute of Carmelite Studies, 1979), 27.5, p. 518.

11. See William James, *The Varieties of Religious Experience* (New York: Collier-Macmillan, 1961); Grace M. Jantzen, "Feminists, Philosophers, and Mystics," *Hypatia* 9 (1994), pp. 186–206; Grace M. Jantzen, *Power, Gender and Christian Mysticism* (Cambridge: Cambridge University Press, 1995); William Johnston, *Mystical Theology: The*

Science of Love (Maryknoll, NY: Orbis, 1995); Steven T. Katz, "Language, Epistemology and Mysticism," in *Mysticism and Philosophical Analysis*, ed. Steven T. Katz (New York: Oxford University Press, 1978), pp. 22–74; Steven T. Katz, ed., *Mysticism and Philosophical Analysis* (New York: Oxford University Press, 1978); Steven T. Katz, ed., *Mysticism and Religious Traditions* (New York: Oxford University Press, 1983); Steven T. Katz, *Mysticism and Language* (Oxford: Oxford University Press, 1992); Celia Kourie, "Mysticism: A Survey of Recent Issues," *Journal of the Study of Religion* 5 (1992), pp. 83–103; Bernard McGinn, *The Foundations of Mysticism: Origins to the Fifth Century* (New York: Crossroad, 1991); Bernard McGinn, *The Growth of Mysticism: Gregory the Great Through the Twelfth Century* (New York: Crossroad, 1994); Bernard McGinn, *The Flowering of Mysticism: Men and Women in the New Mysticism—1200–1350* (New York: Crossroad, 1998); Mark A. McIntosh, *Mystical Theology: The Integrity of Spirituality and Theology* (Malden, MA: Blackwell, 1998); Steven Payne, "The Christian Character of of Christian Mystical Experiences," *Religious Studies* 20 (1984), pp. 417–27; Nelson Pike, *Mystic Union: An Essay on the Phenomenology of Mysticism* (Ithaca and London: Cornell University Press, 1992); Denys Turner, *The Darkness of God: Negativity in Christian Mysticism* (Cambridge: Cambridge University Press, 1995); Evelyn Underhill, *Mysticism* (New York: E. P. Dutton, 1911, 1961).

12. Evelyn Underhill, *Mysticism* (New York: E. P. Dutton & Co., Inc, 1911, 1961), p. 81.

13. William James, *The Varieties of Religious Experience* (New York: Collier-MacMillan, 1961), pp. 299–301.

14. Underhill, *Mysticism*, p. 81.

15. Ibid.

16. See Chapter 6: "Evelyn Underhill: A Practical Mysticism."

17. Underhill, *Mysticism*, p. 81.

18. Ibid.

19. The title is given by Harvey D. Egan, SJ, and cited by Bernard McGinn, *The Foundations of Mysticism* (New York: Crossroad, 1991), p. 286.

20. Karl Rahner, "Experience of Self and Experience of God," in *Theological Investigations*, vol. 13, trans. David Bourke (London: Darton, Longman & Todd, 1975), p. 124.

21. Ibid., p. 128.

22. Karl Rahner, "Reflections on the Unity of the Love of Neighbour and the Love of God," in *Theological Investigations*, vol. 6, trans. Karl-H. and Boniface Kruger (London: Darton, Longman & Todd, 1969), pp. 231–49. This essay is discussed in the concluding chapter. McIntosh, using the thought of Levinas, describes this unity in postmodern terms: "My love for my neighbour is what constitutes me as a human person" (*Mystical Theology*, p. 215) for "I am never more myself than when I give myself away for my neighbour in love" (p. 216).

23. Karl Rahner, *The Practice of Faith*, ed. Karl Lehmann and Albert Raffelt (New York: Crossroad, 1986), p. 70.

24. Ibid., p. 84.

25. McGinn, *The Foundations of Mysticism*, p. 288; Rahner, *The Practice of Faith*, p. 81.

26. McGinn, *The Foundations of Mysticism*, p. 288.

27. Lonergan's most important works are *Insight* (London: Darton, Longman & Todd, 1957) and *Method in Theology* (New York: Herder & Herder, 1972). Intellectual conversion is the recognition and awareness that one's knowing and choosing follow an ordered set of operations: experience, understanding, judging, deciding (*Method in Theology,* pp. 6–20). Moral conversion "changes the criterion of one's decisions and choices from satisfaction to values" (*Method in Theology,* p. 240).

28. Lonergan, *Method in Theology*, pp. 240, 105.

29. Ibid., p. 241.

30. Ibid., pp. 105–7.

31. James R. Price III, "Lonergan and the Foundation of a Contemporary Mystical Theology," in *Lonergan Workshop*, vol. 5, ed. Fred Lawrence (Chico, CA: Scholars Press, 1985), p. 170.

32. Lonergan, *Method in Theology*, p. 176.

33. Louis Dupré, "The Christian Experience of Mystical Union," *Journal of Religion* 69 (1989), p. 8.

34. Ibid.

35. Dorotheus of Gaza, *Instructions*, quoted in Olivier Clément, *The Roots of Christian Mysticism*, trans. Theodore Berkeley, OCSO (London: New City, 1993), p. 272.

36. Isaac of Nineveh, *Ascetic Treatises* 34, quoted in Clément, *The Roots of Christian Mysticism*, p. 275.

37. Underhill, *Mysticism*, p. 428.

38. Teresa of Avila, The Interior Castle," in *The Collected Works of St. Teresa of Avila*, vol. 2, trans. Kieran Kavanaugh, OCD, and Otilio Rodriguez, OCD (Washington, DC: Institute of Carmelite Studies, 1980), VII.4.7, p. 446.

3

Catherine of Siena:
The Two Feet of Love

To grasp the quality of presence and influence Catherine had in her lifetime, we would have to imagine a young woman about twenty-five to thirty, with no formal education but known for her holiness, who is simultaneously a roving ambassador for the United Nations and an adviser to the pope, the archbishop of Canterbury, and the World Council of Churches.

Catherine lived in a century "when the Church and society and her own Dominican order were in chaos."[1] The fourteenth century saw the world breaking away from the medieval framework of a Europe united under one emperor and one pope. In Catherine's Italy independent states vied with one another for supremacy and Catherine attempted to make peace between them. In her lifetime she knew the ravages of the Black Plague (which began a year after her birth), the scandals of the Avignon papacy, and the Great Schism, which was not resolved until after her death.

Her era was also a time of mystical fruitfulness in the Church. In the Rhineland Meister Eckhart, John Tauler, and Henry Suso prayed, preached, taught, and wrote. In England Julian of Norwich prayed in her anchorhold and wrote of the *Revelations* that she had experienced, the monastic author of *The Cloud of Unknowing* produced his treatise on prayer, and Walter Hilton described the "ladder of perfection."

Early Life

Catherine was the twenty-fourth of twenty-five children in the family of Giacomo Benincasa and Lapa Piacenti.[2] Born in Siena in 1347 (possibly on March 25), she became the focus of her mother's attention when her twin sister died early. Her father was a prosperous dyer of cloth and so the family was comfortable economically.

Those who remembered her as a child described her as stubborn with an iron will (this remained characteristic of her throughout her life), but very happy and cheerful; she was nicknamed Euphrosyne because of her sunny nature. She was a charming child. She was very pretty with golden-brown hair, a color considered very desirable in Siena.

The family lived near the Church of St. Dominic, where St. Thomas Aquinas had once preached, and so she was formed in a Dominican environment, attending Mass, going to other services, and absorbing Dominican spirituality through the preaching and teaching of the friars. A foster brother, Thomas della Fonte, became a Dominican priest while Catherine was still a child. He was to be her first confessor and spiritual director.

At the age of six, while returning from visiting her sister Bonaventura with her brother Stefano, she is said to have had a vision of Christ above the church. He looked at her with a loving smile and blessed her as a priest would. After this, her personality changed and she became quiet and withdrawn and tried to spend long times in prayer in the church (which her mother did not allow her to do). She no longer played games with other children and began to fast and deny herself food.

At the age of seven she made a vow of virginity and consecrated herself to Christ, but with no thought of becoming a nun. When she was twelve, her family began to prepare her for marriage but Catherine wanted none of this. The family sent her to live with her married sister Bonaventura with the hope of changing her mind. Indeed, for a while, she learned to enjoy dressing nicely and arranging her hair. But when Bonaventura died in 1362 she returned home. One day she overheard her family discussing the husband-to-be they had selected for her. Her iron will asserted itself as she told them absolutely *no*—she would *not* marry anyone!

Her foster brother, Father Della Fonte, told the family that they could not force Catherine into marriage and he advised her to enter a convent. This would have been the normal course of events for a pious young woman, especially someone who had vowed virginity at such a young age. But Catherine had no desire for cloistered religious life. One day he told her that one way to thwart her family's plans was to cut off her long, beautiful hair, which she promptly did. The cries of anguish from her family were heard in the whole neighborhood, for now she was not suitable for marriage.

Her furious parents dismissed the servants and ordered Catherine to do all the cooking, washing, and cleaning in the house. This she did with a joyful, peaceful heart that eventually won her father over. She was allowed to live at home with no prospect of marriage.

Dominican Life

While Catherine did not want to enter a convent, she did want to become part of the Dominican family. In her parish there was a group of women known as the Mantellate, whose name came from the black Dominican cloak they wore as they visited the poor and the sick. They lived in their own homes, wore the Dominican habit, and lived lives of prayer and charity. Catherine was not yet twenty; these women were widows. It was unheard of for such a young woman to enter this branch of the Dominican family, but Catherine's determination prevailed and she was clothed with the Mantellate habit at the age of eighteen. The habit gave Catherine an official tie to the Church and the protection of the Dominican Order. Both would be very significant when she began her active life of ministry in the Church and society.

But first came three years of solitude and prayer in her family home. She lived in a little room (more like a cupboard) under a stairway. There she prayed constantly, fasted rigorously (so much so that her ability to digest food was permanent impaired),[3] and did severe penances. She learned to read so that she could read the psalms in the Divine Office.

In 1368, when she was twenty-one, she experienced a mystical espousal to Christ. This momentous grace signaled the end of her days of solitary life. She left her life of seclusion in obedience to Christ who had told her, "Love your neighbor as yourself." This she did as she began to visit the poor and sick in the hospitals of Siena. She gave alms so freely that more than once she totally emptied the family larder.

Gradually a circle of friends, both women and men, formed around her. Her years of prayer had not changed her winning and charming personality (her friends always spoke of her beautiful eyes and delightful smile). This group, which became known as the Family or the Fellowship, was composed of some of the Mantellate, some wealthy young men who acted as her secretaries, and several priests. Though she was the youngest among them, they affectionately called her "Mamma." In 1374 the Dominican chapter appointed Raymond of Capua as her confessor. This served the purpose of giving her a holy theologian as her personal guide and also helped the Dominican Order keep an eye on her since her reputation for holiness had begun to spread. Catherine and Raymond became very close friends, and he wrote the first account of her life.

After three years of constant service to those in need in Siena, Catherine suffered a severe illness in 1370 in which she experienced a "mystical death"—four hours of ecstasy while her body appeared lifeless. In returning to consciousness she understood that she was to spend the rest of her life bringing others to God. Catherine's public life now began in earnest.

Catherine's Public Life: Prayer and Action

Catherine had three major desires in the public and ecclesial spheres. First, she entreated the various popes who lived during her lifetime to preach a Crusade to the Holy Land in order to bring Christendom back to a sense of purpose. In her eyes such a war would be a profound conversion experience for those who fought and for the whole Church. Today this seems incredible but it was a common way of thinking in the Middle Ages. This Crusade did not happen during her lifetime.

Second, she worked tirelessly for the reform of the Church. There were specific evils such as nepotism and laxity in punishing the guilty. Many bishops and priests led scandalous lives. Catherine wrote many letters to the pope, bishops, and other influential Church personnel. In a letter in 1372 to the nephew of Pope Gregory XI she wrote:

To reform the whole, you must destroy right down to the foundations. I beg of you, even if you have to die for it, to tell the Holy Father to remedy all this iniquity and when the time comes to make ministers and cardinals, not to make them for flattery, nor for money, nor for simony. But, with all your power, implore him to look for virtue and good repute in the man, not whether he is noble or plebian; for it is virtue that makes a man noble and pleasing to God.[4]

Third, she worked for the return of the pope from Avignon in France. The popes had begun to live in Avignon in 1305. Because strong French kings controlled weak French popes, there had been little inclination on the part of these popes to return to Rome. In 1376 she began to write to Pope Gregory XI, urging him to return to Rome. Her letter reads in part: "I implore you on the part of Christ Crucified to make haste. Use a holy deceit; that is, appear to defer the day and then go quickly and soon and you shall escape the sooner from this anguish and travail. Let us go quickly, my sweet Babbo, without any fear. If God is with you, no one else shall be against you."[5]

Gregory entered Rome on January 17, 1377, but he died the following year on March 27. While historical sources demonstrate that he was beginning to decide to return before Catherine intervened, her determination certainly helped to speed his decision.

Catherine entered into Italian diplomatic life by working for peace between the city-states of Lucca, Pisa, and Florence and the papal states. Her efforts did not bear much fruit but they were not a total waste.

After Gregory XI's death in 1378 the archbishop of Bari was elected as Pope Urban VI. His autocratic ways alienated the French cardinals and they declared his election invalid. A second pope, the antipope Clement VII, was elected in September 1378, thus plunging the Church into schism. Catherine worked tirelessly to halt the schism, pleading with Raymond of Capua to go to the French king and ask him to end the schism (which he did not do). She wrote to Urban VI in order to strengthen him, appealing for the creation of a papal council of holy persons to advise the pope and end the schism. But to Catherine's intense distress the schism widened along national lines. Her own Dominican Order also split. She wrote letters all over Europe—to France, Perugia, Queen Joanna of Naples, and others—trying to heal the schism. The schism was not resolved until 1417 (thirty-seven years after her death), when two of the three claimants stepped down. The new pope was Martin V, who was elected on March 11, 1417.

Catherine's Personality

Catherine's strong will, which was so evident in her childhood, remained a determining characteristic of her adult personality. She was often heard to say, "I will and I must," or, to others, "You must and you will." Yet her personality involved many opposite elements: she was iron-willed yet vulnerable, passionate yet gentle, volatile yet tender, self-willed yet surrendered, independent yet critical, and "more than a little mad with love."[6] She could talk for hours and more than once Raymond of Capua fell asleep from sheer exhaustion as she talked on and on.

In addition to her diplomatic efforts for peace and reconciliation in the Church and civil society, her ministry included preaching. Her presence was said to be so powerful that people would bring family members who were in need of conversion to her and they would experience a powerful grace of change just by being near her. There were numerous stories of healings and miracles during her life and afterward.

Her intense life of prayer was lived publicly: she prayed in the churches where she lived or traveled. To her embarrassment her prayer frequently included ecstasies. On April 1, 1375, she received the stigmata as the five wounds of Christ appeared on her hands, feet, and side. Although she felt their excruciating pain, she asked Christ that these signs would not be visible to others.

Her Writings

Catherine wrote one major treatise on prayer and the Christian life that is titled *The Dialogue*.[7] We also have many of her letters and some of her prayers.[8] Hagiography boasts that she dictated *The Dialogue* in three days (September 9–13, 1378) to three secretaries writing simultaneously. But in reality she most probably began to write it in 1377 (she had suddenly learned to write shortly before). The impetus for her book was a profound mystical experience, which Raymond of Capua describes:

nearly two years before she died such brightness of light was revealed to her from heaven that she felt constrained to spread it abroad by means of writing, begging her secretaries to be on the alert to take down whatever issued from her mouth as soon as they saw that she was going into an ecstasy. In this way there was composed within a brief space of time a certain book, which consists of a Dialogue between a soul that asks the Lord four questions, and the Lord Himself who replies to the soul and enlightens it with many useful truths.[9]

By 1378 she was referring to the book in her letters. It must have been finished before she was called to Rome in November 1378 to deal with the schism because there is no mention of the schism in it though she writes much about the corruption in the Church. The style does not reflect ecstatic dictation but a great deal of painstaking editing done by Catherine herself. Raymond and others would have written in a more sophisticated style, but her friends were too in awe of her holiness to edit what she wrote.

The book is framed by four petitions: for herself, for the reform of the Church, for the whole world in general and in particular for Christians in rebellion against the Church, and for divine providence to supply in general what is needed.[10] She used metaphors highly effectively, such as the central image of Christ as the Bridge, and wove together her understandings of the Christian life, prayer, and discipleship in which we can hear her voice entreating, demanding, praying, and instructing. She wrote it as one continuous whole, but later her disciples overcame their scruples and did the minimum amount of editing by dividing it into 167 chapters.

Final Years

Catherine came to Rome in 1378 at the request of Pope Urban VI in the early years of the Great Schism. She wanted to work for the unity of the Church until her death, and this wish was granted. Beginning in January 1380, her health began to decline dramatically as she suffered convulsions and paralysis. Even in her physical agony she would literally drag herself from her lodgings to the Basilica of St. Peter for Mass each day until late

February. She died at dawn on April 29, 1390, age thirty-three, calling out for the mercy of Jesus' blood upon her. She was canonized a saint in 1461 and in 1970 was declared a Doctor of the Church (together with St. Teresa of Avila), the first two women so designated in the Catholic Church.[11]

Contemplation in Action

As we consider Catherine's teaching and the relevance it has for us today, there are three themes that are primary: contemplation in action, the interweaving of truth and love, and the unity of the love of God and the love of neighbor.

Catherine was a woman possessed by God and on fire with God's truth and love for the salvation of the world. Her own life of prayer was the source from which all her energy flowed. From the testimony of Raymond of Capua and other friends, we learn something of the external elements of Catherine's prayer. Her favorite times for prolonged prayer were after the morning liturgy and in the early evening, as well as during the night when she hardly slept. She would frequently interrupt business and conversations to "consult with God." Often she would be transported in her prayer into an ecstatic trance, losing the use of all of her senses except speech and in these trances she would pray aloud. Her disciples would write down these prayers as she prayed. When she prayed alone, especially in the garden, she liked to sing.

Her prayer was formed in the liturgy and the Divine Office. From the extant daily readings in the liturgy of her time, we can see that she had deeply appropriated and integrated them into her spiritual vision. Some of her recorded prayers obviously flow from the readings of the liturgy of that day.

Her prayers are not spoken in the language of a "dark night" or intense spiritual darkness, but since she speaks knowingly of this kind of experience in *The Dialogue,*[12] we can infer that she had experienced this during her three years of solitude. The themes of her prayer interweave themselves into a beautiful gospel pattern: knowledge of God as loving Savior and of herself as a loved sinner, the centrality of truth and love, the primacy of desire. Prayer and life were always joined for Catherine and her concerns are readily apparent in her prayers that have come down to us, especially for the specific needs of the Church.

What are the signs of authentic prayer? Catherine was convinced that good feelings and consoling thoughts were not necessary, but that the long-term fruits of growing in love and compassion were most significant. Catherine teaches us to distinguish between our desires for gifts and our desires for the Giver of these gifts. Those who are sincere, "afire as they are with love, look only to [God] the Giver, and not to the gift. They love the gift because of [God] the Giver, and not because of their own consolation."[13] The sign of true prayer is the desire for virtue that remains in the person after the consoling feelings have dwindled away, especially if the person is "anointed with the virtue of true humility and set ablaze with divine charity."[14]

Catherine was convinced that God calls each of us to mystical union, no matter how weak and imperfect we are, if only we will surrender to the fire of divine love. As we grow in prayer and union with God, "God becomes the home we never have to leave; as water surrounds and embraces the fish, becoming its very life, we begin to live in God like the fish in the sea and the sea in the fish."[15]

Living in this sea of love, our prayer becomes constant. We can be occupied with many external things, yet we continue to swim in the sea of the Beloved. Catherine was most certainly a contemplative in action. After her three precious years of solitude, she never again had the luxury of prolonged times of seclusion. Her life and her prayer became one, and her love for the Church, her desire for its reform, and her activities of peacemaking were all fed from the same source: profound union with her Beloved in prayer.

Thus true ministry, whether in the fourteenth century or today, flows from intimacy with God, while this intimacy continually pushes us into the heart of the world. False prayer can be recognized by seeking our own consolation, and helping others out of necessity and not out of love. Catherine became very upset when one of her friends, the English hermit William Flete (c. 1310–82), refused to leave his solitude and help her in Rome at the time of the Great Schism.

Intercessory Prayer

The fruit of union with God is twofold: loving action and intercessory prayer. Catherine's cry was for "mercy upon the world" and her world was certainly in need of an abundance of God's mercy. The motive for intercession is love: since love binds us to those who are beloved to us, we must join ourselves to the intercession of Jesus and intercede for those in need. Catherine knew the truth of the Scripture text, "He always lives to make intercession for them" (Heb 7:25). She discovered that the power of intercessory prayer did not depend on her virtue (or that of anyone else); it depended on the power of God to whom she was united in love. She understood Christ to say to her, "The more you offer me sorrowing and loving desires for them, the more you will prove your love for me."[16] Catherine became increasingly bold in her intercessory prayer and demanded much of God. She was heard to pray "I beg you—I would force you even!" to have mercy on the world. On feast days she would pray with even greater audacity.

Thus for Catherine, the loving union she experienced with God flowed forth in bold and courageous intercessory prayer. There was nothing that she would not ask of her Beloved. Her love for God increased her desire for God's love and mercy on the world and gave her constantly growing apostolic zeal—for the conversion of sinners, for the reform of the church, for peace in civil society. In Catherine's life, prayer and action were one movement of love.

Truth and Love

Living the Dominican charism of truth, Catherine joined it to the fire of divine love. Catherine spoke of God as "gentle first Truth."[17] She made her own the texts from John's Gospel: "You will know the truth, and the truth will make you free" (8:32) and "For this was I born, and for this I came into the world, to testify to the truth. Everyone who belongs to the truth listens to my voice" (18:37).

Her *Dialogue* begins and ends with her understanding of God as Truth. In the first chapter we already see the interweaving of truth and love that marks Catherine's spirituality:

> A soul rises up, restless with tremendous desire for God's honor and the salvation of souls. She has for some time exercised herself in virtue and has become accustomed to dwelling in the cell of self-knowledge in order to know better God's goodness towards her,

since upon knowledge follows love. And loving, she seeks to pursue truth and clothe herself in it.[18]

The final words of *The Dialogue* are a passionate plea to the Truth, who is God: "Clothe me, clothe me with yourself, Eternal Truth."[19] Catherine lived the reality of the words of Jesus, "I am the way, and the truth, and the life" (John 14:6), and she was aflame with the desire to see truth lived in the Church and her society.

Catherine's time, like our own, was full of deceit. She knew well the lies and treachery that were the stuff of the politics of her day. As the Great Schism began to tear Western Christendom asunder, she wrote to three Italian cardinals: "On what side soever, I find nothing but lies . . . (some of the cardinals have proclaimed Urban VI to be anti-pope) . . . But anyone who says it . . . lies up to his eyes."[20]

Catherine asserted that the treachery and falsehood that filled the Church and civil society had its origins in selfishness that acted as a poisonous cloud that seduces and enslaves. This selfishness pushes "us away from the truth that nothing created can be God for us, and open[s] us to a living hell on earth."[21]

As we reflect on the situation of the world today, Catherine's words are as fresh as the headlines in the newspapers. The unmasking of the lies of racism, sexism, and violence is a mammoth task and the responsibility of each believer. Each of us is called to reflect on how we have absorbed and lived the lives of our culture and society. As we begin to unmask the power of the lies that have shaped their lives, we will experience the power of the Spirit to live the truth in love.

And what is truth? This was Pilate's cynical question to Jesus on trial before him (John 18:38). For Catherine the truth is God's love for us. Truth gives birth to love and love continues the birthing. For as we live in love we understand how things really are: the truth of all persons created in love by God and destined for eternal life in God. Love and truth form an unending circle, leading us to the truth of ourselves and the world in God: "For love follows upon understanding. The more they know, the more they love, and the more they love, the more they know. Thus each nourishes the other. By this light they reach that eternal vision of me in which they see and taste in me in truth when soul is separated from body."[22] Catherine's unity of loving and knowing recalls the classic definitions of mystical knowledge: a knowledge through love, a sweet and loving knowledge.

How does one live the truth in love? Catherine insists that it is the gift of the Holy Spirit. The Spirit given in baptism is an inner light that gives a taste and desire for the truth of God's love for us and all people. Catherine, perhaps unconsciously reflecting her own experience, stresses that learning by itself does not lead to truth: "I tell you, therefore, it is far better to walk by the spiritual counsel of a humble and unschooled person with a holy and upright conscience than by that of a well-read but proud scholar with great knowledge. For one cannot share what one does not have in oneself."[23]

As a Dominican, Catherine participated in the charism of sharing with others the fruits of her contemplation, her pondering of the mystery of God who is Truth and Love. The purpose of the Dominican ministry of preaching was to share the truth of God's love in order that people might experience themselves and come to inner freedom and joy in the saving gift of Jesus the Christ. Catherine lived and died for the Truth who is Jesus. Her every effort—in word, letters, prayer, entreaty—was to urge, command, demand that people know and see the truth in Christ. She knew that the truth was saving truth and that the world's redemption comes through the Truth who is Love. Clothed as she was in the Truth, she was totally free to speak the truth: "It is your truth that offers truth, and with your truth I speak the truth."[24]

Catherine's teaching on truth and love thus recalls us to the heart of the gospel: to know Jesus Christ who is grace and truth (John 1:14), who leads us to all truth, and thus living in truth we are set free to love with the gift of the Spirit has been poured into our hearts (Rom 5:5).

Love of God and Love of Neighbor

When Catherine began to leave the solitude that she had cherished for three years in response to the Lord's call, she protested: "I have already divested myself of all worldly cares; now that I have cast them aside, must I return to them again? I have washed the feet of my affections clean of every stain of sin and vice, must I then befoul myself again with the dust of the earth?"[25]

Catherine told Raymond of Capua, her confessor and first biographer, that when she was obliged to leave her seclusion and go to talk to someone, "she felt such a sharp pain in her heart that it seemed as though it was about to break."[26] It was only the Lord who could persuade her to go and eat with her family and then return to prayer. She cried bitterly and the Lord said to her:

> Be quiet, sweetest daughter; it is necessary for you to fulfill your every duty, so that with my grace you may assist others as well as yourself. I have no intention of cutting you off from me; on the contrary, I wish to bind you more closely to myself, by means of love of the neighbor. You know that the precepts of love are two: love of me, and love of the neighbor; in these, as I have testified, consist the Law and the Prophets. I want you to fulfill these two commandments. You must walk, in fact with both feet, not one, and with two wings fly to heaven.[27]

Catherine's active life thus was to be lived on the two feet of love of God and neighbor and her journey would take her to places in Europe that she could not have dreamed of during her years of solitude. Catherine came to realize that "love of [God] and love of neighbor are one and the same thing: Since love of neighbor has its source in me, the more the soul loves me, the more she loves her neighbor."[28] Her life was a living parable of the unity of the love of God and neighbor, the two great Gospel commandments (Mark 12:28–31).

The central image of Catherine's *Dialogue* is that of Christ the Bridge (chaps. 26–87). This Bridge stretches from heaven to earth, from God to the human person. To travel on it is to find Truth and Love Who is the Bridge. The call to travel this Bridge is for *all*. In her imperative style Catherine declares: "This is the way you must all keep to no matter what your situation, for there is no situation that rules out either your ability or your obligation to do so. You can and you must, and every person gifted with reason has this obligation."[29]

The journey on the Bridge is one of love, and once again we hear of the indissoluble bond of love of God and neighbor: "you should love your neighbor with the same love with which you love me."[30] After Catherine reluctantly left the cloister of the cupboard-room in her family home, she learned by experience the inseparable bond between these two loves. And she had harsh words for those who refused to serve others lest they lose time for prayer or disturb their inner peace:

These people find all their pleasure in seeking their own spiritual consolation—so much so that often they see their neighbors in spiritual or temporal need and refuse to help them . . . But they are deceived by their own spiritual pleasure, and they offend me more by not coming to the help of their neighbors' need than if they had abandoned all their consolations.[31]

It is one thing to try to love God, but usually much more difficult to love other people with their faults and foibles. We are made in the image of God, who is Love, and we find our deepest happiness in and through the love of God and each other. Catherine uses the beautiful image of a "chain of charity"[32] to describe the unity of persons with one another. Even if we wished, we cannot break the bonds that unite us to one another.

Because we are each different, with diverse strengths and weaknesses, we need each other, exactly as the parts of the human body rely on each other (1 Cor 12:14–26). Catherine expands this understanding using the example of an orchestra: God is the conductor and each of us plays a different instrument, under the guidance of our loving maestro.[33] We come to God in and through the love we have for each other, and not alone.

Thus, the teaching of Scripture that we are to love God and each other completely and totally became the guiding principle for Catherine's life of ministry and service. Though she would have preferred to remain in prayerful solitude, she left those delights in obedience to her Spouse who called her to live the truth in love by serving her sisters and brothers. And this she did in both very simple and very dramatic ways.

Catherine's Ministry of Love

On fire with divine love and passion for the truth, Catherine exercised a wide-ranging ministry, from direct care of the poor and sick to audacious denunciation of injustices in the Church and her society.

Catherine both served the sick and the poor personally and urged others to do so. When the plague broke out again in 1374, she gave an an example of unending service and self-sacrifice. An eyewitness, Thomas Caffarini, described her work: "She was always with the plague-stricken; she prepared them for death, she buried them with her own hands. I myself witnessed . . . the wonderful efficacy of her words which made many people repent."[34]

She urged almsgiving even as she gave away her own family's food and clothing to the poor. Her encouragement to give alms is based on basic Christian charity, the imperative to give to others in need, declaring that "the poor are the hands which will open the gates of eternal life to you if you give alms with whole hearted love."[35]

At other times she describes the institutional dimension of the poverty of her own day and demands that rulers act for justice. In a letter to the king of France, Charles V, she tells him:

> Do not close your eyes to the wrongs which your officials commit through bribery or neglect of the poor. Be a father to the impoverished as an almoner of what God has given you. See to it that the crimes committed in your kingdom are punished and that good deeds are exalted and rewarded. All this is a part of divine justice.[36]

For Catherine, authentic justice "seeks the common good and not that of an individual."[37]

Catherine was aflame with zeal for the conversion of sinners. This included those individuals who were notorious public sinners, rulers who led scandalous lives, causing feuds and wars, and Church leaders who were unfaithful to their charge as shepherds of the flock.

In 1375, a young man, Niccolo di Toldo, was condemned to death for making inflammatory remarks against the government of Siena. Catherine exerted much energy in bringing him to true conversion. His cries of hatred and revenge turned to a desire for martyrdom. Catherine kept her promise to be with him at his death and received his head into her hands at the moment of his execution. Writing to Raymond of Capua, Catherine said, "First Truth[38] showed me that he was saved, not by any works, but only by God's grace and mercy . . . It seems that the first stone is already in place."[39] Catherine interpreted his death as the firstfruits of those who would give their lives for the reform of the Church.

Her efforts were also directed to those involved in family and political feuds. These intractable battles caused the death of many men in fights and battles. Although she was first scorned for her efforts (what right did this young woman have to interfere, they cried), her efforts often led to successful mediation of bitter quarrels. Writing to two brothers of the

Belforti family, she stressed that "sin establishes a feud between man and his creator. . . . He who kills his enemy kills himself first . . . Be reconciled both to God and to your enemies . . . and then come and see me as soon as you can."[40]

To political leaders, often in conflict with the Church, she was equally forceful, as a letter to the duke of Milan, Bernabo Visconti, demonstrates. He had seized papal lands, slaughtered clergy and laity, and disregarded the entreaties of the pope's legate for peace. In 1372 Pope Gregory XI declared war on him and Visconti amazingly turned to Catherine in the hope that she would defend him from the pope. But this was a vain entreaty, for she wrote:

> I tell you—I beg you in the name of Christ crucified—never meddle in this again. Keep your own cities in peace, passing sentence on your own subjects when they are at fault. But never, never pass sentence on these others, for they are ministers of this glorious precious blood.[41]

Catherine's voice was also raised in denunciation of the scandals in the Church. Writing to Pope Urban VI at the time of the schism, she was outraged at the abuses and scandals in the Church: simony, avarice, neglect of the poor, and luxurious living. This young woman told the pope:

> The world can tolerate no more. Vices abound, especially among those who were put in the garden of holy church to be fragrant flowers, sending the fragrance of virtue, and we see instead that they revel in wretched and hateful vices so that the whole world reeks! . . . Where is the generosity and care of souls, the distribution of alms to the poor? You know well that men are acting otherwise. With grief I say that your sons nourish themselves on the wealth they are accumulating by their ministry of the blood of Christ . . . nor are they ashamed to be such money-changers.[42]

Catherine not only denounced injustice and scandal; she described what true justice should be. In a letter to the king of Hungary, she implores him to be a just ruler: "Exercise justice toward the great as well as toward the powerful, to the poor as to the rich. Do not compromise, do not allow yourself to be intimidated by flattery, by threats, by a desire to please."[43]

Her letter to the rulers of Bologna has a contemporary ring as she describes the reasons for injustice:

> When one is in charge, one (often) fails in true justice. And this is the reason: one is afraid of losing one's status, so, in order not to displease others, one keeps covering and hiding their wrong-doing, smearing ointment on a wound which at the time needs to be cauterized . . . What is the reason for such injustice? Self-centered love. . . . In order to remain in true holy justice, rendering to all their subjects their due, they need to show mercy to those who deserve mercy, not on sudden impulse but out of truthful conviction . . . Their motivation will be not what people say but holy true justice, and they will be concerned not for any private good but for the common good.[44]

Where did a young woman with no formal education get such wisdom and insight into the human heart and social evils? Her understanding of the evils of human life and the remedies needed for true justice and peace came from the wisdom of the Spirit, communicated to her in prayer by the One who is Truth, Justice, and Love. In her love of Christ, Catherine would never spare herself. She died at thirty-three, worn out physically by her efforts but still longing to do more for the Church and the society of her day.

Catherine and the Contemporary Context

While more than seven hundred years separate Catherine's era from our own, her life and teaching have much to say to us today. The problems of poverty, injustice, feuds, scandal, and disunity that she denounced remain part of human reality today. The difference is that they have become ever more complex since we now are able to analyze their global dimensions, while Catherine knew only their local and European dimensions.

Catherine's life and ministry has a fourfold message to us. First is her insistence on truth as central to life. The world hears many lies today: some people are of more dignity than others, some have the right to more of the world's resources than others. Catherine's stress on truth and love calls us to ensure that the efforts to bring about a just and peaceful world are built on the solid foundations of the equality and dignity of each human person.

Second, Catherine's life of prayer vividly illustrates the bond between contemplation and action. Though she most probably would have chosen to live a life of prayer and seclusion, she found herself in the midst of a society and Church whose very foundations were cracking. Her experience of God in prayer gave her the wisdom in the Spirit to denounce injustice and announce what true justice is and how to attain it. Catherine is sometimes called a "social mystic" and that is correct. But even more her life demonstrates clearly and convincingly that authentic prayer leads to care for the poor and action for justice.

Third, Catherine's call to walk on the two feet of the love of God and the love of neighbor describes the perennial Christian vocation, to be lived today as truly as she lived it in fourteenth-century Italy. We have no choice: we cannot choose either a private spirituality or an activism that is not animated out of the love of God who is truth. Love of God, First Gentle Truth, impelled Catherine's efforts in love and service; and all her exertions inflamed her love of God even more.

Fourth, Catherine speaks to our efforts for unity as we strive to become a just and loving society and world. Catherine worked for peace and reconciliation among the political leaders of the city-states and in the Church itself, divided by schism and hemorrhaging from scandal. Catherine urged people to reconcile and forgive each other on the basis of their common dignity as daughters and sons of the one God. This is the most solid basis for unity since we can affirm the uniqueness of each person who has something irreplaceable to contribute to the good of all, each gift making the whole greater than the sum of its parts.

Notes

1. Suzanne Noffke, "Introduction," in *Catherine of Siena: The Dialogue*, trans. Suzanne Noffke (New York: Paulist, 1980), p. 1.

2. An early source of Catherine's life is the biography written by her confessor Blessed Raymond of Capua, *The Life of St. Catherine of Siena,* trans. George Lamb (London: Harvill, 1960). Other biographical sources are Johannes Jorgensen, *Saint Catherine of Siena*, trans. Ingeborg Lund (New York, London, and Toronto: Longmans, Green, 1938); Catherine M. Meade, *My Name is Fire* (New York: Alba, 1991); Sigrid Undset, *Catherine of Siena*, trans. Kate Austin-Lund (New York: Sheed &

Ward, 1954); Richard Woods, *Mysticism and Prophecy: The Dominican Tradition* (Maryknoll, NY: Orbis, 1998), pp. 92–108. Suzanne Noffke includes a comprehensive bibliography of works by and about Catherine in *Catherine of Siena: Vision Through a Distant Eye* (Collegeville, MN: Liturgical, Michael Glazier, 1996), pp. 233–67.

3. Grace M. Jantzen comments that "by modern standards Catherine of Siena would be classified as suffering from anorexia nervosa" (*Power, Gender and Christian Mysticism* [Cambridge: Cambridge University Press, 1995], p. 216). But Catherine's fasting is much more complex than a medical diagnosis. Jantzen interprets her inability to eat as an extreme form of identification with the suffering of Christ and relying on the work of Caroline Walker Bynum (*Holy Feast and Holy Fast: The Religious Significance of Food to Medieval Women* [Berkeley, CA: University of California Press, 1987]), states that "women are linked with the humanity of Christ, who suffered to save the world, and therefore in their suffering flesh they find their true holiness" (p. 222). Such extreme fasting is not the male route to holiness.

4. Alice Curtayne, *Saint Catherine of Siena* (London: Sheed & Ward, 1934), p. 167.

5. Ibid., p. 110.

6. Mary Ann Fatula, *Catherine of Siena's Way* (London: Darton, Longman & Todd, 1987), p. 19.

7. Quotations from *The Dialogue* are from the edition translated by Suzanne Noffke (New York: Paulist, 1980).

8. See *I, Catherine: Selected Writings of Catherine of Siena*, trans. Kenelm Foster and Mary John Ronayne (London: Collins, 1980), which contains nineteen letters; *The Letters of St. Catherine of Siena*, vol. 1, trans. Suzanne Noffke (Binghamton, NY: Medieval & Renaissance Texts & Studies, 1988); *Letters of Catherine of Siena: Letters 1–70*, trans. Suzanne Noffke (Ithaca: Cornell University Press, 1999); *Letters of Catherine of Siena: Letters 71–144*, trans. Suzanne Noffke (Ithaca: Cornell University Press, 1999); *The Prayers of Catherine of Siena,* trans. Suzanne Noffke (New York: Paulist, 1983); Mary O'Driscoll, ed., *Catherine of Siena: Passion for the Truth, Compassion for Humanity* (New Rochelle, NY: New City, 1993), which is an edited collection of some of her letters and prayers, together with selections from *The Dialogue*.

9. Raymond of Capua, *The Life of St. Catherine of Siena*, p. 320.

10. *The Dialogue*, 1, p. 26.

11. St. Therese of Lisieux (1873–97), a French Carmelite, was the third woman to be named a Doctor in the Church in 1997.

12. Raymond of Capua describes a period of time shortly before the end of her three-year period of seclusion when she experienced severe temptations of all kinds. When she asked, "My Lord, where were you when my heart was disturbed by all those temptations?" the answer was "I was in your heart . . . and I, who was defending your heart from the enemies, was hidden there all the time" (*The Life of St.*

Catherine of Siena, p. 94). In *The Dialogue* Catherine writes of what she learned about self-knowledge in these trials: "And this knowledge is more perfectly gained in time of temptation, because then you know that you are nothing, since you have no power to relieve yourself of the sufferings and troubles you would like to escape" (chap. 43, p. 88) and "at no time does the soul know herself so well, if I am within her, as when she is most beleaguered" (chap. 90, p. 168). The edition cited is the translation by Suzanne Noffke (New York: Paulist, 1980).

13. *The Dialogue,* 106, p. 200.

14. Ibid., 106, p. 198.

15. Fatula, *Catherine of Siena's Way,* pp. 105–6.

16. *The Dialogue*, 129, p. 255.

17. Ibid., 87, p. 160.

18. Ibid., Prologue, p. 25.

19. Ibid., 167, p. 366.

20. Quoted in Fatula, *Catherine of Siena's Way,* pp. 61–62.

21. *Letter T 299,* quoted in ibid., p. 64.

22. *The Dialogue*, 85, pp. 157–58.

23. Ibid., 85, p. 157.

24. Quoted in Fatula, *Catherine of Siena's Way,* p. 74.

25. Raymond of Capua, *The Life of St. Catherine of Siena*, p. 106.

26. Ibid., pp. 107–8.

27. Ibid.

28. *The Dialogue*, 7, p. 36.

29. Ibid., 55, p. 110. Note Catherine's typical expression: "You can and you must."

30. Ibid., 64, p. 121.

31. Ibid., 69, pp. 130–31.

32. Ibid., 148, p. 311.

33. Ibid., 147, pp. 310–11.

34. Quoted in Mary Jeremy Finnegan, "Catherine of Siena: The Two Hungers," *Mystics Quarterly* 17 (1991), p. 173.

35. Piero Misciatelli, ed., *Le Lettere di S. Caterina da Siena* (Florence, 1940), IV, #304, quoted in Carola Parks, "Social and Political Consciousness in the Letters of Catherine of Siena," in *Western Spirituality: Historical Roots, Ecumenical Routes*, ed. Matthew Fox (Santa Fe, NM: Bear & Co., 1981), p. 254.

36. Misciatelli, IV, #235, quoted in ibid., p. 254.

37. Misciatelli, IV, #268, quoted in ibid., p. 255.

38. Catherine often used this phrase to refer to God.

39. *Letter 273*, quoted in *Catherine of Siena: Passion for the Truth, Compassion for Humanity*, ed. Mary O'Driscoll (New Rochelle, NY: New City, 1993), pp. 42–43.

40. Quoted in Finnegan, "Catherine of Siena," p. 174.

41. Quoted in ibid., p. 175.

42. Misciatelli, IV, #291, quoted in Parks, "Social and Political Consciousness," pp. 255–56.

43. Misciatelli, V, #357, quoted in ibid., pp. 256–57.

44. *Letter 268*, quoted in O'Driscoll, *Catherine of Siena,* p. 39.

4

Ignatius of Loyola:
Finding God in All Things

Ignatius was born in 1491, a little over one hundred years after the death of Catherine of Siena. At the time of his death in 1556, the Church in the West had suffered its most severe rupture since apostolic times due to the Protestant Reformation. He left as his legacy his *Spiritual Exercises* and the Society of Jesus.[1]

Early Years

Inigo[2] of Loyola was a Basque, from the northeastern part of the Iberian peninsula. His family was wealthy enough to have their own castle, in which he was born. When he was about fifteen he went to be trained for court life in the home of the high treasurer of King Ferdinand and Queen Isabella, Juan Velaquez de Cuellar. There the teenage Inigo was dazzled by the fine clothes worn at court, the deeds of chivalry to be done, and the lovely ladies to be won. His personality at early manhood included the desire for worldly praise and glory, eagerness to distinguish himself by reckless deeds, and tenacity in reaching his goal once he had decided upon it. These characteristics, transformed by his conversion, were to be his throughout his life.[3]

His life at the court gave him some military skills although he was not trained as a professional soldier. But he took part in various military expeditions, including the siege of Pamplona on May 17, 1521, in which he was wounded by the French. His leg was shattered by a cannonball. Because of his bravery he was treated well by the French and was carried to the family castle in Loyola to recover.

As his leg began to heal it became obvious that it would not be straight. Inigo told the doctors to rebreak the leg and reset it in the hope that he would regain full use of it. This they did while Inigo, the brave soldier, bit his lips but did not cry out in pain. The leg never did heal well and he walked with a limp for the rest of his life.

Conversion (August 1521–February 1522)

At twenty-six Inigo was a practicing Catholic but definitely not a devout Christian. His life was about to change radically as he recovered from his leg injury. To pass the time he asked his sister-in-law for some of the romantic novels of which he was so fond. But no novels could be found, only the *Lives of the Saints* and Ludolph of Saxony's *Life of Christ*. These were better than nothing, so Inigo read and reread them.

As he did so, he became aware of the movements of his own heart. When he imagined doing the kind of great deeds that St. Francis of Assisi or St. Dominic had done he felt an initial repugnance followed by a great feeling of joy and peace. When he thought about doing brave deeds for "his lady love" he felt an initial joy but this later changed to a sense of depression. Gradually he learned to interpret these feelings and realized that living as the saints did, while difficult, would bring him joy, while doing courageous deeds for a young woman would not bring lasting peace. He began to ask himself, "What if I should do what St. Francis did, and what St. Dominic did?" and then told himself, "St. Dominic did this, therefore I have to do it; St. Francis did this, therefore I have to do it."[4]

When he was sufficiently recovered he went to the shrine of Our Lady at Montserrat and made a general confession of his sins (which took him three days!). He spent the night of March 24, 1522, in vigil, as a young man would do the night before he was knighted. In the morning this new knight of Christ stripped off his fine clothing, replaced it with a pilgrim's robe, laid his sword before Mary's altar, and formally dedicated himself to serving the Eternal King, under Mary's protection.

On Retreat at Manresa

Ignatius went to the small village of Manrea, a few miles from the shrine at Montserrat. His first intention was to spend a short time in retreat and then leave for the Holy Land. But he ended up spending eleven months living in a cave, begging for food, praying, and fasting. During this time he began to sketch out the outline of his *Spiritual Exercises,* which would be based on his own experiences of prayer and discernment.

He learned much in a very practical way about what he would later term the *good* and *evil spirits.* For example, he was fascinated by a vision of a bright serpent but later realized it was not a good spirit.[5] He also learned that the intense consolations that severely limited his sleep were not necessarily sent by God.

One day while he was sitting by the banks of the River Cardoner in Manresa he had a profound mystical illumination in which he said that he gained great clarity of understanding about the Trinity, the creation of the world, the incarnation, and the role of Mary.[6] All these insights found their way into the *Spiritual Exercises.*

The Pilgrim

Inigo left Manresa in March 1523 and went on pilgrimage to Jerusalem (September 1523), visiting all the holy places. He wanted to remain there but this proved impossible and he returned to Spain. He realized that if he was going to help others he needed to study and so at the age of thirty-three he began to learn Latin in Barcelona, sitting with young boys in a primary school. He began to give the *Spiritual Exercises* to individuals and people came to him for advice and counsel, seeing in him someone of remarkable spiritual insight and gifts.

In 1526 he went to Alcala to study philosophy, but his part-time ministry of direction and retreats began to attract too much attention (remember, he was a layperson, not a cleric) and so he went to the University of Salamanaca in 1527. In 1528 he went to Paris, where he stayed until 1535. Here he studied theology at the University of Paris, earning a master's degree.

Beginnings of the Society of Jesus

During his travels from one city to another Ignatius began to gather around him a circle of friends, both men and women, to whom he gave the *Exercises*. On August 15, 1534, Ignatius and seven of these friends[7] made a vow to be together in community and to meet in Venice the next year. From there they pledged themselves to go on pilgrimage to Jerusalem. If this proved impossible, they would go to Rome to offer themselves to the pope so that he could send them wherever he thought best.[8]

Ignatius went to Venice, where he studied theology, waited for his companions, and worked on the *Spiritual Exercises*. His companions arrived on schedule but they were unable to go to the Holy Land because of war with the Turks. With six others Ignatius was ordained a priest on June 24, 1537. After a year of ministry in the Venice area, they went to Rome to offer themselves to the pope.

As they walked to Rome, Ignatius had a profound mystical experience at a small wayside chapel near Rome called La Storta. He asked Mary to "place him with her Son" and he heard Christ say to him, "I shall be propitious to you in Rome." He experienced a profound sense of being "with Christ" and he saw Christ carrying a cross on his shoulder and the Father saying to Christ, "I want you to take this man for your servant."[9]

Years in Rome

Ignatius was never to leave Rome. Pope Paul III assigned him and his companions to apostolic ministry there, where they preached, heard confessions, began classes for adults, worked with prostitutes, and began to open schools.[10]

The Society of Jesus was approved by Pope Paul III on September 27, 1540. Ignatius was elected superior for life on April 6, 1541. During his lifetime the Society spread rapidly throughout Europe and in India and Brazil; at his death there were approximately one thousand members. From a small apartment in the Jesuit house in the center of Rome Ignatius worked on the Constitutions of the Society of Jesus, wrote letters to his increasingly far-flung brothers, and administered the Society.

His own life of prayer continued to grow and deepen during these years. He experienced the gift of tears when he celebrated Mass. Ignatius learned and taught from his own experience what it means to "find God in all things." He died on July 31, 1556, and was canonized together with his dear friend Francis Xavier (whom he had sent to India and the East in 1542) on March 12, 1622.

Ignatius the Mystic

While there is a pervasive Christology in the spiritual teaching of Ignatius, he was a mystic whose experience of God was primarily Trinitarian.[11] His experiences at Manresa, especially the grace he encountered by the banks of the River Cardoner, gave him an inner knowledge of "the manner in which God created the world,"[12] so that he was able to consider and judge all things as proceeding from the Triune God. This grace was the foundation of his vision to "seek and find God in all things."

Ignatius's mystical vision has four components.[13] First, it is a Trinitarian vision of all of creation coming forth from the Trinity and all things returning to God. Second, it is profoundly Christological. The election, the radical decision to follow Christ, is the pivotal point of the *Spiritual Exercises* (169–89) and the Christ one is called to follow is Jesus, humble, poor, and on his way to the cross. For Ignatius, the person and mission of Jesus are inseparable: one chooses to follow Christ in mission.

Thus, the third dimension of Ignatius's mystical vision is its apostolic character. Those who are called to follow Christ and who answer the call do not sit on the sidelines and observe him; they cooperate in the task of leading all of creation back to God. Gervais Dumeige comments: "This mystique has not, and will not have, nuptial overtones either; it is and will be rather a mystique of service. In other words, the Trinity that reveals itself to St. Ignatius is not only 'contemplated'; it reveals itself actively, as a source and principle of apostolic action."[14]

Finally, Ignatius's apostolic vision is centered in the Church, the Mystical Body. As Christ was sent to bring "good news to the poor . . . [and]

release to the captives" (Luke 4:18–19), so those who follow Christ share in his mission within the Christian community. Ignatius understood this to be the Catholic Church with a special bond of obedience to the pope. In a wider perspective today, we can describe this communitarian sense as the Christian community as a whole, seen in a variety of traditions and ecclesial bodies. We cooperate in the work of God with other disciples.

Ignatius's vision thus leads to a synthesis of the great themes of Christian belief: the Triune God as Creator of all things, the incarnation of the Word/Sophia of God in Christ, the redeeming mission of Christ to bring all people back to the original unity in Christ. Because Ignatius saw everything in the light of God, he was singularly able to find God in all things.

Ignatius's Legacy

Ignatius has left us a singular legacy in the *Spiritual Exercises,* which has profoundly influenced the history of Christian spirituality. In the *Exercises* we find three themes that are significant in the integration of prayer and social commitment. These are: (1) the call to make all choices in life in relation to the "end" for which we are created, seen in the "Principle and Foundation" of the *Exercises*; (2) the "Rules for Discernment of Spirits," which give us a guide for the interpretation of the movements of our hearts within the dynamics of choice; and (3) the understanding of the unity of all things in the love of God described in "The Contemplation to Attain the Love of God." The inner dynamism of the *Exercises* is to "find God in all things," a challenge and gift as needed today as it was in the time of Ignatius.

The *Spiritual Exercises*: Structure and Dynamics

The *Spiritual Exercises* first took shape during the eleven months Ignatius spent in Manresa. He wrote them in the little cave that was his home during this very long retreat. Their essential structure was completed during that time and while Ignatius refined them in the years that followed as he directed many persons in the making of the *Exercises*, he did not radically revise them.

The *Exercises* are a school of prayer in which to find God and find oneself in God. While they are structured in four "weeks" and often are the basis of a thirty-day retreat, the actual length is determined by the needs of a particular retreatant. No "week" is necessarily seven days in length.

They begin with the "Principle and Foundation," which is the bedrock experience for all that will follow since it orientates the exercitant to the need for choice in the light of God's creative purpose. Each of the following weeks has a specific grace for which the person prays earnestly:

The First Week is focused on oneself as a sinner and God's love for oneself as a sinner. At the beginning of each meditation Ignatius instructs the person to "ask for what I desire" and during this Week the principal grace is to ask for "a growing and intense sorrow and tears for my sins"[15] now seen in the light of God's overwhelming love.

The Second Week is focused on Christ: hearing his call to discipleship, considering his life as depicted in the Gospels, and deciding to follow him completely and totally. In Ignatian language, this choice is "the election." The principal grace of the Second Week is to desire to "ask for an intimate knowledge of our Lord, who has become man for me, that I may love Him more and follow Him more closely."[16]

During the Third Week the exercitant follows Christ to the cross, participating in his passion through compassionate presence and praying for "sorrow, compassion and shame because the Lord is going to His suffering for my sins."[17] The final week is spent with the Risen Lord and one prays "for the grace to be glad and rejoice intensely because of the great joy and the glory of Christ our Lord."[18] The concluding meditation of the *Exercises* is the "Contemplation to Attain the Love of God," often termed the "Contemplatio" (230–37). It is both a synthesis of the graces of the *Exercises* as a whole and the first step to living the grace of "finding God in all things." One prays for a comprehensive vision that gives one "an intimate knowledge of the many blessings received, that filled with gratitude for all, I may all in all things love and serve the Divine Majesty."[19]

This sketch of the dynamics of the graces of the *Exercises* is like a manual about how to swim. One can read about how to do the crawl or the backstroke but eventually one has to find some water and dive in. So it is with the *Exercises*: one must do them, pray them, and experience the dynamic of the grace that they contain for those who ask and receive.

The Principle and Foundation

In the "Principle and Foundation," which begins the *Exercises*, we observe from the very beginning Ignatius's understanding of the relationship between God as Creator and all of creation.

The "Principle" answers the following questions:

Why have we been created? "Human persons are created to praise, reverence, and serve God the Lord and by this means to attain salvation."[20]

Where have we come from? While not explicitly stated, Ignatius implies the traditional belief of God as Creator.

How are we to relate to the rest of the world? "The other things on the face of the earth are created for us, to help us to attain our purpose, and we should rid ourselves of them insofar as they hinder us from attaining it."

How do we do this in practice? "Thus we should make ourselves indifferent to all created things, insofar as we are allowed free choice and are not under any prohibition. Consequently, as far as we are concerned, we should not prefer health to sickness, riches to poverty, honor to dishonor, a long life to a short life. The same holds for all other things."

And how can we judge how well we are doing? "Our one desire and choice should be what will best help us attain the purpose for which we are created."[21]

Desire is a crucial dimension of the *Exercises* and of the life of the Spirit as whole.[22] As we have already seen, Ignatius instructs those making the *Exercises* to ask specifically for what they want at the time they are praying. In his *Autobiography*, Ignatius speaks of desire eighteen times.[23] He took his desires seriously because he considered them graces from God. Thus he instructed members of the Society of Jesus to "endeavor to conceive great resolves and elicit equally great desires."[24]

The "Principle and Foundation" contains in miniature the major themes of the *Exercises* and of Ignatius's mystical vision. It describes how we are related to God (creature to Creator), how we are related to the rest of creation (always seen in view of our end, who is God), the need for choice, and how to use created things to serve God. It thus anticipated the dynamics of the "Election" and the "Rules for the Discernment of Spirits" that are to guide all our choices. The final vision of the *Exercises* in the "Contemplatio," the union of the person and God in Christ through love, is first seen in the "Principle and Foundation," in which the end of all of our striving, couched in the traditional language of "saving one's soul," is stated.

The Dynamics of Commitment

There is a saying attributed to the theologian Harvey Cox: "Not to decide is to decide." Ignatius certainly would agree, for the whole orientation of the *Exercises* is to choose to follow Christ completely and then to specify one's commitment in a particular way of life.

In the Second Week the retreatant prays several unique and creative meditations that Ignatius composed, all of which involve the dynamic of conscious choice. In the "Call of an Earthly King" (*SpEx* 91–99), Ignatius presents the call of a human ruler who issues a summons to follow him. Ignatius instructs the exercitant to compare the call of this king[25] with the invitation of Christ who says, "whoever wishes to join me in this enterprise must be willing to labor with me, that by following me in suffering, he may follow me in glory."[26]

Once this choice has been made (if it cannot be made, then the retreat ends at this point), the Second Week continues with meditations on the life of Christ, beginning with the annunciation to Mary. But Ignatius's intention is clear: the goal is to choose to follow Christ completely and to discover how to do that in a particular way of life. We are not praying simply for the sake of prayer, but with the motive of radical decision. Ignatius states: "While continuing to contemplate His life, let us begin to investigate and ask in what kind of life or in what state His Divine Majesty wish to make use of us."[27]

Three more challenging meditations continue the movement toward total commitment to Christ. In the "Two Standards" (*SpEx* 136–48) the contrast is drawn between two armies, that of Christ and that of Lucifer or Satan. The intentions of both are exposed: Lucifer to ensnare with riches, honor, and pride, and Christ to call disciples to poverty, insults, and humility. The retreatant is again confronted with choice.

The following meditation, "The Three Classes of Persons" (*SpEx* 149–57), directs the person to pray "for the grace to choose what is *more* [italics mine] for the glory of His Divine Majesty and the salvation of my soul."[28] The word *more* (*magis* in Latin) is a favorite Ignatian term, urging the person never to be content with the minimum but rather to desire to give without counting the cost. Using the example of the money of his day, Ignatius describes three persons who each have acquired ten thousand ducats, but not entirely justly. They each wish to rid themselves of this burden, each in their own way. One person delays until the hour of death and never accomplishes his mission. The second wants to have both the money and serve God, but obviously on his own terms. The third person seeks first the will of God in all things. Then it does not matter if he has or does not have the money: what is essential is to be better able to serve God. Thus Ignatius continues to lead the exercitant along the road of decisive choice.

We choose according to what attracts us. Ignatius inverts the logic of the "the world" when he presents the "Three Kinds of Humility" (*SpEx* 165–68) and invites the retreatant to discover the depth of his or her motivation for commitment at this time. The "first degree" is to obey the commandments and never to commit a mortal sin. This is necessary for salvation. The "second degree" reflects the "indifference " of the "Principle and Foundation": it matters little whether one is rich or poor, honored or disgraced, lives a long life or dies young. What is essential is to serve God and save one's soul. This leads to the decision never to commit a venial or less serious sin.

What Ignatius hopes the person will be moved to is desire for the "third degree" of humility: to "choose poverty with Christ poor, rather than riches; insults with Christ loaded with them, rather than honors; I desire to be accounted as worthless and a fool for Christ, rather than to be esteemed as wise and prudent in this world."[29] The motivation is not self-contempt but the desire to be with Christ.

If retreatants have been faithful and generous in the Second Week, they have followed the call of Christ along the path to whole-hearted commitment. Their priorities are now aligned with those of Christ and they are ready to specify their commitment in a particular way of life, or to rechoose the commitment that they have previously made (e.g. marriage), but now in the light of their desire to live the *magis* of zealous service of Christ.

The "Election"

Ignatius repeatedly calls us back to first principles. So in deciding how to live my life (or how to live the choices I have already made), "I must consider only the end for which I am created, that is, for the praise of God our Lord and for the salvation of my soul."[30] My lifestyle, vocation, profession must be chosen in the light of this ultimate goal, and not outside of it since "my first aim should be to seek to serve God, which is the end, and only after that, if it is more profitable, to have a benefice or marry, for these are means to the end,"[31] or, in contemporary terms, to study for a particular profession, run for political office, enter a religious congregation, or make any other choice in life.

But *how* does one make that particular choice? Ignatius describes three times and ways for making a choice that is in accord with the leading of the Spirit, or what has traditionally been termed "the will of God." The first is the easiest and the rarest: when a person's heart is moved so spontaneously that he or she is able to choose "without hesitation, or the possibility of hesitation."[32] A prime example is the response of Matthew who, on hearing Jesus say, "Follow me" (Matt 9:9), left his money-changer's table and followed him.

The second time is through sifting through the "experience of desolations and consolations and discernment of diverse spirits."[33] It is here that Ignatius's "Rules for the Discernment of Spirits" demonstrate their importance. The third time or way of making a choice is "a time of tranquillity" in which one considers the end for which one has been created—the praise and glory of God and one's salvation—and chooses in accord with this end.[34]

Ever the practical director and guide, Ignatius suggests several ways to consider the matter at hand in the "third time" if the choice is not clear. The first is to use one's "understanding to weigh the matter with care and fidelity" and to list the advantages and disadvantages of the particular matter, considering every aspect of the choice to be made (*SpEx* 180–81). For example, a young woman is trying to decide what to study during her university years. A business degree appeals to her because of the possibilities of earning a good deal of money. But she also ponders earning a degree in psychology and imagines herself counseling women and children who have been sexually abused. Both are equally possible and equally attractive. Ignatius would advise her to draw up a list of the advantages and disadvantages of both courses of study, to choose with the prayer that God will "confirm it for His greater service and praise."[35]

If this exercise in assessing the various aspects of the matter to be decided does not yield a peaceful decision, Ignatius suggests three other strategies, all involving the imagination (*SpEx* 185–87). One can imagine advising another person on what to do in this situation, and then to follow the same advice. Another tactic is to imagine oneself at the hour of death: what would one have chosen? Ignatius says: then do it! Finally, one considers the time of judgment after death: in the light of being "judged" by God, what would one have done? Ignatius then counsels the person to choose.

Discerning the Spirits

As we reflect on the circumstances of life at the beginning of a new century, with so much that needs to be done, Ignatius's counsels on decision making have contemporary relevance. Now that there are so many more choices in life, especially for younger people, a way through the forest of possible paths is more necessary than ever. Especially crucial is the gospel call to enflesh justice and peace in one's society.

At the heart of the dynamic of choice in Ignatius's vision of discipleship is observation of the movements of one's heart in response to the experiences of consolation and desolation. Attention to his own affective experience over the years, beginning with the attraction and aversion he experienced for various courses of action as he recovered from his battle injuries, led to his structuring of the "Rules for Discernment of Spirits," the principles of judgment of the diverse movements of one's heart (*SpEx* 313–36).[36]

Ignatius divides the Rules into two parts: those for the First Week and those for the Second Week. The distinction is in terms of the degree of conversion and commitment of the person. In the First Week the person is engaged in responding to God's merciful love and is beginning to refocus her or his life in the light of that love. In the Second Week (and following) the person is responding to the call to total commitment to Christ.

Thus in the Rules for the First Week Ignatius contrasts the sinner with someone who has begun to be serious about living a Christian life. The action of the "good spirit" and "evil spirit"[37] is decidedly different. In persons who are habitual sinners, "the enemy is ordinarily accustomed to propose apparent pleasures," filling their minds with the delight of their usual vices. In contrast, the "good spirit" will "rouse the sting of conscience and fill them with remorse."[38]

But once a certain degree of conversion has occurred, the tactics change: "Then it is characteristic of the evil spirit to harass with anxiety, to afflict with sadness, to raise obstacles backed by fallacious reasonings that disturb the soul. Thus he seeks to prevent the soul from advancing."[39]

The strategy of the good spirit is completely different, for this spirit gives "courage and strength, consolations, tears, inspirations, and peace,"[40] making everything easy and allowing the person to go forward in peace.

Ignatius coined the technical terms of *consolation* and *desolation* to describe the affective experiences at the heart of discernment. Both are distinguished by the direction of the heart's movements and it is that intentionality that is so crucial.

Consolation is the experience of feeling one's heart aflame with love for God, of shedding tears for the sheer love of God and sorrow for one's sins and "every increase of faith, hope and love, and all interior joy that invites and attracts to what is heavenly and to the salvation of one's soul by filling it with peace and quiet in its Creator and Lord."[41] Ignatius insists that this is a real experience: one is not thinking about being peaceful, loving God, feeling joy. One is experiencing this.

Desolation is the affective opposite: "darkness of soul, turmoil of spirit, inclination to what is low and earthly, restlessness rising from many disturbances which lead to want of faith, want of hope, want of love . . . (the person is) separated, as it were, from its Creator and Lord."[42] Ignatius warns strongly that we are not to make any change or any decision when we are experiencing desolation. Rather, we are to stand firm in the resolutions and commitments we have already made (*SpEx* 318–19). We are to be patient and to realize that one day consolation will return.

Ignatius gives three strategies for dealing with the movements of the "evil spirit." Though they are framed in language that is both culture-bound and patriarchal, the underlying truths remain valuable today.[43] First, the "enemy" is compared to woman, who is "a weakling before a show of strength, and tyrant if he has his will."[44] The person is counseled to be strong in the face of temptation and so defeat the enemy. Second, the tactics of the evil spirit are like those of a false lover who does not want to be discovered. The strategy here is very simple: to reveal one's disquiet of soul "to a confessor, or to some other spiritual person who understands his deceits and malicious designs"[45] in order to unmask the face of temptation. Lastly, the enemy uses tactics similar to that of a military commander who studies the position of the enemy and chooses the weakest point to attack. Similarly, "the enemy of our human nature investigates from every side all our virtues . . . Where he finds the defenses of eternal salvation weakest and most deficient, there he attacks and tries to take us by storm."[46] The need of self-knowledge, a counsel of all the great teachers of prayer, finds its place here. If we know our strengths and weaknesses we will be better able to distinguish the leadings of the good spirit from that of "the enemy of our human nature."

In the Second Week the dynamics of discernment become more intricate, for both the good spirit and the evil spirit may give consolation. The "good angel consoles for the progress of the soul, that it may advance and rise to what is more perfect"[47] but the evil spirit "consoles" in order to misdirect the person.

Ignatius demonstrates his acute psychological insight by instructing us to "carefully observe the whole course of our thoughts. If the beginning and middle and end of the course of thoughts are wholly good and directed to what is entirely right, it is a sign that they are from God."[48] But if our thoughts lead to a desire to do something evil, or even less good, or distract us from our purpose to serve Christ, then they are not of God. In like manner if the thoughts and ideas "weaken the soul, or disquiet it . . . destroying the peace, tranquillity and quiet it had before . . . these things are a clear sign that the thoughts are proceeding from the evil spirit."[49]

In the Second Week Ignatius uses the principle of "like to like" in discerning the spirits. If one is growing in love and commitment to Christ and others, "the action of the good angel is delicate, gentle, delightful . . . (like) a drop of water penetrating a sponge," while the action of the evil spirit is "violent, noisy and disturbing . . . like a drop of water falling upon a stone."[50] If a person is going from bad to worse, the movements of the spirits are the reverse.

> When the disposition is contrary to that of the spirits, they enter with noise and commotion that are easily perceived. When the disposition is similar to that of the spirits, they enter silently, as one coming into his own house when the doors are open.[51]

These are the basic principles of discernment that Ignatius learned through his own experience, refined through a lifetime of prayer and guidance of others, and structured into the *Exercises*. They are essential tools for Christian decision making and for the attitude of heart that desires to "find God in all things."

One learns to discern by doing it. The Rules give us the bare-bones structure of how the good and evil spirits can affect human beings. Growing self-knowledge and self-awareness of one's strengths, weaknesses, patterns of sinfulness, and receptivity to grace all help a person to discern correctly if she or he is being urged toward light and God or toward darkness and sin. The assistance of another person in spiritual direction or the help of a group of friends with whom one shares one's experience of the leadings of the Spirit are time-honored ways to learn how to discern well.[52]

The Contemplation to Attain the Love of God

The final meditation of the *Exercises* brings together the graces of the Four Weeks in a condensed form. The "Contemplatio" (*SpEx* 230–37) "is not only the culmination of the retreat, but the state of transition from the desert to real life, from contemplation to praxis."[53] Ignatius first invites us to consider that "love ought to manifest itself in deeds rather than in words"[54] and that love consists in mutual sharing: what one has, one shares.

From this perspective, Ignatius structures a four-part meditation focused on asking for the grace of "an intimate knowledge of the many blessings received, that filled with gratitude for all, I may in all things love and serve the Divine Majesty."[55] All things come from God as loving Creator and all things are to be seen in the light of God who is Love.

In the first part of the "Contemplatio" we are invited to remember all the blessings of creation and redemption and all that we personally have received from God. Ignatius instructs the person to "ponder with great affection how much God our Lord has done for me, and how much He has given me."[56] In the light of this what can one do but give oneself completely to this loving God? And so the retreatant is directed to pray:

Take, Lord, and receive all my liberty, my memory, my understanding, and my entire will, all that I have and possess. Thou hast given all to me. To Thee, O Lord, I return it. All is Thine, dispose of it wholly according to Thy will. Give me Thy love and Thy grace, for this is sufficient for me.[57]

In the second part of this meditation we reflect on how God dwells in all of creation—the elements, plants, animals, human beings—and so God dwells in me. The only response that can be made to the God of Life is to give my life to God and thus the person prays, "Take, Lord, receive . . ." again. The third movement of the "Contemplatio" focuses on God at work in all of creation, giving being and life. God works *for me*: my response is again one of total self-giving. The fourth and final section describes the incredible generosity of God's goodness since "all blessings and gifts (descend) from above,"[58] including one's own gifts and powers, together with justice, goodness, and mercy "as the rays of light descend from the sun, and as the waters flow from their fountains."[59] One's final prayer in the retreat is a repetition of the response already made: "Take, Lord, and receive all that I am and will ever be."

The "Contemplatio" leads the person back to the "Principle and Foundation" and the graces of the Four Weeks of the *Exercises*. The First Week considered creation and one's history of salvation; the first point of the "Contemplatio" also "moves from creation to redemption and expands all these personal graces."[60] The parallel continues as we observe that in the Second Week the focus had been on the Incarnate Word, Jesus the Christ, in the world and one's total commitment to him. Similarly, the second section of the "Contemplatio" emphasizes that God dwells in all of creation.

The Third Week, focused on the passion, was an intense experience of being with Christ as he labored for our salvation and liberation. Thus the third movement of the final meditation invites us to consider how God labors in all of creation. The Fourth Week, in which we rejoiced with Christ risen, finds its counterpart in the concluding section of the "Contemplatio" with its emphasis on God as the origin of all goodness: "As the risen Christ is the source of all consolation, that is, of the holy Spirit, so God is the source of all that is."[61]

The dynamic of the "Contemplatio" moves from the exterior to the interior: from the gifts God has given to God who is Gift. It is a movement into the depths of God in which one will find all that God has given. But the purpose of the "Contemplatio" is "not contemplation simply, but a contemplation that transcends itself and moves into the decisions and directions of a man's life."[62] It leads the person from the solitude of the days of prayer into the challenges of everyday life.

The graces given are two: vision and union. Through the whole process of the *Exercises*, culminating in this final intricate meditation, one has struggled to see the world as God sees it, to view it in terms of the principle and foundation. Now, at the end, one sees God "in all things." This is the graced seeing of everything in God and God in everything. This, Ignatius trusted, would transform the "seeing" of every moment of life as God is "discovered" in all things.

The depth of love is measured by what one shares with the Beloved. God has given the immensity of divine love and goodness; the person responds with her or his own gift of self. In this exchange of love comes the grace of union, as God and the person surrender to each other. One now understands all things as good, as holy, as coming from God. Ignatius is not concerned here with the problems of evil and suffering seen in the light of God's love. Rather, his intention is to lead the retreatant to the vision of being able to find God in all things, including suffering.

The goal of the *Exercises* is surrender to God's love, to the call of Christ. Without the election that precedes the "Contemplatio," the final surrender in loving self-giving is impossible. But the surrendered heart wants to give without limit. And in giving everything one finds everything in God.

The grace of the "Contemplatio" is the foundation and source of the ability to "find God in all things." Ignatius began the meditation with the statement that love proves itself in deeds, not in empty words. As one recognizes and experiences the depth of divine love, the response is to be generous and totally self-giving. In the *Exercises* Ignatius bids us to ask ourselves: "What have I done for Christ? What am I doing for Christ? What ought I to do for Christ?"[63] However, other key questions are: Where will I find Christ? Who is the God I seek?

It is important to note that while Ignatius uses the phrasing "to seek and find God in all things" he usually means Jesus Christ.[64] Phrases such as "Eternal Lord of all things" and "Divine Majesty" are applied to Christ. In one of his letters to scholastics about the relationship of prayer and studies (in which Ignatius states that the students should not spend long hours in prayer but should study), the original text states that they are to seek "the presence of our Lord" in all things.[65] While one can infer the presence of God in all of creation, Ignatius focuses on the presence of Christ who has become one with us in the incarnation and thus is present in all things and can thus be "found" by those who have given their lives to him.

"Finding God in All Things"

When Ignatius founded the Society of Jesus, he broke with the thousand-year tradition of Western monasticism whose Benedictine motto was *ora et labora*: to pray and work in an enclosed monastic setting. He began something new: an apostolic body who lived in community but did not pray the Divine Office in choir and whose rule of life was based on Ignatius's own charism: to seek God in all things, to find God in all things.

This became not only the central principle of this new form of religious life, it also gave the laity "an anxiously awaited method of unifying his faith and his everyday living."[66] This ideal, which was the foundation of Ignatius's mysticism, was to be extended not only to the members of the Society of Jesus but to all those who would be influenced by Ignatian spirituality.

Ignatius speaks of his own experience in his *Autobiography*: "He had always grown in devotion, that is, ease in finding God, and now more than ever in his whole life. Every time, any hour, that he wished to find God, he found him."[67] Written toward the end of his life, this is a truly remarkable statement. His contemporaries stated that "nearly always he was directed to God, even if at times he seemed to do something else."[68]

The source of this grace was Ignatius's constant union with the Trinity, a grace that had its origin in the experience at the River Cardoner in which he saw all things in the light of God. This transforming experience became the basis of all his decisions and actions. Jerome Nadal, an important early member of the Society of Jesus, testified that "we saw with deep amazement and sweet consolation how this grace, which was a light in his soul, manifested itself in the wisdom and sureness of all his actions. It was as if a light shone over his countenance."[69]

What Ignatius experienced in his personal relationship with God he communicated to his followers through the dynamic of the *Spiritual Exercises*. The lasting fruits of the *Exercises* in the life of the person who makes them is to seek in all things the presence of God, to find God in all things, to live with God ever before one's eyes, and to always direct one's self to God.[70]

The Foundations of "Finding God in All Things"

There are five foundational understandings that undergird the experience of seeking and finding God in all things. They flow from Scripture and the theology of the *Exercises*. First, we are to understand creation from the perspective of faith: all things and all history are to be seen in the light of the divine presence. God is not remote from human history, but involved with humanity. This is the unfolding of the meaning of the incarnation in each era and culture.

Second, building on Matthew 25:31–46, we can find Christ in other people through our concrete service to them. Active love and service are thus imbued with the Christocentric vision of the presence of Christ in one's neighbor. Finding God in prayer is good but not sufficient, for Christ is present in those in need. This establishes ever more firmly the call to do the works of peace and justice as a constitutive dimension of following Christ.

Third is the continual search for the call of God, the leading of the Spirit. As we have seen, a central concern of the *Exercises* has been to discern the will of God in one's life and to make an "election," a graced choice, according to the principles of discernment. But one choice is not enough, even if it becomes the primordial commitment of one's life. Each day, each hour, gives opportunity to discern whether what is being experienced, thought, or felt is leading one toward God and the service of others or away from God and those in need.

Fourth, we are called to clear away the underbrush of mixed motivations in our lives and, as Ignatius wrote, "to seek solely the things of Jesus Christ."[71] The purity of intention that Ignatius speaks of so often in his writings is that of seeking the glory of God and the good of the persons one serves. This echoes the motto he adopted: "All to the greater glory of God" (*ad majorem gloriam Dei*). Focusing on the glory of God and not on one's own self-will and finding God in all things were intrinsically linked in Ignatius's spiritual vision.

Finally, since one is on fire with love of God, the culminating grace of the "Contemplatio," one is to be eager to serve with unselfish love. Because God as love is at the heart of all creation, all reality, then the lover seeks the Beloved with ever-increasing zeal and enthusiasm, giving love in return for love.

How to Find God in All Things

The theory is clear but the practice of "finding God in all things" still remains challenging. The Ignatian spiritual tradition emphasizes four means to this end. First is continual mortification and self-denial. To find God one cannot be centered on one's selfish desires. Ignatius was convinced that a Jesuit did not have to pray for many hours each day. Discussing the needs of the young students in the Society, Ignatius said that "his opinion, from which no one would ever move him, was that for the scholastics one hour of prayer is sufficient, it being supposed that they are practicing mortification and self-denial."[72] The discipline of self-denial was not an exercise in itself but directed toward true inner freedom: the grace of desiring only the will of God in order to do it.

While Ignatius did not want the members of his Society to engage in long hours of prayer, he most definitely wanted them to pray. Without formal prayer at regular times a person simply cannot come to know God and the ways of God. Regular times of prayer are to overflow into a continuous attitude of prayer, which is not restricted by time or method. The *Exercises* are for beginners, those who are learning how to pray and how to follow Christ. After making the *Exercises*, they must grow and develop the life of prayer, nourished by the Scriptures, prayerful reading, and, above all, the desire to seek and find God.

Third, Ignatius knew that one would learn how to "find God in all things" if during each day one regularly recalled the presence of God, much as a person in love delights to recall the voice and person of the beloved. To a Jesuit who complained that people constantly at the door disturbed his interior union with God, Ignatius replied:

> You should always receive with great charity those who come to you
> to obtain spiritual help and consolation. But after you have been
> called, or while you are on the way, make use beforehand of some
> ejaculatory prayer.[73] Beg God that he may deign to help that person
> through you. Then you should direct all your thoughts and conver-
> sations towards helping the visitor make spiritual progress.[74]

Finally, Ignatius recommended the regular practice of examining one's conscience as a sure means of discovering whether one had been faithful to the presence of God discovered in the midst of life. Such an examination was to be made twice a day and was, in his view, actually more important than a formal time of meditation, since its aim was to discern whether one had been faithful to the promptings of the Spirit. This exercise gradually acquired a very negative connotation of only looking for sin in one's life. However, in our own day it has been revived under the title of the "Awareness Examen" or "Consciousness Examen."[75] In its new incarnation it is a fivefold prayer of:

1. Asking for the light of the Spirit to see the day as God has seen it.
2. Reviewing the day (or part of the day), asking myself where God had been present and how I had responded: with generosity or selfishness. Or perhaps it is only now that I recognize the presence of God in an event or conversation.
3. Thanking God for the ways I have found the divine presence in all things.
4. Praying in sorrow and repentance for the ways I was not aware of God's presence and so did not find God in all things.
5. Praying for the grace needed to respond to God during the next day.

This exercise, done regularly, teaches the person the sensitivity needed to find God in all things.

Prayer and Action

Jerome Nadal, considered the best interpreter of Ignatius's spirit and vision, wrote that "the action of charity, when united to God, is perfect action."[76] The discerning heart who finds God in all things finds God *in the world*, and not apart from it, as if living in some hot-house dwelling and as if God could not be present in ordinary life experience.

The key to this for Ignatius was the vision of truly finding God in all things. It was from this perspective that he instructed the early members of the Society to lift their minds to God in the midst of studies and action "and by means of this directing everything to the divine service, *everything is prayer*" (italics mine).[77] But how is this possible?

If we look at prayer and action as two distinct activities, we see that they have different objects. Prayer is directed to God and nurtures the vision necessary to "find God in all things." Action is oriented to the world but "this action constitutes our relationship to God, and if it is performed within the context of the Christian vision, it aims at nothing less than making the relationship with God that is nurtured in prayer a real and actual relationship."[78] This becomes a continual dance of love: prayer extends vision and action makes concrete the desire to do the works of love.

Speaking of prayer and action, Ignatius used the traditional image of "Martha and Mary," which often describes the superiority of contemplation (Mary) over action (Martha) in terms of unity, not opposition, although he still shared the view that contemplation was more important: "In this way, Martha and Mary are united; and through their giving mutual aid to each other not one part of the Christian life (even though it be the better one, contemplation) is embraced; rather, with the anxiety and trouble over many things now banished, Mary helps Martha and is united with her in our Lord."[79]

This is the Ignatian vision of service with Christ in the world. The experience of loving union in Christ, of being rooted and grounded in him (John 15:1–7), provides the energy and vision for the works of justice and peace. Action brings one into contact with the realities of social sin—the oppressive social structures of one's culture and society—and through one's contemplative union in God a person can judge the truth or error of the values one confronts.

The search for the will of God to be made as an "election" in the *Spiritual Exercises* is interpreted according to the "signs of the times" of one's own context.[80] Certainly one of the most important ecclesial signs is the call to do the works of justice and peace in one's own day. This can be understood as the will of God for the world: that justice be done. Roger Haight describes the three types of union with God that occur when a person works for justice: "he or she becomes one with God in three ways: morally, by a union of wills; contemplatively, by possessive knowledge of the God who wills justice; ontologically, by cooperative response to the intimate presence of God's personal Spirit."[81]

The Ignatian vision of "finding God in all things" thus demolishes the false dichotomies between prayer and action that have so undermined an authentic Christian praxis of loving action. His insistence that God is truly found in the world enables Christians to discern and act confidently in the power of the Spirit, seeking to do the "more" for the glory of God, which will make the world a more just and peaceful place.

Wherever the works of the gospel are done—whether feeding the poor and hungry or clothing the naked (Matt 25:31–46) or bringing liberty to captives (Luke 4:18)—there is the Spirit of God at work. And there is the call to Christians to decide to follow Christ, poor, humble, and suffering, to the cross and beyond, always seeking to find God in all things, animated by love and zeal for the things of God.

The fullness of God's *shalom* in every country, North and South, is still to be accomplished. It is brought to ever greater fullness by both individual and corporate actions inflamed with the love of God who has created all, sustains all, labors for all, and is found most especially in the poor and abandoned.

Conclusion

In Ignatius we see a synthesis of three central themes in Christian spirituality. The first understands God's creative presence as not limited to past "created acts" but vital and real in the present situation, in everyday life. The second focuses on Christ and his call to discipleship; for Ignatius this is a call whose response can only be total commitment. The "election," the conscious choice to follow Christ, poor and humble, is the underlying dynamic of the *Spiritual Exercises*. Lastly, the disciple enters into the creative work of God by loving action, seeking to find God in all things. And where God seems not be present, in situations of war, violence, and injustice, the disciple is called to work in the power of the Spirit of God to transform social structures into realities that mediate the values of the kingdom—love, justice, peace, reconciliation.

Notes

1. For background on Ignatius's life and spirituality, see the introduction in George E. Ganss, ed., *Ignatius of Loyola: Spiritual Exercises and Selected Works* (New York: Paulist, 1991), pp. 9–63, which contains his *Autobiography*, selections from the *Constitutions*, and selected *Letters*. Quotations from the *Autobiography* are from this edition. Harvey D. Egan analyzes Ignatius's mystical experience in *Ignatius Loyola the Mystic* (Collegeville, MN: Liturgical, Michael Glazier, 1987).

2. He was baptized "Inigo" and used this name until between 1535 and 1540, when he began to call himself "Ignatius." This change occurred because "a registrar at the University of Paris mistakenly translated his name into the Latin 'Ignatius'" (Robert Bireley, *The Refashioning of Catholicism, 1450–1700* [Washington, DC: The Catholic University of America Press, 1999], p. 29).

3. W. W. Meissner, *Ignatius of Loyola: The Psychology of a Saint* (New Haven, CT: Yale University Press, 1992), presents a psychological interpretation of Ignatius's personality from a Freudian perspective.

4. Ignatius of Loyola, *Autobiography, in Ignatius of Loyola: Spiritual Exercises and Selected Works*, ed. George E. Ganss (New York: Paulist, 1991), no. 7, p. 70.

5. Ibid., no. 19, p. 76, no. 31, p. 81.

6. Ibid., no. 30, pp. 80–81.

7. Nicolas Bobadilla, Jean Codure, Peter Faber, Diego Lainez, Simao Rodrigues, Alfonso Salmeron, and Francis Xavier.

8. This was the motivation behind the "vow of obedience" to the pope that later became part of Jesuit life. Ignatius reasoned that since the pope knew best the needs of the Church, he could send them where they were truly needed.

9. *Autobiography*, 96, p. 109.

10. See John W. O'Malley, *The First Jesuits* (Cambridge, MA: Harvard University Press, 1993), which describes and analyzes the initial years of Jesuit ministry.

11. For theological analysis of Ignatius's mystical experience, see Adolf Haas, "The Mysticism of St. Ignatius According to His *Spiritual Diary*," in *Ignatius of Loyola: His Personality and Spiritual Heritage, 1556–1956,* ed. Friedrich Wulf (St. Louis: Institute of Jesuit Sources, 1977), pp. 164–99; John O'Donnell, "The Trinitarian Vision of Ignatius Loyola in Contemporary Theological Perspective," in *Some Theological Aspects of Ignatian Spirituality* (Rome: Centrum Ignatianum Spiritualitatis, 1985), pp. 25–76.

12. *Autobiography*, 29, p. 80.

13. John O'Donnell, "The Trinitarian Vision of Ignatius Loyola in Contemporary Theological Perspective," in *Some Theological Aspects of Ignatian Spirituality* (Rome: Centrum Ignatianum Spiritualitatis, 1985), pp. 26–28.

14. Quoted in ibid., p. 27.

15. *Spiritual Exercises* 55. All references to the *Spiritual Exercises,* other than the "Principle and Foundation," are from the edition edited by Louis J. Puhl, SJ (Chicago: Loyola University Press, 1951).

16. Ibid., 104.

17. Ibid., 193.

18. Ibid., 221.

19. Ibid., 233.

20. The text of the "Principle and Foundation" is from the translation by Elisabeth Meier Tetlow, *The Spiritual Exercises of St. Ignatius of Loyola* (Lanham, MD: University Press of America, 1987).

21. Ibid., p. 11.

22. See William A. Barry, *What Do I Want in Prayer?* (New York: Paulist, 1994); Susan Rakoczy, "Discernment and Desire," *The Way* 39 (1999), pp. 269–80; Philip Sheldrake, *Befriending Our Desires* (Notre Dame, IN: Ave Maria, 1994).

23. Edward E. Kinerk, "Eliciting Great Desires: Their Place in the Spirituality of the Society of Jesus," *Studies in the Spirituality of Jesuits* 16 (November 1984), p. 6.

24. Ibid., p. 5.

25. Throughout the *Exercises,* Ignatius uses images and symbols from his culture, especially those of a military nature. This naturally reflects his experience. While the symbols may be awkward for us in our specific culture and milieu, the dynamic of choice—whatever the symbols used—remains true.

26. *Spiritual Exercises* 95.

27. Ibid., 135.

28. Ibid., 152.

29. Ibid., 167.

30. Ibid., 169.

31. Ibid.

32. Ibid., 176.

33. Ibid.

34. Ibid., 177.

35. Ibid., 183. Some Ignatian commentators see the "third time" as really a variant of the second because of the need to have the decision *confirmed*, and this is done through the experience of peace, which is the most crucial sign of "finding" the will of God.

36. See Thomas S. Green, *Weeds Among the Wheat* (Notre Dame, IN: Ave Maria, 1984); Jules J. Toner, *A Commentary on Saint Ignatius' Rules for the Discernment of Spirits* (St. Louis: Institute of Jesuit Sources, 1982); Jules J. Toner, *Discerning God's Will: Ignatius of Loyola's Teaching on Christian Decision Making* (St. Louis: Institute of Jesuit Sources, 1991); Jules J. Toner, *Spirit of Light or Darkness: A Casebook for Studying Discernment of Spirits* (St. Louis: Institute of Jesuit Sources, 1995); Jules J. Toner, *What is Your Will, O God? A Casebook for Studying Discernment of God's Will* (St. Louis: Institute of Jesuit Sources, 1995).

37. Toner discusses the various theological opinions on the existence of Satan and demons in his *Commentary on Saint Ignatius' Rules for the Discernment of Spirits*, pp. 260–70. He comments, "Those who wish to leave Satan and demons out of the picture when discerning spirits can read Ignatius' references to these as personifications of the power of evil in self and the world. Only let it be clear that this is a practical decision which in no way decides the theological question about the reality of what is left out of consideration" (p. 35).

38. *Spiritual Exercises* 314.

39. Ibid., 315.

40. Ibid.

41. Ibid., 316.

42. Ibid., 317.

43. In their book on the *Spiritual Exercises*, Katherine Dyckman, Mary Garvin, and Elizabeth Liebert comment on Ignatius's negative use of "woman" in the Rules: "In choosing 'woman' as a metaphor for the way the enemy works, Ignatius unwittingly employs a deadly stereotype of women, implying that they are vacillating, seductive, cowardly or, at best, weak. Against strong men they wilt, but they turn on weak men. A metaphor must work not only for the teller; it must also function for the receiver. Such a metaphor, reinforcing as it does the worst gender stereotypes, serves neither men nor women" (*The Spiritual Exercises Reclaimed: Uncovering Liberating Possibilities for Women* [New York: Paulist, 2001], p. 259).

44. *Spiritual Exercises* 325.

45. Ibid., 326.

46. Ibid., 327.

47. Ibid., 331.

48. Ibid., 333.

49. Ibid.

50. Ibid., 335.

51. Ibid.

52. The resources in spiritual direction are numerous. Among them are William A. Barry and William J. Connolly, The *Practice of Spiritual Direction* (New York: Paulist, 1982); Rose Mary Dougherty, *Group Spiritual Direction: Community for Discernment* (New York: Paulist, 1995); Tilden Edwards, *Spiritual Director, Spiritual Companion* (New York: Paulist, 2001); Kathleen Fischer, *Women at the Well: Feminist Perspectives on Spiritual Direction* (New York: Paulist, 1988); Margaret Guenther, *Holy Listening: The Art of Spiritual Direction* (Boston, MA: Cowley, 1992); Gerald May, *Care of Mind, Care of Spirit: A Psychiatrist Explores Spiritual Direction* (San Francisco: HarperSan Francisco, 1982, 1992); Susan Rakoczy, ed., *Common Journey, Different Paths: Spiritual Direction in Cross-Cultural Perspective* (Maryknoll, NY: Orbis, 1992); and Janet Ruffing, *Spiritual Direction: Beyond the Beginnings* (New York: Paulist, 2000). A helpful journal is *Presence*, the publication of Spiritual Directors International.

53. Gregory D'Costa, *The Practice of Love* (Gujarat, India: Gujarat Sahitya Prakash, 1991), p. 248.

54. *Spiritual Exercises* 230.

55. Ibid., 233.

56. Ibid., 234.

57. Ibid.

58. Ibid., 237.

59. Ibid.

60. Michael Buckley, "The Contemplation to Attain Love," *The Way Supplement* 25 (1975), p. 101.

61. Ibid., p. 103.

62. Ibid., p. 96.

63. *Spiritual Exercises* 53.

64. See Haas, "The Mysticism of St. Ignatius," pp. 196–98, for commentary on this understanding.

65. Cited in ibid., p. 197.

66. Josef Stierli, "Ignatian Prayer: Seeking God in All Things," in *Ignatius of Loyola: His Personality and Spiritual Heritage (1556–1956)*, ed. Friedrich Wulf (St. Louis, MO: Institute of Jesuit Sources, 1977), p. 136.

67. *Autobiography,* 99, p. 111.

68. Stierli, "Ignatian Prayer," p. 142.

69. Quoted in ibid., p. 142.

70. Phrases from the letters of Ignatius, quoted in ibid., pp. 143–44.

71. Quoted in ibid., p. 157.

72. Quoted in ibid., p. 159.

73. This is a brief prayer such as "Jesus have mercy on me" or "Come, Holy Spirit."

74. Quoted in Stierli, "Ignatian Prayer," pp. 161–62.

75. The contemporary form of this practice is described in the paradigmatic article by George Aschenbrenner, "Consciousness Examen," *Review for Religious* 31 (1972), pp. 14–21.

76. Quoted in Stierli, "Ignatian Prayer," p. 163.

77. Ibid., p. 148.

78. Roger Haight, "Foundational Issues in Jesuit Spirituality," *Studies in the Spirituality of Jesuits* 19/4 (1987), p. 38.

79. Quoted in Stierli, "Ignatian Prayer," pp. 149–50.

80. E.g. "the Church has always had the duty of scrutinizing the signs of the times and of interpreting them in the light of the gospel" (*GS* 4). Cf. *Pacem in terris*, the twentieth-century encyclical that described the signs in 1963: workers claiming their rights (*PT* 40); women becoming conscious of their human dignity and claiming their rights (*PT* 41); the conviction that all persons are equal (*PT* 43–44); and the beginning of a global awareness of human rights (*PT* 75–79).

81. Haight, "Foundational Issues in Jesuit Spirituality," p. 42.

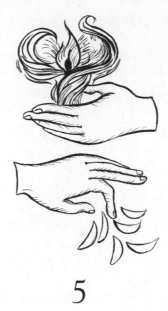

5

Martha and Mary: Sorting Out the Dilemma

A number of years ago I was part of a team giving a retreat for a group of lay leaders in the Catholic charismatic renewal in the United States. During one of the evening sessions we focused the discussion on efforts to promote the works of justice and peace in prayer groups. One woman stood up and, with great agitation, said, "All my life I was a Martha. Now I am a Mary. Don't you dare tell me I have to go back now and be a Martha too."

Her statement illustrates well the dichotomy that has often been part of Christian spirituality: either one is engaged in active works as a "Martha" or one is a "Mary," spending much time in prayer. The text on which this tension is based is that of Luke's description of the two sisters and their attitudes toward Jesus:

Now as they went on their way, he entered a certain village, where a woman named Martha welcomed him into her home. She had a sister named Mary, who sat at the Lord's feet and listened to what he was saying. But Martha was distracted by her many tasks, so she came to him and asked, "Lord, do you not care that my sister has left me to do all the work by myself? Tell her then to help me." But the Lord answered her, "Martha, Martha, you are worried and distracted by many things; there is need of only one thing. Mary has chosen the better part, which will not be taken away from her." (10:38–42)[1]

Approaching the Problem

In the history of Christian spirituality we find three approaches.[2] In one hierarchical approach "Mary" and the contemplative life are judged superior to "Martha" and the active life. This is exemplified in the writings of Origen, John Chrysostom, Augustine of Hippo, Gregory the Great, Bernard of Clairvaux, and the anonymous author of *The Cloud of Unknowing*. A second hierarchical approach is to judge Martha superior to Mary. Meister Eckhart and John Calvin demonstrate this view. The third is that of integration: Mary and Martha as one in the life of the person. Aelred of Rievaulx, Thomas Aquinas, Francis of Assisi, and Teresa of Avila describe this unity. We will analyze these approaches and also offer a feminist interpretation from the work of Elisabeth Schüssler Fiorenza.

Mary as Superior to Martha

This has been the usual interpretation of the story throughout Christian history. The writers who adopt this approach do not all have the same emphasis but they are united in asserting the superiority of Mary's contemplative stance over and against the activity of Martha.

Origen (185–255)

Origen, Christian philosopher and theologian, was born in Alexandria and studied there. Alexandrian thought was distinguished by its Platonism, including its spirit/matter and mind/body dualism, with matter and the body held to be of lesser value. This is readily apparent in Origen's writings, especially in his interpretation of the Martha-Mary dynamic.

Together with his teacher, Clement of Alexandria, Origen is the founder of the allegorical school of scriptural interpretation. In his *Commentary on John* he states several times that Mary is the symbol of the reflective life and Martha of the active life:

> One could say that Mary is a symbol of the people of the nations, while Martha [is a symbol] of people of the circumcision . . . And not unpersuasively do they say, because of the way of life in the law of Moses, that it is said to Martha: "Martha, you worry about many things, but few things are necessary." For many commandments according to the letter of the law are needed for salvation, but few, upon which hang the whole law and the prophets, are needed that are legislated about love.[3]

Origen stresses that Mary stands "highest" over Martha and their brother Lazarus (cf. John 11:1–44) since she is more enlightened; Martha understands less and thus is more worldly.[4] Though his treatment of Martha and Mary is clearly hierarchical, Origen's description of the relationship of prayer to life is more nuanced. He states that "the entire life of the saint taken as a whole is a single great prayer. What is commonly called prayer, is then, a part of this prayer."[5] However, Origen's allegorical interpretation of the relationship of prayer and the active life influenced many Christian writers in the following centuries.

John Chrysostom (c. 349–407)

John Chrysostom follows Origen in praising Mary over Martha in every comparison that is made between the sisters.[6] However, he uses a literal or historical approach in contrast to Origen's allegorical method. In *Homily LXII* he speaks of Martha as the weaker of the two even though she appears more zealous (2).

Chrysostom also contrasts the two women as disciple and minister in *Homily LXIII*. Mary is a disciple, one of the inner circle of Jesus' closest friends, while Martha is described as "ministering" (Greek *diakonein*), giving service. He approves of this type of activity but stresses that Mary's role as disciple is greater. Jesus' presence signaled the presence of the kingdom and Mary recognized this, while Martha, still busy serving, did not.

Augustine of Hippo (354–430)

The most important commentator on this theme in the patristic period is Augustine of Hippo, who discusses the relationship of Martha and Mary in several sermons.[7] He stresses that Mary's role is better than Martha's and builds his case in several ways.

In *Sermon 103* on Luke 10:38–42 Augustine contrasts feeding Christ in the flesh with being fed by him in the Spirit. Martha is busy with many things while Mary is gazing "on the one thing."[8] Christ admonishes Martha and calls her attention to the fact that Mary has chosen "only one thing" (Luke 10:42).

Augustine stresses that deeds done for the poor are truly good and must be done (5). Yet the dichotomy remains since "all this is good, yet what Mary chose is better."[9] Actions done in love are good but are insufficient since it is gazing at the Lord, being nourished by his Word, which is the truly good. Augustine places the relationship between serving and listening to the Word in an eschatological perspective. When Martha comes to "her home country,"[10] that is, heaven, there will not be anyone to feed, clothe, and assist. But those who have been like Mary, who have chosen what she chose, will find that their choice "will be full and complete there."[11] Therefore, we need to prepare for dwelling in the "home country" by learning how to be fed by the Lord. Being fed (Mary's choice) is thus better than "feeding others" (Martha's role), even though Martha's role is necessary. However, this emphasis does lead one to be somewhat disheartened since the active life is interpreted as distinctly second-best.

In *Sermon 104*, which also focuses on this text, Augustine makes a rhetorical statement: if Jesus was really reprimanding Martha for her service, then "let people all give up ministering to the needy; let them all choose the better part, which shall not be taken away from them . . . Let the works of mercy be laid aside, everything be concentrated on the one science,"[12] for after all, the Gospel itself says that Jesus judged Mary's part to be better.

But it is not that simple. We need to look at what Martha was doing: a long list of chores that are never-ending in this life. But Mary had chosen one thing and that thing would last in the world to come: "the single unity of charity."[13] In the next life active service will be taken from us but the "one thing necessary" will be ours forever: "Toil, you see, will be taken away from you, so that rest may be given you. You, my dear, are still on the high seas; she is already in port."[14]

In these two women, says Augustine, we find two kinds of life: "present and future life, toilsome and restful, miserable and beatific, temporal and eternal life."[15] Martha's life is the image of "things present, in Mary that of things to come."[16] Both are necessary, each in their own time, but Mary's choice has to begin here in this life in our contemplation of the Word. But even though Martha's service is judged as not as ultimately important in relation to Mary's, still it is not without merit. The need for Martha-type service will eventually end: "The hard work will be taken away, but the reward will be paid."[17]

Augustine reminds his people that the service of hospitality and the works of mercy are done to Christ: "When you did it for one of these least of mine, you did it for me (Matt 25:40)."[18]

Quoting Matthew 5:6, "Blessed are those who are hungry and thirsty for justice, because they shall be satisfied," Augustine describes Mary, seated at the feet of the "the storehouse of justice," receiving some crumbs, for "she was enjoying truth, listening to truth, avid for truth, longing for truth. In her hunger she was eating truth, drinking it in her thirst."[19] The crumbs Mary was receiving will eventually be fed to us from the full table of the Lord in the next life.

"The one thing necessary, the better part" of which Jesus speaks, is God. In *Sermon* 255 Augustine states this plainly: "So we shall not be in need of anything, and that's why we shall be blessed. We shall be full, you see, but of our God; and all these things that we desire here as being so important, that's what he will be for us."[20] All earthly needs will be gone and God will satisfy us utterly and completely.

Augustine presents Martha and Mary in a hierarchy of values, with Mary's part as more valuable, because of his eschatological vision. Martha represents the Church of the present and Mary the Church of the future.[21] This world will pass away and with it the call to minister to the hungry, the cold, the imprisoned, and all those in need. Mary's choice, to listen to the Word and be nourished, begins here and will come to its fullness after death, when we will see God face to face.

What Mary learns, truth and justice, is the foundation of what Martha is doing: acts of mercy and justice, doing the truth in love. Augustine's dualistic vision thus contains a seed of unity: the works of Martha are undergirded by the understanding of Mary of the Word who is Truth, Justice, and Love. This insight most probably comes from his own experience, since as a busy pastoral bishop Augustine lived a life of prayer and intense activity. Perhaps he "envied Mary's repose, her quiet and not her perfection, which is for the Parousia."[22] The result was that his interpretation became the normative one in the history of Christian spirituality even to our own day.

Gregory the Great (540–604)

It is from Gregory the Great, theologian and pope, that we receive a clear description of the two lives, active and contemplative:

> The active life is: to give bread to the hungry, to teach the ignorant the word of wisdom, to correct the erring, to recall to the path of humility our neighbor when he waxes proud, to tend the sick, to dispense to all what they need, and to provide those entrusted to us with the means of subsistence. But the contemplative life is: to retain indeed with all one's mind the love of God and neighbor, but to rest from exterior action, and cleave only to the desire of the Maker, that the mind may now take no pleasure in doing anything, but having spurned all cares, may be aglow to see the face of its Creator.[23]

Following Augustine, he asserts that the contemplative life is superior to the active life: "The active life has much merit, [though] the contemplative life has more."[24] While the active life is not bad there is more merit in the contemplative one. For Gregory, the mixed life of action and contemplation is actually higher, though he generally restricts it to clerics and monks[25] and he does not mention women. Martha and Mary are symbols of these two ways: Martha's way is good but not best because it will cease with this life, but Mary's way begins here and "may be perfected in the heavenly country, because the fire of love which begins to burn here, when it sees Him whom it loves, will in His love blaze up the more."[26] Although the contemplative life is higher we do not remain continually in it on this earth and Gregory also speaks of the passing from one state back to the other:

> But we must know that just as it is the right order of living to pass from the active life to the contemplative, so usually it is useful for

the mind to turn back from the contemplative to the active, that by the very fact that the contemplative has inflamed the mind, the active might be more perfectly held.[27]

While Gregory's position on the symbolism of Martha and Mary is hierarchical, his teaching on the relationship of the two lives is actually more subtle since he also asserts that the mixed life of contemplation is actually the best. Here he foreshadows the thinking of Thomas Aquinas on this subject. We return to Gregory's position when we consider writers who speak of the unity between action and contemplation.

Bernard of Clairvaux (1090–1153)

Bernard—monastic reformer, mystic, and writer—dominated twelfth-century Europe in a dramatic way. His Cistercian reform of monastic life spread very quickly and he also preached the Second Crusade. He inherited and emphasized the patristic era's teaching that the contemplative life is higher than the active life.

In *Sermon 57 on the Song of Songs* Bernard describes the joys of the contemplative life as symbolized in Mary:

> And we have the contemplative, Mary, in those who, as time has passed, and God's grace has worked with them, have managed to reach a better and happier stage . . . they take insatiable delight in meditating on God's law day and night, and now and then, when the Bridegroom's countenance is unveiled, they gaze on it with a joy that cannot be told, and are transformed into its image, changed from glory into glory, by the Lord, the Spirit.[28]

Bernard continues Augustine's stress on the eschatological fulfillment that is found in Mary's contemplative life: "Martha is preoccupied with a whole lot of service, Mary is intent on the Lord's words. To Martha belongs the preparation, but the fulfillment belongs to Mary."[29] He also states that the active and contemplative lives have nothing to do with each other:

> Those who give their leisure to God should never under any circumstances aspire to the noisy life of their brethren who have duties

to perform. Let Mary always seem short of resources, and less adequate, and let her opt for her administration to be placed in other
tasks . . . A Pharisee gets cross, her sister complains, even the disciples mutter: in each case, Mary holds her peace, and Christ speaks
up for her.[30]

Perhaps Bernard's teaching also reflects the tensions in his own life:
called to monastic life he also was immersed in the political and social
affairs of his day and most probably yearned for the peace and quiet of
the monastery at Clairvaux.

The Cloud of Unknowing

There is no ambivalence in the teaching of the anonymous author of *The
Cloud of Unknowing*, a fourteenth-century English treatise on prayer.
The monastic author, possibly a Carthusian, was absolutely clear that the
contemplative life is higher and more important than the active life.

> Let me begin by saying that in the Church there are two kinds of
> life, active and the contemplative. The active life is lower, and the
> contemplative life is higher Within the active life there are two
> degrees, a lower and a higher, and within the contemplative life are
> also two degrees, a lower and a higher.[31]

These are not independent of each other but complementary since "neither can exist completely independent of each other."[32]

The author's description of the two is traditional: the active life
begins and ends on earth while the contemplative life begins on earth but
will end in eternity. The active life is troubled and busy with many things
but the contemplative life "sits in peace with the one thing necessary."[33]

In chapters 17–21 the author comments at length on the Lucan story
of Martha and Mary. The two sisters are the models of the active life and
the contemplative life for Christians and since the contemplative life is
higher, persons should not be criticized for following that path, whether
they are moving from one state of life to another or are young people
choosing this way.

While the two types of life are complementary, they cannot be combined successfully, that is, one cannot be a pure contemplative and active

at the same time. Commenting on Christ's words, "But only one thing is necessary," the author states:

> Surely he was referring to the work of loving and praising God for his own sake. There is no work greater. Finally, he wanted Martha to understand that it is not possible to be entirely dedicated to this work and the active work at the same time. Everyday concerns and the contemplative life cannot be perfectly combined though they may be united in some incomplete fashion.[34]

Though there are only two ways of life, there are three stages: the good and upright Christian life "in which love is predominantly active in the corporal works of mercy,"[35] then a second stage in which persons begin to meditate on spiritual truths (e.g., one's own sinfulness, the passion of Christ, the joys of eternal life). The first life is good and the second is better but the third, that of the contemplative life, is best of all. In this third stage "a person enters the dark cloud of unknowing where in secret and alone he centers all his love on God."[36]

The author reflects the intricate exegetical conflation of the figures of Mary of Bethany, Mary Magdalene, and the unnamed sinner of Luke in speaking of "this" Mary. He reverses the usual medieval emphasis on contrition and states that "Christians should follow Mary in devoting themselves to contemplation out of fervent love for Christ, rather than from a sense of penitence and remorse."[37]

Summary

The authors we have surveyed established the primacy of Mary's contemplative posture in contrast to Martha's role of active service. All were male authors, a sign of the dominance of male thought in spirituality during the patristic and medieval eras. This interpretation established the hierarchy of vocations in the Church and within religious life itself. Religious life and priesthood were "higher" ways of life than marriage and family life with its immersion in activity; within religious life the contemplative life was higher than any active form of ministry. In the medieval ages the Franciscan and Dominican mendicant orders for men offered a new way of combining contemplation and action in caring for the pastoral needs of the people, especially through evangelical preaching.

Women's desires to collaborate in this work were frustrated and they were confined to cloistered convents as Poor Clares and second order Dominicans.[38]

The hierarchy of vocations remained firm even in the twentieth century. Vatican II brought a fresh insight by asserting that "all the faithful of Christ of whatever rank or status are called to the fullness of the Christian life and to the perfection of love."[39]

The paradigm of the contemplative life as more valuable than the active life becomes the norm against which other voices with different views will be contrasted. It is to a second theme, the superiority of Martha over Mary, that we now turn.

Martha as Superior to Mary

The interpretation of Meister Eckhart (1260–1328), Dominican theologian, teacher, and preacher, is unique since he asserts that Martha is superior to Mary, "for she is far more spiritually advanced than Mary and is only trying to help her sister progress."[40] Martha asked Jesus to have Mary help her with the work "because she loved Mary and wished to make her more perfect."[41]

Eckhart's teaching on the roles of these two women is found in three sermons, two of which are on Luke 10:38–42. In *Sermon 2* he uses the images of virgin and wife to describe the roles of Martha and Mary. He translates verse 38 as "Our Lord Jesus Christ went up into a little town, and was received by a virgin who was a wife."[42] A virgin is one who is perfectly detached and receptive to God. But this is not enough. To remain a virgin, says Eckhart, is never to bear fruit: "If he is to become fruitful, he must of necessity be a wife."[43]

> A virgin who is a wife is free and unpledged, without attachment; she is always equally close to God and to herself. She produces much fruit, and it is great, neither less nor more than is God himself. This virgin who is a wife brings this fruit and this birth about, and every day she produces fruit, a hundred or a thousand times, yes, more than can be counted, giving birth and becoming fruitful from the noblest ground of all—or, to put it better, from that same ground where the Father is bearing his eternal Word.[44]

By joining the two seemingly contradictory roles of virgin and wife in one person, Eckhart anticipates the interpretation he will offer in *Sermon 86*, also on the same text.

He describes Mary and Martha as both having three distinct characteristics:

> Three things caused Mary to sit at the feet of Christ. The first was that God's goodness had embraced her The second was ineffable longing: She longed for she knew not what, and she wanted she knew not what. The third was the sweet consolation and delight she drew from the eternal words which flowed from the mouth of Christ.
>
> Martha, too, was drawn by three things which caused her to go about and wait on our dear Christ. The first was her respected age and a ground very rich in experience. This made her think that no one could do the work as well as she. The second was a mature power of reflection which enabled her to accomplish external works with the perfection that love demands. The third was the dignity of her great guest.[45]

Eckhart says that Martha asked for assistance not out of frustration because of the amount of work she had to do but because of endearment. She knew Mary better than Mary knew herself: "She realized that Mary had been overwhelmed by a desire for the complete fulfillment of her soul . . . Martha had lived long and well; and living gives the most valuable kind of knowledge."[46]

Martha feared that Mary was at Jesus' feet more for enjoyment than spiritual profit. The developing Christian tradition interpreted Jesus' words to Martha—"Martha, Martha, you are worried and distracted by many things; there is need of only one thing. Mary has chosen the better part, which will not be taken away from her" (Luke 10:41–42)—as a rebuke. In contrast, Eckhart asserts that Mary has chosen the better part because "she will become as happy as you."[47] In Eckhart's view, Martha had already attained great virtue and "was so grounded in being that her activity did not hinder her. Work and activity led to eternal happiness."[48] She was already superior in virtue and her fear was that "her sister would remain clinging to consolation and sweetness, and she wished her to become as she herself was."[49] So Martha was asking Mary to get up in order to become perfect.

This is indeed a reversal of the teaching we saw in Augustine, Gregory, Bernard, and others. As a Dominican whose charism was to share with others the fruits of one's contemplation, Eckhart realized that good works do not of themselves hinder the life of prayer. Thus Martha symbolizes the perfect interior freedom in which one's work does not impede progress in prayer and union with God.

Two additional sources in his writings point toward the integration of prayer and action. In *Sermon 33* Eckhart responds to Aquinas's teaching that the active life is better than the contemplative, "for in it one pours out the love he has received in contemplation" by asserting that "yet it is all one; for what we plant in the soil of contemplation we shall reap in the harvest of action and thus the purpose of contemplation is achieved."[50] Eckhart is thus moving toward a harmony of contemplation and action:

> In this life no person can reach the point where he is excused from outward works. Even if someone follows the contemplative life, he cannot altogether keep from flowing out and mingling in the life of action . . . What I say is that someone who lives the contemplative life may, indeed, must, be absolutely free from outward works when engaged in the act of contemplation, but afterwards his duty lies in doing outward works. For no one can live the contemplative life without a break, and an active life bridges the gaps in the life of contemplation.[51]

Eckhart's originality reflects the impetus of Western Christian spirituality in the High Middle Ages to begin to bring the sacred and secular together and his insights "represent the epitome and finest fruits of this tradition."[52] His dramatic reversal of the tradition gives hope and courage to the majority of persons who live in the world, not in the cloister, that one can live a life of deep prayer and intense activity. He can also be said to anticipate the core of the Ignatian vision of "seeking God in all things" and is not far from John Calvin's interpretation, which rejected the traditional active/contemplative dichotomy.[53]

Martha and Mary as One

A third theme in the tradition of Christian spirituality presents Martha and Mary, symbols of the active and contemplative lives, as one. Some writers who have previously emphasized the primacy of Mary over Martha, such as Gregory the Great and the author of *The Cloud of Unknowing*, nuance their interpretation when describing their mutual relationship. Thomas Aquinas makes an important contribution here. Francis of Assisi discusses the relationship of the two in the language of complementarity. Two writers, Aelred of Rievaulx and Teresa of Avila, describe the relationship in terms of the union of the two lives.

Mutual Relationship

Although Gregory the Great is quite firm in emphasizing the superiority of the contemplative over the active life, when he begins to apply this principle to the lives of preachers and pastors, he speaks of the "higher life," which combines both action and contemplation. He bases this on the example of Christ himself: "The contemplative life is far from the active, but when our incarnate Redeemer came, showing both lives, he united them in himself. When he worked miracles in the city, he spent the night in continuous prayer on the mountain."[54] The contemplative life will be aided by the active life, as love of neighbor increases one's love for God. Gregory urges us to "love God and our neighbor from the bottom of our heart."[55]

Gregory's conclusion is that a "mixed life" of contemplation and action is the best for preachers and pastors; next best is the contemplative life of those who practice chastity and silence; and lastly married people who lead good lives in the world.[56] He thus anticipates the teaching of Thomas Aquinas on the superiority of the mixed life in religious orders.

The monastic author of *The Cloud of Unknowing* had also stressed that the contemplative life is higher than the active life. But he also modifies his position by describing how both lives have a higher and a lower degree:

> Within the active life there are two degrees, a lower and a higher, and within the contemplative life there are also two degrees, a lower and a higher. But these two lives are so complementary that although they are quite different from one another, neither can exist completely independent of the other . . . In the lower degree of the active life a person does well to busy himself with good deeds and works of mercy. In the higher degree of the active life (which

merges with the lower degree of the contemplative life) he begins to
meditate on the things of the spirit. . . . But in the higher degree of
contemplation—such as we know it in this life—all is darkness and
a cloud of unknowing.[57]

A life of pure activity leaves much of human potential untapped. But
the unity of the higher degree of the active life with the lower degree of
the contemplative life leads to a person becoming, on the human level,
one's real self. The person "becomes increasingly interior, living more
from the depths of himself and becoming, therefore, more fully
human."[58] The higher degree of the contemplative is beyond nature
since one achieves this by grace, not by human effort.

These two writers thus allow for a mutual relationship between the
active and contemplative ways that is very beneficial both to the growth
of persons and to their ministry in the Christian community.

Francis of Assisi (1182–1226) uses the language of complementarity,
not hierarchy, in discussing the roles of Martha and Mary for the brothers who live in hermitages:

> Those who wish to live religiously in hermitages should be three
> brothers or four at the most; two of these should be mothers and
> they may have two sons or at least one. The two who are mothers
> should follow the life of Martha, while the two sons should follow
> the life of Mary (cf. Lk. 10:38–42) . . . The sons, however, should
> sometimes assume the role of the mothers, as from time to time it
> may seem good to them to exchange [roles].[59]

Francis makes a small but important contribution to this discussion by
introducing the practical instruction of exchanging the roles of active
servant and contemplative hermit.

The Mixed Life

The most significant writer on the mutual relationship of the active and
contemplative lives is Thomas Aquinas (1225–74). In the *Summa Theologica* (II.II) he discusses the division of life into active and contemplative
dimensions (q. 179), the meanings of the contemplative life (q. 180) and
the active life (q. 181), and the relationship between the two (qq. 182, 188).

Thomas both upholds the traditional understanding that the contemplative life is better than the active one and goes beyond this to assert the primacy of the "mixed life." The contemplative life is higher because it pertains to the intellectual life (not external things), can be more continuous, is more delightful, requires fewer external things, is loved for its own sake, is focused on the divine, and is commended by Christ in Luke 10:38–42.[60] The active life is the servant of the contemplative life, for it "prescribes certain works of the active life as dispositions to the contemplative life; which it accordingly serves rather than commands."[61] Moreover, the active life assists the contemplative life by quelling the internal passions of the soul: "Hence the work of the active life conduces to the contemplative, by quelling the internal passions which give rise to the phantasms whereby contemplation is hindered."[62]

For Thomas, the relationship between the two is complex. On the one hand, he speaks of the active life as preceding the contemplative in the order of generation,[63] but he also sees the active life as deepening one's aptitude for contemplation: "those who are more adapted to the contemplative life can take upon themselves the works of the active life, so as to become yet more apt for contemplation."[64]

His conclusion is that the mixed life of both action and contemplation is superior to a life of pure contemplation. Here he reflects the charism of his Dominican experience. His statement is placed within the context of discussing the merits of different types of religious orders:

> Accordingly we must say that the work of the active life is twofold. One proceeds from the fullness of the contemplation, such as teaching and preaching . . . And this work is more excellent than simple contemplation. For even as it is better to enlighten than merely to shine, so is it better to give to others the fruits of one's contemplation than merely to contemplate. The other work of the active life consists entirely in outward occupation, for instance almsgiving, receiving guests, and the like, which are less excellent than the works of contemplation, except in cases of necessity, as stated above. (q. 182, art. 1)[65]

Since he is speaking of religious orders, this is applied to their works. Thomas makes no application to the lives of the laity. But the implications are there: prayer and action are not necessarily only seen in terms of good and better, but in reference to the fruitfulness of sharing the fruits of prayer with others in loving action.

Martha and Mary United

Two authors speak of the unity of Martha and Mary. Aelred of Rievaulx (1110–67), English monk and writer, was convinced that contemplation and action were to be seen as a unity in the life of a person. Neither is to be neglected:

> For in no way should you neglect Mary for Martha, nor Martha for Mary. If you neglect Martha, who is to feed Jesus? If you neglect Mary, what use is it to you that Jesus has entered your house, if you do not savour his sweetness? Be sure, brethren, that in this life these two women should never be separated.[66]

Aelred especially stresses the need to do the corporal works of mercy: to feed the hungry, give drink to the thirsty, and to see in those in need Christ himself (Matt 25:31–46): "So, brethren, all the while that Christ is poor, and walks about the earth, and is hungry and thirsty, and tempted it is essential to have both these women in the house, i.e., to have both these activities in a single soul."[67] He is aware that this unity is for this life only and that in the life to come "Mary, i.e. spiritual work, will take complete possession of our house, which is our soul."[68]

Aelred's insistence on the unity of Martha and Mary is echoed by Teresa of Avila (1515–82), Carmelite mystic, reformer, and writer. Her presence in this analysis of the Martha and Mary text amid the many men who commented on the text reflects the situation of the Church down through the ages since women had few opportunities for education and those who wrote, such as Teresa, Hildegard of Bingen, and Catherine of Siena, wrote from their experience of prayer and life.[69]

In *The Interior Castle* Teresa describes progress and growth in prayer as moving from one mansion to another, until one reaches the seventh mansion, that of mystical union and spiritual marriage. It is here that Teresa speaks of the unity of Martha and Mary.

After describing in detail in the preceding six mansions the many extraordinary experiences of her prayer, we might think that Teresa will say that the end of prayer is enjoyment of God. That is far from her thought, for she states plainly that the aim of prayer is to show God how much one loves the Divine Spouse by doing good works and good works alone. Her principle of discernment is that authentic prayer bears fruit in love of God and neighbor "manifested in determination and active self-giving. Without that as their center, Teresa's cornucopia of experiences would be nothing more than a wild ride through the outer (or inner) reaches of the psyche."[70]

In the seventh mansion God has "now fortified, enlarged, and made the soul capable"[71] of birthing good works, which is the purpose of spiritual marriage.[72] Now Martha and Mary are one:

> Believe me, Martha and Mary must join together in order to show hospitality to the Lord and have Him always present and not host Him badly by failing to give Him something to eat. How would Mary, always seated at His feat, provide Him with food if her sister did not help her? His food is that in every way possible we draw souls that they may be saved and praise Him always.[73]

The person thus lives a unity of prayer and action, for "Martha and Mary never fail to work almost together when the soul is in this state. For in the active—and seemingly exterior—work the soul is working in interiorly. And when the active works rise from this interior root, they become lovely and very fragrant flowers."[74] In order to please God one puts aside desires for rest and ease in order to serve others, forgetting oneself for the sake of one's neighbor.

Teresa discusses this unity of contemplation and action as a fruit of union with God, the goal of our lives. Because it is placed at the end of the journey through the mansions, we might be tempted to think that few will experience this. However, Teresa states clearly many times that the goal of prayer is loving service, doing good works, growing in virtue.[75] Although we observe these fruits "at the end" of the journey, they are to be anticipated all along the way. The whole journey of faith and prayer is to be animated by loving service, thus a concrete demonstration of the unity of the love of God and love of neighbor.

A Contemporary Feminist Interpretation

As has been apparent, all the interpretations of the Martha-Mary text that we have considered have been by men, with the exception of Teresa of Avila.[76] This reflects the androcentric bias of Christian theology down the ages to our own century, for it has been men who have written the theology books and Scripture commentaries. The voice of women has been muted when heard at all.[77]

However, in our own era, the development of feminist theology, including feminist biblical hermeneutics, has added a distinctly new language to theology. In discussing the dilemma of Martha and Mary—the relationship of prayer and action—the literal and allegorical interpretations of male writers are no longer sufficient.

A significant voice in feminist theology is that of Elisabeth Schüssler Fiorenza,[78] and it is to her interpretation of the Martha-Mary text that we now turn.[79] She presents a fourfold strategy for reading this text and others: a hermeneutics of suspicion, a hermeneutics of remembrance, a hermeneutics of evaluation and proclamation, and a hermeneutics of imagination.[80] These strategies "are not undertaken in a linear fashion . . . but as critical movements that are repeated again and again in the 'dance' of biblical interpretation."[81] Use of her methodology will reveal a clearly different interpretation of this text than has been traditionally presented.

A Hermeneutics of Suspicion

The watchword of this moment is "what you see and read is not necessarily what is actually there" since the basic assumption of feminist hermeneutics is that the Scriptures, which were written by men, have an androcentric bias. Thus this hermeneutic "seeks to detect and analyze not only the androcentric presuppositions and patriarchal interests of the text's contemporary interpretations and historical reception but also those of biblical texts themselves."[82]

The Martha and Mary story is not assumed to be a feminist liberating text just because women are its central characters. Fiorenza rejects two interpretations: an abstractionist approach and an apologetic feminist reading. The first reduces the two women to theological principles and types, which is the classic symbolization of the women as representing the active and contemplative lives. She also discards a contemporary interpretation in which Mary is praised by Jesus for choosing to listen to his teaching in the posture of a disciple, instead of doing traditional women's work in the kitchen.[83] Fiorenza excludes this second interpretation because it highlights Christian women's role as disciples at the expense of Jewish women who continued to do the work of the house, forgetting that both Martha and Mary were Jewish women.

The use of the Greek word *diakonein* (service) (v. 41) is usually interpreted to mean "serving at table." The text reflects the postresurrection context of the early Christian community, seen in the use of the word *kyrios* (Lord) in verse 40. However, *diakonia* also means service to the community, including service of the word (Acts 6:5), and had "already become [a technical term] for ecclesial leadership in Luke's time."[84]

Our natural sympathies lie with Martha, who is being chided by Jesus; most people, especially women, would feel that Mary should be assisting her sister in the work of hospitality. But Fiorenza points out that the women are not the center of the story. It is the Lord's intervention that is the key: he chides Martha and praises the silence of Mary, which is the posture of a disciple who listens but does not proclaim.[85] Thus women are included in the circle of disciples but their ministry is to be limited.

A Hermeneutics of Remembrance

The second moment in the interpretation of the Martha-Mary text involves trying to reconstruct early Christian history in order to show the memory and heritage of women for the Church of today. Because Luke uses the word *kyrios* he is appealing to the authority of the risen Lord for what occurs in the story.

The early Christian community gathered in house-churches and so Martha welcomed the Lord into her house. *Diakonia* referred to the eucharistic table-service in the house-church and also included proclamation of the word. Does the story then imply that Martha was leading the small Christian community in *diakonia?*

Fiorenza's position is that Luke's interest in the text is to downplay the leadership roles of women and to use the authority of *kyrios* to silence Martha. She states:

> Luke 10:38–42 stresses that the *diakonein* of Martha is not the "one thing needful" and hence must be subordinated to "listening to the word." However, it must not be overlooked that the "good portion" chosen by Mary is not the *diakonia* of the word: it is not the preaching but rather the listening to the word. The characterization of

Mary as a listening disciple corresponds to the narrative's interest in playing down the leadership role of women.[86]

Luke, also the author of Acts, minimizes the role of women in the early Christian community.[87] While both women and men listen to the proclamation of the gospel and become disciples (Acts 8:3; 9:2; 17:12; 22:4), Luke tells us no stories about women preachers, missionaries, prophets, and founders of house-churches.

A hermeneutics of remembrance as applied to the Martha-Mary text demonstrates, says Fiorenza, that Luke's interests are to "silence women leaders of house-churches who, like Martha, might have protested, and to simultaneously extol Mary's 'silent' and subordinate behavior."[88] This can explain why women usually identify more with Martha than with Mary, suspecting that there was more going on than the text presents. This moment of "remembrance" casts a light into the deep shadows of the past to reveal that indeed there had to be significant ministry being done by women if Luke tried to curb their *diakonia* by appealing to the authority of the Lord.

A Hermeneutics of Evaluation and Proclamation

This hermeneutical task has two dimensions: to assess critically the values and visions the text enshrines in order to assist women today to name their alienation from and oppression within the biblical tradition and also to determine how the text is read and heard today.[89] Even though this text contains much that is oppressive to women, Fiorenza does not think that it should not be used in preaching and teaching. Rather, it must be presented in a new way to explore the hidden levels of oppression.

She gives four examples of how the text can function to critique the situation of women.[90] First, Mary's silent listening is a liberating example of how women can take time from "work" for themselves. Second, Martha is not described as the kind of self-sacrificing figure that has been the traditional role of women. Third, Fiorenza asserts that a theological reinterpretation of the meaning of service and servanthood must assert that disciples are no longer divided into those who serve and those who are served. Fourth, ministry should not be regarded as service but as an "equality from below," as a democratic practice of solidarity with all those who struggle for survival, self-love, and justice."[91] Women's ministry has to be reenvisioned as a practice of solidarity and justice since the category of service does not function as a liberating concept in a patriarchal Church that does not promote a discipleship of equals.

A Hermeneutics of Imagination

The final moment in this hermeneutical task is to articulate alternative liberating interpretations "which do not build on the androcentric dualisms and patriarchal functions of the text."[92] This can happen with the help of historical imagination, amplifications of the narrative, artistic re-creations, and liturgical celebrations. Fiorenza gives an example of this from the work of one of her students, Gena Marie Stinnett. The text is written from the perspective of Martha; she describes the conversation Jesus had been having with her and Mary and the others who had gathered in her house:

> By the time the teacher finished this story, evening had approached and it was time for sharing the meal. I asked Jesus if he would stay to eat with us. He said yes, and added: "Martha, don't go to a lot of trouble. Whatever you were going to have will be fine. Let me help you." We started toward the kitchen when one of the males hollered: "The women can go but you Jesus, stay here. After all we have important things to talk about and they don't really understand theology."
>
> But an Essene who had become one of the disciples travelling with Jesus said: "Isn't God's word for all people? Before I joined your movement I had always studied the Torah with other women. Are we women disciples to be excluded?" . . . And Jesus replied: "Susanna thank you for speaking out. You are much blessed by Holy Wisdom, for you are right." And he asked me to preside at the breaking of the bread and invited Susanna to say the blessing and to teach the Torah lesson for the day. There was grumbling among the men, but we women were excited by the new possibilities God had opened up for us.[93]

Evaluation

Fiorenza's methodology challenges biblical scholars, theologians, teachers, and preachers in the Christian community to take seriously the socio-political background of Scripture texts, their religious contexts, and their rhetorical interests.[94] The word of God is not immune from the conscious and unconscious use by the authors with an androcentric bias that is oppressive to women.

The use of this methodology as applied to the Martha-Mary text casts a different light on the traditional interpretation of the two women as symbolic of the active and contemplative lives. The challenge remains for all disciples, both women and men, to discover ways of integrating both dimensions in their daily lives, even as Fiorenza's reading of the text makes us aware that there is a great deal more to the text than the traditional approaches have included.

Conclusion

The Martha-Mary text is a good analogy of the struggles of the life of discipleship in finding ways to unite prayer and active service. A hierarchical approach that values one over the other is not useful because both have intrinsic worth. Eckhart's interpretation of exalting Martha over Mary, while attractive, still suffers from this dualism.

What is needed is a "both/and" dynamic of uniting prayer and action, of Mary and Martha becoming one in the life of a person. Though Teresa of Avila places this unity in the seventh mansion, the time of spiritual marriage and thus intense union with God, a more inclusive vision is to see the entire life journey of a person in faith, hope, and love as a conscious effort to combine intense prayer and loving action for justice, peace, and reconciliation.

Elisabeth Schüssler Fiorenza's interpretation of the text adds a caution to any simple reading of the classic story. Her feminist reconstruction reminds us that persons must do this from within the realities of their context, with attention to its socio-political-economic realities, whether of systemic injustice or an individual experience of oppression. What gives energy to the work of transforming the world, more specifically, the place in which we each live the gospel? It is living at the center of our being, who is God, as we act in the power of the Spirit to do the works of God, which are justice, love, compassion, and reconciliation.

Notes

1. The text used is the New Revised Standard Version Bible: Catholic Edition (Nashville, TN, 1993, 1999).

2. A very fine and useful study that surveys the interpretation of Mary and Martha together with their brother Lazarus, beginning with the Scripture texts through medieval writings is Heather Jo McVoy, "Those Whom Jesus Loved: The Development of the Paradigmatic Story of Lazarus, Mary and Martha Through the Medieval Period" (PhD diss., Florida State University, 1992). The aim of McVoy's study is broader than this chapter, for she also investigates the conflation of the several "Marys" in the Gospels (Mary of Bethany, the woman who anointed the feet of Jesus as depicted in Mark 14:3–9, and Mary of Magdala) in a broad survey of patristic and medieval writers.

3. Origen, *The Commentary on St. John's Gospel*, vol. 1, ed. A. E. Brooke (Cambridge: Cambridge University Press, 1896), no. 78, pp. 287–88. Private translation by Edward Dougherty, SJ. See also IV.10, XIX.4, XX.

4. McVoy, "Those Whom Jesus Loved," p. 79.

5. Origen, "On Prayer," in *Origen: An Exhortation to Martyrdom, Prayer, First Principles: Book IV, Prologue to the Commentary on the Song of Songs, Homily XXVII on Numbers,* trans. Rowan A. Greer (London: SPCK, 1979), XII.2, p. 104.

6. McVoy, "Those Whom Jesus Loved," p. 85.

7. These are *Sermons 103, 104, 169, 179,* and 255.

8. Augustine of Hippo, "Sermon 103," in *Sermons III/Vol. 4 (94A–147A) on the New Testament*, trans. Edmund Hill, OP, ed. John E. Rotelle, OSA (New Rochelle, NY: New City, 1992), no. 3, p. 77.

9. Ibid., no. 5, p. 78.

10. Ibid., no. 6, p. 79.

11. Ibid.

12. Augustine of Hippo, "Sermon 104," in *Sermons III/Vol. 4 (94A–147A) on the New Testament*, trans. Edmund Hill, OP, ed. John E. Rotelle, OSA (New Rochelle, NY: New City, 1992), no. 2, p. 82.

13. Ibid., no. 3, p. 83.

14. Ibid.

15. Ibid., no. 4, p. 83.

16. Ibid.

17. Augustine of Hippo, "Sermon 179," in *Sermons III/Vol. 5 (148–153) on the New Testament*, trans. Edmund Hill, OP, ed. John E. Rotelle, OSA (New Rochelle, NY: New City, 1992), no. 4, p. 301.

18. Ibid., no. 3, p. 300.

19. Ibid., no. 5, p. 301.

20. Augustine of Hippo, "Sermon 255," in *Sermons III/Vol. 7 (230–272B) on the New Testament*, trans. Edmund Hill, OP, ed. John E. Rotelle, OSA (New Rochelle, NY: New City, 1993), no. 7, p. 162.

21. Anne-Marie La Bonnardière, "Les Deux Vies, Marthe et Marie (Luc 10:38–42)," in *Saint Augustin et la Bible*, ed. Anne-Marie La Bonnardiere (Paris: Beauchesne Editions, 1986), p. 412.

22. Ibid.

23. Gregory the Great, *Homilies on Ezekiel* II.ii.8, quoted in Cuthbert Butler, *Christian Mysticism* (London: Armstrong, 1922, 1967), pp. 171–72.

24. Gregory the Great, *Moralium in Jacob* VII.VIB, quoted in McVoy, "Those Whom Jesus Loved," p. 123.

25. Bernard McGinn, *The Growth of Mysticism* (New York: Crossroad, 1994), p. 76.

26. Gregory the Great, *Homilies on Ezekiel* II.ii.9, quoted in Butler, *Christian Mysticism*, p. 172.

27. Ibid., II.ii.11, p. 173.

28. Bernard of Clairvaux, *Sermon 57 on the Song of Songs*, no. 11, PL 1463. The translations of the quotations from Bernard's writings were done by Nicholas King, SJ.

29. Bernard of Clairvaux, *Sermon II on the Assumption*, no. 7, PL 2143.

30. Bernard of Clairvaux, *Sermon III on the Assumption*, no. 2, PL 2144–46.

31. *The Cloud of Unknowing,* ed. William Johnston (Garden City, NY: Double-day Image, 1973), 8.3, p. 58.

32. Ibid., 8.3, p. 58.

33. Ibid., 8.4, p. 58.

34. Ibid., 20.2, p. 75.

35. Ibid., 21.2, p. 76.

36. Ibid., 21.3, p. 76.

37. McVoy, "Those Whom Jesus Loved," p. 191.

38. Caroline Walker Bynum, "Religious Women of the Later Middle Ages," in *Christian Spirituality: High Middle Ages and Reformation*, ed. Jill Raitt (New York: Crossroad, 1989), p. 121; J. A. Wayne Hellman, "The Spirituality of the Franciscans," in *Christian Spirituality: High Middle Ages and Reformation*, ed. Jill Raitt (New York: Crossroad, 1989), pp. 36–37; Grace M. Jantzen, *Power, Gender and Christian Mysticism* (Cambridge: Cambridge University Press, 1995). Jantzen describes Francis as placing Clare in a convent against her will since she and her companions wanted to join the men in the work of preaching: "Even so radical a man as Francis did not see his way clear to allow women to be unenclosed. Clare insisted that she had not left her home to become a Benedictine nun but to become a follower of Francis and of Christ in evangelical poverty," pp. 199–200. In contrast, Gabriel O'Donnell presents

the traditional view that women's participation in the new evangelical movements was always seen as cloistered life: "The 'second order' was made up of cloistered women who withdrew totally from the ordinary pressures and demands of human society in order to become perfect imitators of Christ" ("Mendicant Spirituality," in *Spiritual Traditions for the Contemporary Church*, ed. Robin Maas and Gabriel O'Donnell [Nashville: Abingdon, 1990], p. 88). This applied to both Franciscan and Dominican women.

39. *Lumen gentium,* no. 40.

40. McVoy, "Those Whom Jesus Loved," p. 183. In his *Commentary on John* (#130) Eckhart does present the traditional interpretation of Martha and Mary: "As long as we are not like God or are still undergoing the birth by which Christ is formed in us (Gal 4:9), like Martha (Luke 10:41) we are restless and troubled about many things" (*Meister Eckhart: The Essential Sermons, Commentaries, Treatises and Defense*, trans. Edmund Colledge, OSA, and Bernard McGinn [New York: Paulist, 1981], pp. 172–73).

41. John D. Caputo, "Fundamental Themes in Meister Eckhart's Mysicism," *The Thomist* 42 (1978), p. 204.

42. Meister Eckhart, "Sermon 2," in *Meister Eckhart: The Essential Sermons, Commentaries, Treatises and Defense,* trans. Edmund Colledge, OSA, and Bernard McGinn (New York: Paulist, 1981), p. 177.

43. Ibid., p. 178.

44. Ibid., pp. 178–79.

45. Meister Eckhart, "Sermon 86," in *Meister Eckhart: Teacher and Preacher*, ed. Bernard McGinn (New York: Paulist, 1986), p. 338.

46. Ibid., pp. 338–39.

47. Ibid., p. 342.

48. Ibid., p. 343.

49. Ibid., p. 342.

50. *Meister Eckhart: A Modern Translation*, trans. Raymond Blakney (New York: Harper Torchbooks, 1941), p. 111. Blakney numbers this sermon as *Sermon 3*, pp. 109–17.

51. "Saying 18," In *The Best of Meister Eckhart*, ed. Halcyon Backhouse (New York: Crossroad, 1995), p. 137. The text appears also in the "Fragments" section in Blakney's translation, p. 238. Richard Woods, OP, a scholar of Eckhart's works, in private correspondence stated that Blakney tended "to cite spurious works once attributed to Eckhart but rejected by more recent critical authorities . . . The teaching is certainly not alien to Eckhart's thought, and that may be the important point."

52. Blake R. Heffner, "Meister Eckhart and a Millennium with Mary and Martha," in *Biblical Hermeneutics in Historical Perspective*, ed. Mark S. Burrows and Paul Rorem (Grand Rapids, MI: Eerdmans, 1991), p. 130.

53. Commenting on Luke 10:38–42, Calvin stated: "Now this passage has been wickedly perverted to commend what is called the contemplative life. But if we aim

at bringing out the genuine sense, it will appear that Christ was far from intending that His disciples should devote themselves to idle and frigid speculations . . . But we know that men were created to busy themselves with labour and live well for the common good" (*A Harmony of the Gospels Matthew, Mark and Luke* 2.89–90 quoted in Alexander Loveday, "Sisters in Adversity: Retelling Martha's Story," *Women in Biblical Tradition*, ed. George J. Brooke [Lewiston, NY: Edwin Mellen, 1992], p. 174).

54. *Moralia in Job* 28, quoted in McGinn, *The Growth of Mysticism,* p. 78.

55. *Homilies on Ezekiel* II.ii.15, quoted in Butler, *Christian Mysticism,* p. 181.

56. He also allows that the grace of contemplation may sometimes be even given to those who are married. See *Homilies on Ezekiel* II.v.19, quoted in McGinn, *The Growth of Mysticism,* p. 74.

57. *The Cloud of Unknowing*, 8.3, 5, pp. 58–59.

58. Ibid., 8.6, p. 59.

59. Francis of Assisi, "Rules for Hermitages," in *Francis and Clare: The Complete Works*, trans. Regis J. Armstrong and Ignatius C. Brady (New York: Paulist, 1982), 1, 2, 10, pp. 147–48.

60. Thomas Aquinas, *Summa Theologica (ST)*, trans. Fathers of the English Province (London: Burns Oates & Washbourne, 1934), II.II, q. 182, art. 1, reply.

61. *ST*, q. 182, art. 1, obj. 2, p. 135.

62. *ST*, q. 182, art. 3, reply, p. 139.

63. *ST*, q. 182, art. 4, obj. 1, p. 141.

64. *ST*, q. 182, art. 4, obj. 3, p. 142.

65. *ST*, q. 188, art. 6, reply, pp. 274–75.

66. Aelred of Rivaulx, *Sermon XVII on the Assumption*, PL 195, 306. Private translation by Nicholas King, SJ.

67. Ibid., 306.

68. Ibid., 306–7.

69. See Grace M. Jantzen, *Power, Gender and Christian Mysticism* (Cambridge: Cambridge University Press, 1995), pp. 157–92. She points out that women wrote from the authority of their own experience, since the doors to the universities and theological schools were closed to them. She discusses Hildegard of Bingen, Gertrude of Helfta, Hadewijch of Antwerp, and Julian of Norwich.

70. Mary Frohlich, *The Intersubjectivity of the Mystic: A Study of Teresa of Avila's "Interior Castle"* (Atlanta: Scholars, 1993), p. 217.

71. Teresa of Avila, "The Interior Castle," in *The Collected Works of St. Teresa of Avila*, vol. 2., trans. Kieran Kavanaugh, OCD, and Otilio Roddriguez (Washington, DC: Institute of Carmelite Studies, 1980), VII.3.12, p. 442.

72. Ibid., VII.4.6, p. 446.

73. Ibid., VII.4.12, p. 448.

74. Teresa of Avila, "Meditation on the Song of Songs," in *The Collected Works of St. Teresa of Avila*, vol. 2., trans. Kieran Kavanaugh, OCD, and Otilio Roddriguez (Washington, DC: Institute of Carmelite Studies, 1980), 7.3, p. 257.

75. Teresa of Avila, *The Interior Castle*, VII.1.8, 4.12.

76. Early in his journals, Thomas Merton, Trappist monk and writer (1915–68), wrote: "What is the value of the Martha-Mary story? It seems to me that the literal sense is plain, and that the superiority of contemplation over action is stated there" (entry of August 6, 1949, in *Entering the Silence: The Journals of Thomas Merton,* vol. 2, 1941–52, ed. Jonathan Montaldo [San Francisco: HarperSan Francisco, 1996], p. 347). Merton will later struggle with interpreting his call to monastic life as embracing real concern for the world and its problems, demonstrated in his prayer and writing. See the chapter on Merton, "Speaking from Silence."

77. The three women named as Doctors of the Church by the Roman Catholic Church: Saints Catherine of Siena (1347–80), Teresa of Avila (1515–82), and Therese of Lisieux (1873–97), had at best minimal access to the educational opportunities of their days.

78. Among her many writings are *In Memory of Her* (New York: Crossroad, 1983) and *Jesus: Miriam's Child, Sophia's Prophet* (New York: Continuum, 1994). The development of Fiorenza's hermeneutical method can be charted in the succession of her publications. In *Bread Not Stone: The Challenge of Feminist Biblical Interpretation* (Boston: Beacon, 1984), she outlines a fourfold method: a hermeneutics of suspicion, of proclamation, of remembrance, and of creative actualization (p. 15). She expands this perspective in *But She Said: Feminist Practices of Biblical Interpretation* (Boston: Beacon, 1992) by delineating the historical, political, and theological steps of her hermeneutic and by engaging with particular texts. In this book she begins to use the image of dance that is so central to *Wisdom Ways* (Maryknoll, NY: Orbis, 2001). *Sharing Her Word: Feminist Biblical Interpretation in Context* (Boston: Beacon, 1998) adds a contextual perspective that builds on her insistence that "a critical feminist perspective must focus on those wo/men who struggle at the bottom of the kyriarchal pyramid of domination and exploitation" (pp. 77–78).

79. "Arachne—Weaving the Word: The Practice of Interpretation: Luke 10:38–42," in *But She Said*, pp. 52–76. This chapter is an expansion and revision of two earlier versions of the same material: "A Feminist Critical Interpretation for Liberation: Martha and Mary (Lk 10:38–42)," *Religion and Intellectual Life* 3 (1986), pp. 16–36, and "Theological Criteria and Historical Reconstruction: Martha and Mary (Lk 10:38–42)," in *Protocol of the Fifty-Third Colloquy: 10 April, 1986*, ed. Herman Waetjen (Berkeley, CA: Center for Hermeneutical Studies in Hellenistic and Modern Culture, 1987), pp. 1–12, 41–63.

80. Fiorenza, *Bread Not Stone*, pp. 15–22.

81. Fiorenza, *But She Said*, p. 52.

82. Ibid., p. 53.

83. Ibid., p. 59.

84. Ibid., p. 64.

85. Ibid., p. 62.

86. Ibid., p. 65.

87. She also describes the structural parallels between the Lucan text and Acts 6:1–6, which presents the relationship of listening to the word and *diakonia* (*Sharing Her Word*, p. 65).

88. Fiorenza, *Sharing Her Word*, p. 68.

89. Ibid., pp. 68–70.

90. Ibid., pp. 70–73.

91. Ibid., p. 73.

92. Ibid.

93. Ibid., p. 75.

94. Fiorenza's interpretation has been criticized by other scholars. See W. S. Anderson and the minutes of the overall discussion in *Protocol of the Fifty-Third Colloquy*, pp. 17–20, 41–63, and Adele Reinhartz, "From Narrative to History: The Resurrection of Mary and Martha," in *"Women Like This": New Perspectives on Jewish Women in the Greco-Roman World,* ed. Amy-Jill Levine (Atlanta: Scholars, 1991), pp. 161–84.

6

Evelyn Underhill:
A Practical Mysticism

Evelyn Underhill, an English Anglican, is a unique and significant mystic: a married woman, writer, and spiritual director, whose adult life in the twentieth century included a commitment to pacifism from the 1930s until her death in 1941. Her spiritual journey led her along paths of theological and psychological reflection on mysticism to an ever clearer understanding of the relationship between mysticism and social commitment.

Early Life and Spiritual Development

Underhill was born in Wolverhampton, England, on December 6, 1875, the only child of Arthur Underhill, a distinguished barrister, and Alice Lucy Ironmonger. She was baptized and confirmed as an Anglican, but her family was not interested in religion. The family home was in London. A solitary child, Evelyn made friends with two boys, Jeff and Hubert Stuart Moore, whose mother had died. She married Hubert in 1907.

She was educated at home and at a private school, and later at the Ladies Department of King's College, London, where she studied history, languages, botany, and art. On the eve of her seventeenth birthday she wrote: "I believe in God and think it is better to love and help the poor people around me than to go on saying that I love an abstract spirit whom I have never seen."[1]

Her path to relationship with God began with philosophy, especially Plotinus, and through exposure to the art of Italy during the trips to Europe that she took with her mother beginning in 1898. These experiences began to open her to a world beyond the material, a theme reflected in the three novels that she wrote.[2]

Gradually she began to be attracted to Roman Catholicism. In February 1907 she made a retreat at a Franciscan convent, St. Mary of the Angels, in Southampton. She left the convent midway through the retreat and then had a very powerful religious experience at home in which she "was converted, quite suddenly, once and for all by an overpowering vision which had really no specifically Christian elements, but convinced [her] that the Catholic religion was true."[3]

By this time she and Hubert Stuart Moore were engaged to be married; her desire to enter the Catholic Church distressed him greatly, so she decided to delay her entrance for a year. They were married on July 3, 1907, and later that year Pope Pius X published the encyclical on modernism, *Pascendi Dominici Gregis*. Underhill considered herself a modernist and realized that she could not compromise herself intellectually by becoming a Catholic.

As a married woman she supervised a large London house and entertained her husband's business colleagues and their mutual friends. On the surface she was the model of an early-twentieth-century dutiful wife. But the reality was quite different, for Evelyn Underhill exercised great influence through her writings, the most important of which is the classic study *Mysticism: A Study in the Nature and Development of Man's Spiritual Consciousness* (1911),[4] her ministry as a spiritual director, and her leadership of retreats. After her death in 1941, Archbishop Michael Ramsey said that "she did more than anyone else to keep the spiritual life alive in the Anglican church in the period between the wars."[5]

It is impossible to grasp the widening of Underhill's understanding of the Christian life and the nature of commitment without speaking of the influence of Baron Friedrich Von Hügel in her life. First as a friend who was very interested in her work, and later as her spiritual director from 1921 until his death in 1925, Von Hügel helped her bring her attraction to a "pure mysticism" into a framework in which she could experience the sacramentality of everyday life. She had gradually come to realize that she needed a communitarian structure for her faith, and in 1921 she returned to the Anglican Church as a communicant.

Under Von Hügel's direction she began to visit families in poor areas of London twice a week. From our perspective this might seem a bit patronizing, but Evelyn learned much from the families she grew to know and made real friends. Von Hügel insisted on this kind of visiting as a corrective to living a kind of "hot-house" spirituality, absorbed in the theory of mysticism. Balance in the life of active faith was Von Hügel's hallmark for those he directed: a basic framework of daily prayer, visiting the poor, and developing nondevotional interests (she did gardening and wrote plays).

In the early 1920s her perspective began to shift from writing about mysticism to giving retreats on various themes of the Christian life, first for women, then also for clergy. This was an enormous development in the Anglican Church at the time. Her ministry of spiritual direction, begun even before *Mysticism* appeared, continued to grow.

Her Interpretation of Mysticism

Underhill began to write on mysticism at the beginning of the twentieth century, when this experience was being interpreted in psychological categories.[6] She set out to do both a theological and a psychological analysis, which is demonstrated in her three earliest works: *Mysticism* (1911), *The Mystic Way* (1913), and *Practical Mysticism* (1914).

Mysticism is structured in two parts: the mystic fact and the mystic way. In the first, she defines mysticism, sets out its characteristics, and shows its relationship to vitalism, psychology, theology, symbolism, and magic. The second is a description of the stages of mystic consciousness, with many quotations from the writings of the mystics and an impressive bibliography.

Underhill revised this work in 1930. She deleted some sources, added others, and brought the whole work more into congruence with mainstream Christian theology (twenty years later there was much less concern with vitalism and magic in mysticism). Her own journey is reflected in the new stress on an incarnational mysticism and the emphasis on God as the first cause of mystic experience.

Distancing herself from the views of her contemporaries in 1911, she wrote:

> Mysticism, then, is not an opinion; it is not a philosophy. It has nothing in common with the pursuit of occult knowledge . . . It is the name of that organic process which involves the perfect consummation of the Love of God: the achievement here and now of the immortal heritage of man . . . it is the art of establishing his conscious relation with the Absolute.[7]

In another description she defines mysticism as "the art of union with Reality. The mystic is a person who has attained that union in greater or less degree; or who aims at and believes in such attainment."[8] The contemplative consciousness, which is the link binding all mystics, whether in contemplation of nature, God, philosophy, or in action, is "a faculty which is proper to all men, though few take the trouble to develop it."[9] Such contemplative consciousness is linked with artistic creativity and thus the mystic "is an artist of a special and exalted kind, who tries to express something of the revelation he has received."[10]

Mysticism flows from the deep desire of the human person to surrender to the Mystery of total love. Only Love explains mysticism, for Reality is living and personal. It is a real psychological experience, a transformation of the entire person through union with the living God. True mysticism is never self-seeking, never exhibitionist and self-centered, for one loses one's life in order to gain real Life.

In these earlier works, Underhill is at pains to establish mystical experience as an integral part of Christianity. She asserts that "the examination of Christian origins from the psychological point of view suggests that Christianity began as a mystical movement of the purest kind; that its Founder and those who succeeded Him possessed the characteristically mystical consciousness, and passed through the normal stages of mystical growth."[11]

Christ is the model of mystic experience, for he was "the first person to exhibit in their wholeness the spiritual possibilities of man."[12] Christian life and growth is a movement to attain the reality of the fullness of life, as described in John's Gospel (10:10). Underhill often stressed the theme of life in her writings, that the aim of mystic experience was Life and that the mystic journey is an organic process toward the attainment of the Life of God.[13]

The Mystic Journey

Underhill describes this journey to Life in five stages.[14] The first is *the awakening of the self to consciousness of divine reality,*[15] a sense of call to something radically new. The person's sense of gravity is shifted in an experience of conversion. The inner and outer worlds now look and feel different, "breaking old barriers, overflowing the limits of new conceptions, changing their rhythm of receptivity, the quality of their attention to life."[16] While this experience can happen at any time in life, Underhill focuses on ages eighteen or about thirty as prime moments for conversion, the first "before the crystallizing action of maturity has begun" and the second "at the attainment of full maturity."[17]

Sometimes this conversion is gradual, without any definite crisis. But Underhill sees this as exceptional; the inbreaking of the Divine is full of the "travail [that] is the normal accompaniment of birth."[18] This new consciousness is so sudden and so clearly imposed from without that it appears to have a supernatural character.

The second stage is *purification of the self*, the purgative way of the classic interpretation of spiritual growth.[19] After conversion, there is a great sense of contrast between oneself and God's holiness, a great distance between God and oneself. The response of the person is penance, mortification, and discipline in an attempt to overcome self-love and sin as its consequence. If God is indeed to be the only Reality in one's life, one is to be detached from all that is not God.

While purification is a lifelong process, this stage is the completion of conversion, "the drastic turning of the self from the unreal to the real life: a setting of her house in order, an orientation of the mind to Truth."[20]

Underhill uses the three vows of religious life—poverty, chastity, and obedience—to describe the process of detachment. Poverty is the stripping of the self, a casting off of material things. Chastity is purity of soul, "cleansed from personal desire and virgin to all but God."[21] Obedience, the abnegation of the self, leads to a holy indifference to the circumstances of life.

The companion process is that of mortification, the remaking of the self by breaking up one's egotistical attachments and cravings. The "old" and the "new" cannot coexist in the person and thus the need for penance, especially of the body, in order that there is space only for the new person. This stage can end abruptly and while the mystic's life must always be a disciplined life, he or she no longer needs to practice severe physical mortification.

In the third stage, *illumination of the self* or the illuminative way,[22] the language of betrothal becomes a central image. The person emerges from what is often a long stage of purification to apprehend reality in a new way. This is a "deep, intuitional knowledge of the 'secret plan,'"[23] a pervasive sense of God's transcendence and immanence in the world. The joyful sense of God's presence is that of betrothal, not yet the union of marriage. Yet at times the mystic is sure that the quest is ended. Much of the writings of the mystics describes this stage of the journey.

What the mystic now sees in heart and mind can be found in nature, in music and art, and in the specific quest for God. Now the "practice of the Presence of God" is the mystic's usual consciousness, contemplating the reality of God. Underhill stresses that this is a sense of a real presence, though one that is very difficult to describe.

It is in this stage that many of the phenomena with which mysticism is associated—locutions, auditions, visions—occur. The mystic sees and hears with the physical, imaginative, and spiritual senses. But this journey is not yet completed.

Underhill inserts a fourth stage, the *"dark night of the spirit,"* into the mystic journey, breaking the classic threefold experience.[24] This is the transition to union with God. It is another time of purification characterized by impotence, blankness, and solitude. Psychologically it is "an example of the operation of the law of reaction from stress,"[25] a period of fatigue following the intense mystical experiences of the illuminative stage.

Theologically, it includes the sense of abandonment by God, a sense of sin that is much more acute than experienced in the purgative way. The person is in a stage of "helpless misery"[26] in which one can do nothing. One's intellect and will appear powerless in an experience of emotional boredom and ennui, in which one's longings for the Beloved seem to have vanished.

The focus of the suffering of this stage is "to cure the soul of the innate tendency to seek and rest in spiritual joys; to confuse Reality with the joy given by the contemplation of Reality."[27] One desires to see God as God is and experiences incredible loneliness.

Finally, the path ends in a fifth stage, *union with God*, or the unitive way.[28] Underhill describes two types of this experience. The metaphysical mystic, who has spoken of the Absolute in impersonal and transcendent language, now experiences deification, the "utter transmutation of the self into God."[29] Other mystics for whom God is personal and intimate consummate their communion in spiritual marriage. In both types of union the mystic recognizes with astonishment "the transmutation of his salt, sulphur, and mercury into Spiritual Gold—on the other, the rapturous consummation of his love."[30] Since "the Mystic Way has been a progress, a growth, in love,"[31] the only proper end of love is union.

Underhill explains this experience psychologically as the remaking and transformation of the self, as all the dimensions of the human personality have now achieved light and freedom "and with the cessation of stress, power has been liberated for new purposes."[32]

Paradoxically, and vitally important for a theology of mysticism, Underhill asserts that this experience of union is lived in the world and is demonstrated in the lives of mystics by great fruitfulness and creativity. Union with God gives the mystic authority, conviction, serenity, and joy as one experiences living in God. One is united to God in a bond that will never be broken.

While few attain union with God in love in this stage of the journey, Underhill stresses that it is impossible to overestimate their importance for the rest of humanity. Although they dwell on top of the mountain, breathing a pure air, they are "the pioneers of humanity" and "our ambassadors to the Absolute,"[33] demonstrating that it is possible to attain union with God and that this transcendental experience is practical and enhances the life of others through the power of the love of God.

Mysticism and Action

A constant theme in Underhill's writings on mysticism is the link between contemplation and action, the fruitfulness of mystical experience. Quoting her favorite mystic, Jan Van Ruysbroeck, she stresses that "the truly illuminated man flows out in universal charity toward heaven and upon earth."[34] The aim of mystical experience is life in its wholeness (again echoing John 10:10), in which one looks "with eyes of love toward the world."[35]

Writing at the beginning of World War I in 1914, Underhill raises the question of whether her book *Practical Mysticism* is speaking of a topic utterly at odds with the struggle that the war effort will demand of the English people since many associated mysticism with an attitude of passive self-surrender. The temptation is to reduce mysticism "to the status of a spiritual plaything."[36] Underhill is convinced that

> on the contrary, if the experiences on which it is based have indeed the transcendent value for humanity which the mystics claim for them—if they reveal to us a world of higher truth and greater reality than the world of concrete happenings in which we seem to be immersed—then that value is increased rather than lessened when confronted by the overwhelming disharmonies and sufferings of the present time.[37]

She stresses the practical nature of the spiritual life, emphasizing that it is part of every person's daily life and that without it one is not a complete person. The function of a practical mysticism is to increase the efficiency, wisdom, and steadfastness of persons; it "will help them to enter, more completely than ever before, into the life of the group to which they belong."[38] Practical mysticism gives a new vision of the world, the ability to discern beauty in the midst of violence and war.

The effects of mysticism are twofold: transformation of the person, who becomes more real, and expression "in action something of the real character of that universe within which you know yourself to live."[39] Contemplation and action are *one,* giving a new intensity "wherewith to handle the world of things, and remake it, or at least some little bit of it."[40]

Mystical experience is not an end in itself, but it impels one to action, to creative acts, to be "a living, ardent tool with which the Supreme Artist works."[41] Mystics are artists, and the medium of their work is human life in its richness and complexity. They are healers of "the disharmony between the actual and the real"[42] and Underhill uses the examples of Francis of Assisi, Catherine of Siena, Joan of Arc, Teresa of Avila, George Fox, and Florence Nightingale as persons who were able to unite mysticism and action. In the early twentieth century the call was the same: to "work for mercy, order, beauty, significance: [to] mend where you find things broken, make where you find the need,"[43] to bring *real life* into ordinary life. Mysticism is the science of love and thus the action flowing from contemplation is concrete, practical love.

A Mysticism of Love

Underhill's writings describe a mysticism of love as surrender to the Mystery of love who is God. Such surrender is active and practical, involving the whole person. The search for God can only be explained in terms of Love. Such a mysticism is a real experience, of head and heart, for the person is transformed through union with the living God. While the creed, code, and cult of religion remained important for her, she believed that mysticism "is the intense heart of all practical religion."[44]

The experience of God demands and brings forth conversion, the desire to be like what was experienced, to share in the holiness and love of God. Indeed, what is sought is a like holiness, a desire that echoes the scriptural injunction to be "holy, for I the LORD your God am holy" (Lev 19:2). She wrote, "The difference between the saints and us is a difference in degree, not kind."[45]

Working from the insights of St. Augustine of Hippo, Underhill asserts that the love of God "requires all that they have, not only of feeling, but also of intellect and of power . . . the unflickering orientation of the whole self towards Him, ever seeking and finding the Eternal."[46] The union with God that is desired contains nothing of rapture, ecstasy, or unusual experiences; rather, it is "a union organic, conscious and dynamic with the Creative Spirit of Life."[47]

This union in love is possible only through prayer. The "seeking of the Eternal is actuated by love, the finding of it is achieved by Prayer."[48] Prayer is the beginning, end, and middle of the experience of love and union. The life of the Spirit is a balance between silence and action: silent seeking of the Eternal in prayer and loving action.

The fruit of prayer is seen in love as the cause of action that "urges and directs our behaviour, conscious and involuntary, towards an end."[49] In one of her retreats she cautions those listening to her that "unless we leave the retreat more full of charity, with a wide-spreading, energetic, redeeming love of souls—unless we are more determined to make the daily routine of religion into one of spiritual action—and unless that routine is so transfigured with God that we must do every bit of it as well as we can, we might as well not have had the retreat."[50]

Underhill understood that the unity between the love of God and love of neighbor "at last and at their highest become one love."[51] This is the very practical experience of contributing to the growth of the reign of God, which is not accomplished by humanitarian politics or theological restatement but only by holiness. This is the work of saints, and Underhill was convinced that this is a call for all, not just the canonized.

As one's interior life with God grows, so also should one's compassion and love for humanity. Underhill describes this unity: "They do not stand aside wrapped in delightful prayers and feeling pure and agreeable to God. They go right down into the mess, and there, right in the mess, they are able to radiate God because they possess Him."[52]

Underhill often quoted Teresa of Avila in her writings[53] and Teresa's understanding of Martha and Mary as one[54] is reflected in her image of the need to "knock down the partitions between the living room and oratory, even if it means tobacco smoke and incense get a bit mixed up."[55] She often gave her retreatants some practical questions to take home with them:

> Are we taking back a deepened lowliness, a vivid love of our neighbour, and a keen sense of the holy character of our daily work? Are we looking toward perfection in our daily jobs? These are the only proofs by which we truly find and know that God is present in those neighbours and in that daily work.[56]

The life of prayer and love is to be a fruitful life of service. Underhill asserts that "real growth is toward a life of service penetrated by and utterly united with a life of prayer."[57] Growth and service must not be divided since they are to go together from the beginning.

Underhill refers to the questions that Ignatius of Loyola directs the retreatant to ask: "What have I done for Christ? What am I doing for Christ? What ought I to do for Christ?" (*SpEx* 53). These become central to the life of love and are questions that are only "worth asking when souls are open towards Him. Having asked it with such purity of intention as we are capable of, than that which love makes us really long to do will be right."[58] We are called to use the gifts we have, not to pine after those we do not have.

At the end of her seminal work *Mysticism* she quotes Ruysbroeck on "Divine Fecundity":

> When we unite ourselves to God by love, then we are spirit: but when we are caught up and transformed by His Spirit, then we are led into fruition. And the Spirit of God Himself breathes us out from Himself that we may love, and may do good works; and again He draws us into Himself, that we may rest in fruition.[59]

The Meaning of the Spiritual Life

From the early 1920s on, the spiritual life—a real practical mysticism—and how to live it became the focus of Underhill's teaching and writing. The image of "center" dominates her thinking when she describes the spiritual life. It is "simply a life in which all we do comes from the centre, where we are anchored in God: a life soaked through and through by a sense of His reality and claim, and self-given to the great movement of His will."[60] It is marked by integration of the personality, a living unity between contemplation and action, and a new sense of power and vitality. Life in the Spirit expresses itself in work, prayer, self-discipline, and service.

Underhill believed in simple approaches to living the life of the Spirit. So she recommended to those she directed and in her writings a few basic essentials: unconditional surrender to the Divine (whom she often names Reality); a little silence and leisure for prayer and reflection; and a great deal of faithfulness, kindness, and courage. She stressed that these were possible for all who desired to live a spiritual life.

Yet she is very clear that this is a demanding life, for it is "the loving surrender of the soul to God for all His purposes, a total self-giving that welcomes pain and effort as a privilege to be shared with Christ. Christianity is a heroism. It wouldn't be worth having if it were not. Heroism requires the ingredients of the devoted life."[61]

It is the abundant life, lived in dependence on God. It is not an alternative to one's outward, practical life, but "it is the very source of that quality and purpose which makes my practical life worthwhile."[62]

Underhill never divides life into segments: it is all one. It is the demands of the Spirit that must come first and that must rule the whole of life. First things first, says Underhill, and God is First: "God is the only reality, and we are only real insofar as we are in God's order, and God in us."[63]

It is from the center of the circle that our action proceeds, and such all-embracing love is not possible "unless we have found the centre of the circle first . . . and it is at the centre that the real life of the Spirit aims first; then flowing out to the circumference—even to its most harsh, dark, difficult and rugged limits—in unbroken streams of generous love."[64]

Underhill's spirituality is rooted in that of the seventeenth-century French school of De Berulle and Olier. She pays debt to these mentors by describing the relationship of the person to God as a threefold experience of adoration, adherence (which she sometimes terms *communion*), and cooperation.[65]

Adoration of God is "the first and governing term of the life of prayer."[66] It is exclusive attention to God, "awe-struck delight in the splendour and beauty of God."[67] Adoration is the heart of prayer, not intercession or petition. The adoring surrender of the person to God is the essential foundation of intercessory prayer and action. We are to be totally surrendered to God, open to the Divine Immanence.[68]

The second movement is that of communion. The God whom we adore "pours out His undivided love on each of His creatures, and calls each into an ever-deepening communion with Him, a more complete and confident adherence."[69] Our conscious spiritual life begins when "we become aware of this creative action of God and are therefore able to respond or resist."[70] The inner depths of this communion is transformation in Christ as growth in God.

Such transformation leads to the third dimension: cooperation. Though we distinguish them, Underhill stressed that "communion and collaboration, adherence and intercession, can never be separated in experience."[71] Cooperation includes all the ways Christians make practical in the world their adoration and communion in and with God. The "ultimate object of all prayer is greater efficiency for God,"[72] for "God made us in order to use us."[73] While the word *efficiency* may connote some type of organized, time-managed approach to the work of God in the world, Underhill was stressing that prayer must show itself in the fruit of the works of love.

Prayer and Social Concern

It is from this perspective, worked out especially in the retreats that she gave from 1924 to 1936, that Underhill developed her synthesis of prayer and social concern. The first sign of her developing thought was in 1922, when she gave an address to the International Summer School of Social Services at Swanwick. She stressed that Christian regeneration leads to supernatural and psychological changes in the person. As these are linked, so is the response to God and others.

In the article "The Christian Basis for Social Action" (1925), she emphasized that all is sacred since everything is loved by God. Thus "one could not accept human conditions which made it impossible for others to lead a moral life."[74]

She expressed this integral link between one's spiritual life and the world. The spiritual life

> will be decisive for the way we behave as to our personal, social and national obligations. It will decide the papers we read, the movements we support, the kinds of administrators we vote for, our attitude to social and international justice . . . Therefore the prevalent notion that spirituality and politics have nothing to do with one another is the exact opposite of that truth. Once it is accepted in a realistic sense, the spiritual life has everything to do with politics. It means that certain convictions about God and the world become the moral and spiritual imperatives of our life; and this must be decisive for the way we choose to behave about that bit of the world over which we have been given a limited control.[75]

Commitment to Pacifism

While Underhill became ever clearer about the relationship between one's life of prayer and one's commitment to active charity, she was very reluctant to be associated with specific political or religious causes. Until the early 1930s she stressed that her work was to assist personal transformation.

This changed dramatically to a pacifist commitment in the 1930s as the war clouds first gathered over Europe and then burst forth in 1939.

She had supported Britain's involvement in World War I as an expression of her patriotism, and worked in the office of Naval Intelligence for Africa as a translator and writer of guidebooks.

By 1932 she was supporting European disarmament and in 1936 she became a member of the Peace Pledge Union and the Anglican Pacifist Fellowship. Her patriotism was now expressed as a commitment to pacifism and most of the writing that she did in the final years of her life concerned the Christian's response to war. This was a new approach and a significant development in her constant theme of the human person's relationship with God and with each other.

Underhill made a pacifist commitment and urged other Christians to do so because she came to understand that pacifism in the face of violence is the proper way to express the love of God. To love God means to give ourselves completely in love. She wrote:

> The doctrine of nonresistance is after all merely a special application of the great doctrine of universal charity . . . It is a courageous affirmation of Love, Joy and Peace as ultimate characters of the real world of the spirit; a refusal to capitulate to the world's sin and acquiesce in the standards of a fallen race.[76]

She was truly disturbed by the Church's response to World War II and saw the faith of the Church as very weak in the face of such great evil as the war. Its life of faith was so feeble and ineffective that it sought to please people, especially those in power, not God, and was afraid to risk and to suffer. She wrote, "We are forced to the bitter conclusion that the members of the Visible Church as a body are not good enough, not brave enough to risk everything for that which they know to be the Will of God and the teaching of Christ."[77]

But the mission of the Church is to be in the world to save the world:

> The whole of human life is her province, because Christianity is not a religion of escape but a religion of incarnation; not standing alongside human life, but working in and through it. So, she is bound to make a choice and declare herself on the great issues of that life, and carry through her choice into action, however great the cost.[78]

Pacifism, she wrote, can only be sustained by a supernatural faith that "love is the ultimate reality and must prevail."[79] She wanted every Anglican who believed that Christianity had a commitment to peace to join the Anglican Pacifist Fellowship. Her pacifism had an eschatological vision, for the pacifist was the forerunner and precursor of a world yet to come.

Some of the very last things that Underhill wrote were prayers for a prayer service on peace in the time of war. She died on June 15, 1941, in the midst of World War II in Europe and before the war had spread to the Pacific theater. It is interesting to speculate how she would have responded to the atomic bombing of Hiroshima and Nagasaki and the postwar revelations of the Holocaust. Her insistence on love meeting evil with love would have been challenged by these events, even as they challenge every believer's response to evil.

A Practical Mysticism

Underhill began her studies of mysticism and the mystic way in the early years of the twentieth century as part of her own quest for truth. Gradually she learned that the One she sought was not found in a vague "mystic experience" but is the God of Love. Through the influence of Friedrich Von Hügel her understanding of the Christian life was broadened and deepened into a practical sacramentality of all life in Christ. This experience of Christianity taught her what to do with her knowledge that God is Love and it ultimately led her to a pacifist commitment.

We thus see in her life the progression of faith and commitment from intellectual study of the mystery of God in human experience to her own experience of God in her life as real. She clearly understood that there is no separation of the experience of God from the daily reality of life, including the most pressing social and political problems of the world.

Notes

1. Quoted in Margaret Cropper, *Evelyn Underhill* (London: Longmans, Green, 1958), p. 5.

2. *The Grey World* (1904), *The Lost World* (1907), and *The Column of Dust* (1908).

3. Quoted in Dana Greene, *Evelyn Underhill: Artist of the Infinite Life* (London: Darton, Longman & Todd, 1991), p. 25.

4. Underhill was a prolific writer. In addition to her three novels, she wrote forty books, editions, and collections and more than 350 articles, essays, and reviews (Greene, *Evelyn Underhill: Artist of the Infinite Life*, [Darton, Longman & Todd, 1991, p. 37). *Mysticism* is her best-known work. She also translated and edited critical editions of some of the mystics: *The Cloud of Unknowing* (1912), Richard Rolle's *The Fire of Love* (1914), Jan Van Ruysbroeck's *The Adornment of the Spiritual Marriage, The Sparkling Stone, The Book of Supreme Truth* (1916), and Walter Hilton's *The Scale of Perfection* (1923). Her last major work was *Worship* (1936).

5. Quoted in Greene, *Evelyn Underhill*, p. 2.

6. See Chapter 2, "Mystical Experience: The Common Call," which contrasts Underhill's interpretation of the nature of mystical experience with that of William James, the author of *The Varieties of Religious Experience*.

7. Evelyn Underhill, *Mysticism* (New York: E. P. Dutton, 1911, 1961), p. 81.

8. Evelyn Underhill, *Practical Mysticism* (Columbus, OH: Ariel, 1914, 1986), p. 23.

9. Ibid., p. 28.

10. Ibid., p. 48.

11. Evelyn Underhill, *The Mystic Way* (Atlanta, GA: Ariel, 1913, 1992), p. 7.

12. Ibid., p. 43.

13. Ibid., p. 61.

14. See Underhill, *The Mystic Way*, pp. 48–56, for a concise summary.

15. Underhill, *Mysticism*, Part II, Chapter II, pp. 176–97.

16. Underhill, *The Mystic Way*, p. 51.

17. Ibid., p. 52. She wrote nearly a century ago. Today, perhaps "full maturity" could be dated in a person's forties.

18. Underhill, *Mysticism*, p. 177.

19. Ibid., Part II, Chapter III, pp. 198–231.

20. Ibid., p. 204.

21. Ibid., p. 205.

22. Ibid., Part II, Chapter IV, pp. 232–65.

23. Ibid., p. 233.

24. Ibid., Part II, Chapter IX, pp. 380–412.

25. Ibid., p. 382.

26. Ibid., p. 388.

27. Ibid., p. 395.

28. Ibid., Part II, Chapter X, pp. 413–43.

29. Ibid., p. 415.

30. Ibid.

31. Ibid., p. 428.

32. Ibid., p. 416.

33. Ibid., p. 414.

34. Underhill, *The Mystic Way*, p. 62.

35. Underhill, *Practical Mysticism*, p. 109.

36. Ibid., p. 12.

37. Ibid., pp. 12–13.

38. Ibid., p. 15.

39. Ibid., p. 179.

40. Ibid., p. 180.

41. Ibid., p. 182.

42. Ibid., p. 185.

43. Ibid., p. 186.

44. Evelyn Underhill, *Concerning the Inner Life* (London: Methuen, 1926), p. 31.

45. Ibid., p. 30.

46. Evelyn Underhill, *The Life of the Spirit and the Life of Today*, ed. Susan Howatch (Harrisburg, PA: Morehouse, 1922, 1994), pp. 156–57.

47. Ibid., p. 158.

48. Ibid.

49. Ibid., p. 157.

50. Evelyn Underhill, *The Ways of the Spirit*, ed. Grace A. Brame (New York: Crossroad, 1990), pp. 141–42.

51. Underhill, *Concerning the Inner Life*, p. 91.

52. Ibid., p. 93.

53. See Mary Brian Durkin, "Teresian Wisdom in Selected Writings of Evelyn Underhill," *Spiritual Life* 41 (Spring 1995), pp. 20–31.

54. *Interior Castle* VII.4.12.

55. Evelyn Underhill, *The Letters of Evelyn Underhill*, ed. Charles Williams (Westminster, MD: Christian Classics, 1943, 1989), p. 217.

56. Underhill, *The Ways of the Spirit*, p. 141.

57. Ibid., p. 97.

58. Ibid., p. 98.

59. Jan Van Ruysbroeck, *De Septem Gradibus*, cap. XIV, quoted in *Mysticism*, p. 435.

60. Evelyn Underhill, *The Spiritual Life* (London: Hodder & Stoughton; Harrisburg, PA: Morehouse, 1937, 1955), p. 32.

61. Underhill, *The Ways of the Spirit*, p. 155.

62. Ibid., p. 24.

63. Ibid., p.125. Underhill here attributes this quotation to St. Augustine, but Brame points out that in *Mysticism* she had correctly attributed it to Coventry Patmore's *The Rod, the Root and the Flower* (Grace A. Brame, "Evelyn Underhill: The Integrity of Personal Intellect and Individual Religious Experience as Related to Ecclesiastical Authority," *Worship* 68 [1994], p. 37).

64. Underhill, *The Life of the Spirit and the Life of Today*, p. 227.

65. Underhill, *The Spiritual Life*, pp. 58–59.

66. Evelyn Underhill, *Evelyn Underhill: Modern Guide to the Ancient Quest for the Holy*, ed. Dana Greene (Albany: State University of New York, 1988), p. 151.

67. Underhill, *The Spiritual Life*, p. 61.

68. Underhill, *Concerning the Inner Life*, p. 93.

69. Underhill, *The Spiritual Life*, p. 66.

70. Ibid., p. 44.

71. Evelyn Underhill, *The Collected Papers of Evelyn Underhill*, ed. Lucy Menzies (London: Longmans, Green, 1946), p. 93.

72. Ibid., p. 46.

73. Ibid., p. 75.

74. Greene, *Evelyn Underhill,* p. 95.

75. Underhill, *The Spiritual Life*, pp. 80–81.

76. Underhill, *Evelyn Underhill: Modern Guide to the Ancient Quest for the Holy*, pp. 205–6.

77. Evelyn Underhill, *The Church and War* (London: Anglican Pacifist Fellowship, 1940).

78. Ibid.

79. Underhill, *The Letters of Evelyn Underhill*, p. 288.

7

Thomas Merton: Speaking from Silence

In Thomas Merton we meet a man who was born in France, lived for a time in England, and finally spent his mature years in the United States as a Trappist monk, leading a life of prayer, silence, and penance, yet speaking with a strong and clear voice through his writing.

Merton was born in Prades in southern France on January 31, 1915. His father was from New Zealand and his mother was an American. He was baptized in the Anglican Church but religious practice was only an occasional experience of his youth. In 1918 his brother John Paul was born. When Merton was six his mother died of cancer and the following years found him in schools in France, England, and the United States, traveling with his itinerant painter-father. His father also died of cancer when Merton was sixteen. After a disastrous year at Clare College, Cambridge, he returned to the United States and earned his bachelor's and master's degrees in English from Columbia University in New York.

There he met some people who became friends for life, such as Dan Walsh, who taught philosophy, and Mark Van Doren, a noted poet.

Through their influence and that of others, Merton's search for meaning in life led him to a profound conversion and he was received into the Catholic Church on November 16, 1938.

After his reception he began to desire to become a priest and nearly entered the Franciscan Order. But after a retreat at the Trappist monastery of Our Lady of Gethsemani[1] in Holy Week of 1941, he felt his call was to this monastery near Louisville, Kentucky, which he entered on December 7, 1941. He made his solemn vows in 1947 and was ordained a priest in 1949.

From this point on we would expect that Merton, now Father Louis, would be a silent, prayerful presence in this very strict monastery, unknown to the world except to his family and a few friends. Yet the reality was vastly different, for Merton was extraordinarily gifted as a writer and it was through his books, ranging from his autobiography *The Seven Storey Mountain* and his published journals to studies of the prayer and the life of the Spirit, excursions into Eastern religious thought, and writings on monastic renewal and issues of social and political importance, that his voice was heard around the world.

His great desire, increasing throughout his monastic life, was to be a hermit and he finally began to live as a "full-time hermit" in 1965. He made only one trip outside the United States during his monastic life—to Asia in 1968 for a monastic conference in Thailand. There he died a tragic death from electrocution due to faulty wiring in a lamp on December 7, 1968, twenty-seven years to the day that he had entered Gethsemani.

Merton's Attitudes to the World

Thomas Merton joined the Abbey of Gethsemani full of contempt for the world and everything in it. He entered the Trappist Order the day Pearl Harbor was bombed; he had already had enough of the world's false values, which he had interiorized. Describing himself before his conversion as "a true child of the modern world, completely tangled up in petty and useless concerns with myself,"[2] he had been very depressed by the outbreak of World War II and decided that politics were more or less hopeless. He did have a vague sense of being responsible for the war because of his sins[3] but he did not know what to do except pray.

When he visited Gethsemani for the first time for a retreat during Holy Week of 1941, he was so overcome by the experience that he wrote:

> This is the center of America. I had wondered what was holding the country together, what has been keeping the universe from cracking in pieces and falling apart. It is places like this monastery —not only this one: there must be others . . . This is the only real city in America—and it is by itself, in the wilderness.[4]

He entered the monastery determined to forget about the world and everything in it, delighted to throw away his earthly passport in exchange for a new life. Reflecting on the person he was when he entered, Merton described himself as "a sort of stereotype of the world-denying contemplative—the man who spurned New York, spat on Chicago, and tromped on Louisville, heading for the woods with Thoreau in one pocket, John of the Cross in another, and holding the Bible open at the Apocalypse."[5]

To leave the world physically is one thing; to find the world once again after a period of growth and maturation is another experience all together. His first trip outside Gethsemani was in August 1948, seven years after he entered. In his journal he records a small shift in attitude:

> Going into Louisville the other day I wasn't struck by anything particular. Although I felt completely alienated from everything in the world and all its activity, I did not necessarily feel out of sympathy with the people who were walking around. On the whole they seemed to me more real than they ever had before, and more worth sympathizing with.[6]

By 1949, after the publication of *Seven Storey Mountain*, he is able to realize that his complaints about the world are perhaps a weakness since "the world I am sore at on paper is really a figment. The business is a psychological game I have been playing since I was ten. And yet there is plenty to be disgusted with in the world."[7] Merton comments that "perhaps the things I resented about the world when I left it were defects of my own that I had projected upon it."[8]

After the publication of *Seven Storey Mountain* the "world" reentered his life through the massive correspondence that began and continued for the rest of his life. Requests for prayer and for spiritual direction via letter as well as appreciation of his writings gave him a new sense of the struggles of Christians in the world. He could no longer shut the door of his life upon the cares of the world.

Thus in 1951 Merton was able to write:

> Actually, I have come to the monastery to find my place in the world, and if I fail to find this place, I will be wasting my time in the monastery . . . Coming to the monastery has been, for me, exactly the right kind of withdrawal. It has given me perspective. It has taught me how to live. And now I owe everyone else in the world a share in that life. My first step is to start, for the first time, to live as a member of a human race which is no more (and no less) ridiculous than I am myself.[9]

His journal entries in 1957 now speak of decidedly new topics of interest: modern physics, the communist mentality, history, and economics.[10] He begins to reflect on nuclear war, the Cold War conflict with the Soviet Union, and the need to read and understand the "signs of the times."[11]

But it was in March 1958, on another trip to Louisville, that the eyes of Merton's heart were definitively opened to the world. He stood on a street corner and experienced a profound awakening of sympathy and compassion for the world:

> In Louisville, at the corner of Fourth and Walnut, in the center of the shopping district, I was suddenly overwhelmed by the realization that I loved all those people, that they were mine and I theirs, that we could not be alien to one another even though we were total strangers. It was like waking from a dream of separateness, of spurious self-isolation in a special world, the world of renunciation and supposed holiness. The whole illusion of a separate holy existence is a dream . . . This sense of liberation from an illusory difference was such a relief and such a joy to me that I almost laughed out loud. And I suppose my happiness could have taken form in the words: "Thank God, thank God that I *am* like other men, that I am only a man among others." To think that for sixteen or seventeen years I have been taking seriously this pure illusion that is implicit in so much of our monastic thinking.[12]

Merton now rejoices that he is really a member of the human race in which God became incarnate and realizes that "there is no way of telling people that they are all walking around shining like the sun."[13]

Soon after this powerful experience he writes that he is in the process of coming out of a chrysalis, "fighting my way out into something new and much bigger. I must see and embrace God in the whole world."[14] It was from this vision and his new position of sympathy and compassion for the world that Merton's social voice developed.

Solitude and Compassion

The great thirst in Merton's life was for solitude, both interior and exterior, for God alone. He gradually became aware of the difference between true and false solitude: false solitude separates the person from others so that one can no longer give anything to them from the depths of one's spirit, while "true solitude separates one man from the rest in order that he may freely develop the good that is his own, and then fulfill his true destiny by putting himself in the service of everyone else."[15]

The journey to and in true solitude is the search for the true self, a pervasive theme in Merton's writings. Sanctity and being one's true self are identical: "For me to be a saint means to be myself. Therefore the problem of sanctity and salvation is in fact the problem of finding out who I am and of discovering my true self."[16] This is the task of using the gift of freedom "to share with God the work of *creating* the truth of our identity,"[17] a labor of great sacrifice, anguish, risk, and tears.

The false self wishes to exist outside of God's will and love, apart from reality and life. Thus the false self is an illusion since it is impossible to be "outside God," though persons certainly do try to make themselves the center of the universe. But "the secret of my identity is hidden in the love and mercy of God" and "therefore I cannot hope to find myself anywhere except in Him" and "if I find Him I will find myself and if I find my true self I will find Him."[18]

As Merton began to discover his true self and grow as a whole person, he became more open to the world, less condemnatory of everything outside the monastery, notwithstanding a critical stance toward Western secular values. His understanding of true solitude led him to write that the true self is not awakened "merely by loving God alone, but by loving other men,"[19] and that such solitude "is deeply aware of the world's needs. It does not hold the world at arm's length."[20] He gradually learned that "one's solitude belongs to the world and to God."[21]

The contemplative keeps alive "a little flame of presence and awareness and love in a world where it is very difficult for it to be kept alive."[22] Contemplative prayer transforms our visions so that we "begin to see all human persons, all the history of mankind in the light of God."[23]

In his office as master of novices Merton discovered that caring for the novices did not interfere with his solitude. Instead, "everything you touch leads you further into solitude . . . as long as you do not insist on doing the work yourself."[24] His new desert was called "compassion," in which God "sits in the ruins of my heart, preaching His gospel to the poor."[25]

In 1957 he began to read the works of Albert Einstein and discovered a kindred spirit in this scientist who had both a passionate sense of social justice and social responsibility and the desire for solitude, a need that grew as the years progressed. Merton remarks in his journal that he needs to make these sentiments his own.[26] Shortly thereafter he began to learn that the cares of the world called for his compassion in a striking way as he began to speak from the depths of his solitude.

Gandhi as Mentor

The world honors Gandhi for his courageous life of nonviolent action. It was in Gandhi that Merton found a mentor who taught him that political action was also religious action. His interest in Gandhi dated to his school days in England, when he argued about Gandhi's action with the school prefect: "I insisted that Gandhi was right, that India was, with perfect justice, demanding that the British withdraw peacefully and go home; that the millions of people who lived in India had a perfect right to run their own country."[27]

Years later in Gethsemani his reflections on Gandhi's writings helped to undergird his developing conviction that as a monk he must speak about the problems of the modern world. He discovered that Gandhi believed that "political action had to be by its very nature 'religious' in the sense that it had to be informed by principles of religious and philosophical wisdom."[28] Gandhi combined in his own person the "contemplative heritage of Hinduism, together with the principles of Karma Yoga which blended . . . with the ethic of the Synoptic Gospels and the Sermon on the Mount."[29]

Gandhi focused on truth and the liberation of his people, not the possible success of his tactics. His devotion to truth, *Satyagraha*, was a vow to die rather than to say what he did not mean. Gandhi's life demonstrated that political action can come from a profoundly religious basis, in contrast to the usual understanding of politics as purely secular. Here lies his special importance for Christians, says Merton, for "Gandhi emphasized the importance of the individual person entering political action with a fully awakened and operative spiritual power in himself, the power of *Satyagraha*, nonviolent dedication to truth, a religious and spiritual force, a wisdom born of fasting and prayer."[30] Our actions do speak of our inner being and reveal either our fidelity or infidelity to God and ourselves.

Gandhi was a model of integrity for Merton, since his life was totally committed to the way of love and truth. As a monk Merton recognized that he had to live in the Truth, which is the first essential for being what he is called to be. Writing in 1957 he said: "It is absolutely true that here in this monastery we are enabled to systematically evade our real and ultimate social responsibilities. In any time, *social responsibility is the keystone of the Christian life* (italics mine)."[31]

Thus Merton struggled with whether to speak out on some of the pressing social problems of his time, especially racism and war and nonviolence. On the one hand he writes in 1963 that "I do feel called by God to witness in some sense to His truth in the world, but because I have so badly lacked community I have also lacked direction and spiritual judgment, and when I think I am speaking for God, perhaps I am only after all trying to hear a favorable echo from dissenting groups which are opposed perhaps not to the 'world' but only to the 'establishment.'"[32]

And yet he is convinced that the monk, the solitary one, receives the gift of *parrhesia*, or "free speech," that "enables one to look at the world and state what one sees."[33] Writing in 1963 to Daniel Berrigan, SJ, who was very active in protesting U.S. military policies, Merton said: "What is the contemplative life if one doesn't listen to God in it? What is the contemplative life if one becomes oblivious to the rights of men and the truth of God in the world and in His Church?"[34] And so he spoke and his words encouraged some and outraged others, including his monastic superiors.

The Context of Merton's World

Merton began to write on war, peace, and nonviolence in the early 1960s, a time of heightened world tensions. That time seems very far away now that we live in the postcommunist era following the breakup of the Soviet Union. When Merton wrote, however, the Cold War between the Soviet Union and the West, especially the United States, was increasing in intensity. Each side was developing new and more deadly nuclear arms and competing to be the first with the newest form of mass destruction. The cost of armaments continued to escalate and talk of nuclear disarmament was seen as either foolish or treasonous or both. There was talk of "first-strike capability," that is, the ability of a country to launch nuclear missiles and destroy a good portion of the enemy's arsenal before they could launch their own missiles.

Some Americans built "fall-out shelters"[35] in their backyards, structures dug beneath the ground where the family could live for a time if there was nuclear war until it was "safe" to come out. Moralists and politicians debated whether the right to self-defense included shooting a neighbor who tried to enter a shelter that was only large enough for one family.

In October 1962 the world came very close to nuclear war during the Cuban Missile Crisis. The Soviet Union decided to send nuclear missiles to Cuba, only about 90 miles from the southern state of Florida. President John F. Kennedy threatened to use U.S. nuclear weapons if the ships carrying the missiles to Cuba did not withdraw. After some days of acute international fear of all-out nuclear war, the Soviet ships turned back.

The Church in the United States was not at all open to bishops or priests, let alone a Trappist monk, speaking out against U.S. military policies. Catholics in the United States had tried to be good American citizens, never critical of the government, in order to forestall the threat of anti-Catholic invective that Catholics could not be good citizens since they "took their orders from Rome." Although in the next few years more U.S. Catholic voices would be heard criticizing the country's military policies, and most especially the Vietnam War, in 1961 Merton's first writings on war and peace startled people. What was the author of so many popular books on spirituality doing by getting his hands dirty in secular affairs?

As we have seen, Merton had already undergone a long journey from rejecting and fleeing the world he left in 1941 to realizing that in the monastery he remained a person among others, sharing the joys and sorrows of people. The years of prayer and silence, yet filled with writing and major responsibilities in the monastery including being master of novices, were the fertile soil out of which the fruits of Merton's mature reflection on the urgent issues of the day emerged.

He wrote about racism at a time when the civil rights movement in the United States was at its height, stressing that both blacks and native Americans have had invented identities imposed on them. Echoing one of his most important themes, he emphasized that they needed to claim their "true selves," for the civil rights movement was not only about justice but was also a spiritual crisis in which "the truth and authenticity of the person's spiritual identity are called into question."[36]

But it was his writings about peace and nonviolence that made him most controversial. His views alarmed his superiors who thought that monks should not be writing about this topic, especially American monks. For was it not the patriotic duty of all American Catholics to support their country's policy on nuclear policy and deterrence? Merton said "no" loudly and clearly.

Attitudes toward War

In 1941 Merton had registered for the draft as a noncombatant, intending to serve as a stretcher-bearer or as an orderly in a medical hospital. In *The Seven Storey Mountain* he describes his decision, viewing World War II as a war of self-defense and thus just.[37] However, he was rejected by the Draft Board since he had lost so many teeth.

Gethsemani is located fairly near to a military base, Fort Knox. In 1949, eight years after he entered the monastery, he describes a change in his attitude toward hearing the artillery being fired in practice rounds each day.

For seven years it has given me a feeling of uneasiness in the pit of my stomach. Now I realize the Church's mission in the world. It makes no difference essentially whether the world be at war or at peace because the Church is going to emerge victorious anyway. The Kingdom of Christ is being established, and the crimes and stupidity of men and devils, instead of hindering our progress, is only pushing it forward . . . yet it is no contradiction to pray for peace, as the whole Church does, for peace is the will of God and peace depends on union with His will, war being the fruit of its volition.[38]

By the early 1960s Merton's views had changed considerably. He had begun to write on war and social issues for *The Catholic Worker,* the pacifist newspaper founded by Dorothy Day and Peter Maurin in the early 1930s. Here his views found a happy home. But in early 1962 he published his first piece in a journal with a more diverse audience, *Commonweal,* edited by lay Catholics. He stated that "we are no longer living in a Christian world" and that "the Christian ethic of love tends to be discredited as phony and sentimental."[39] He called for disarmament and for the resumption of moral sense and genuine public responsibility. To those who say, "But when has the Church condemned nuclear warfare?" he answers that total war is murder and thus no formal condemnation is necessary, for what is intended by the destruction of cities is genocide. Calling on Christians to see the danger of the times he wrote:

> We have to make ourselves heard. Christians have a grave responsibility to protest clearly and forcibly against trends that lead inevitably to crimes which the Church deplores and condemns. Ambiguity, hesitation and compromise are no longer permissible. War must be abolished. A world government must be established. We have still time to do something about it, but the time is rapidly running out.[40]

He compared the silence of the Church not speaking out on the evil of nuclear war to the silence of Catholics in Germany before and during World War II.[41] He subsequently invited Daniel Berrigan to speak to the monks at Gethsemani and became his friend and adviser.

Merton had become convinced that the conditions for a just war no longer existed in a world bent on stockpiling nuclear weapons for possible use. Nuclear war made no distinction between combatants and noncombatants (a condition of the "just war" theory) in targeting cities and thus is a radically new kind of war. Merton wrote that "a war of total annihilation simply cannot be considered a 'just war' no matter how good the cause for which it is undertaken."[42] Nuclear war is an offensive war and there is no adequate defense, thus demolishing another tenet of the "just war." The possession of nuclear weapons brings the world to the brink of global suicide, "a moral evil second only to the crucifixion."[43]

Merton and Pacifism

In 1948, reflecting on his reading of some materials on Catholic conscientious objectors, Merton stated that "it seems to me more and more that nowadays a Christian ought to be something very close to an *absolute pacifist*."[44] But in the 1960s Merton did not describe himself as a pacifist. Writing to Dorothy Day, who was a committed pacifist, he said:

> It is true that I am not theoretically a pacifist. That only means that I do not hold that a Christian *may not* fight, and that a war *cannot* be just. I hold that there is such a thing as a just war, even today there can be such a thing, and I think the Church holds it. But on the other hand I think that is pure theory and that in practice all the wars that are going around, whether with conventional weapons, or guerrilla wars, or the cold war itself, are shot through and through with evil, falsity, injustice and sin so much that one can only with difficulty extricate the truths that may be found here and there in the "causes" for which the fighting is going on.[45]

Merton argued for a limited or relative nuclear pacifism, as distinct from absolute pacifism. Aware that pacifists often have a very negative reputation as odd characters or Communists or both, he saw this as a specious argument against pacifism. Catholics should be nuclear pacifists since the nuclear war by definition is unjust and immoral, and he cites statements of Pius XII, John XXIII, and the French bishops condemning the use of nuclear weapons in support of this position.[46] Thus the task of the Christian believer is to protest and oppose their use "even to the point of refusing his cooperation in their unjust and immoral use,"[47] advocate disarmament, and become a peacemaker in thought, word, and action.

In 1962 he was forbidden by his superiors to publish any further writings about nuclear war (his reflections were then mimeographed and circulated as "The Cold War Letters"). But he also chided popes, bishops, and theologians for not condemning nuclear war. He waited anxiously while the bishops at Vatican II debated this issue, hoping that they would include a condemnation of nuclear war in *Gaudium et spes* ("The Pastoral Constitution on the Church in the Modern World").[48]

A Prophetic Voice Speaks of Peace

From his solitude in Gethsemani, Merton described the problems of his time as "basically spiritual"[49] since Christians did not live lives transformed in the charity of Christ. Thus they were acquiescing to a nuclear morality that said "better dead than Red." A mature moral conscience is not one that is formed only on external moral directives but "above all from an inner spiritual connaturality with the deepest values of nature and of grace . . . Such a conscience is rooted and grounded in human compassion and in the charity of Christ."[50] This is a view of conscience that is as relevant today as it was in the 1960s. We are called to make moral decisions with a conscience that judges in terms of love and not violence. Thus Merton wrote that it is

> above all vitally necessary to cultivate an inner ground of deep faith
> and purity of conscience, which cannot exist without true sacrifice.
> Genuine Christian action has, in fact, to be based on a complete sac-
> rificial offering of our self, and our life, in the service of truth.[51]

Merton asserted that without this specific moral basis we will betray Christ and the Church, thinking that we are defending the truth when we are only defending our wealth and security, both personal and national. He called Christians to a renewed moral sense and the resumption of genuine responsibility for the world.

He wrote of peace as living the Truth. The roots of war lie in fear, fear of the "enemy" but also fear of one's self.[52] Trust is gone since people cannot be sure that someone will not turn and kill them. Thus the enemy is a scapegoat who symbolizes all the evil in the world. Such scapegoats can be racial or ethnic or political or all of them together. Our minds are "just as filled with dangerous power today as the nuclear bombs themselves."[53]

Merton spoke clearly and with fervor of the Christian's moral duty to seek peace, pursue it, act for it, and pray for it. In 1957 he was already writing of his responsibility "to be a peacemaker in the world, an apostle, to bring people to truth, to make my whole life a true and effective witness to God's truth."[54]

The call of the Christian is to be a peacemaker (Matt 5:9), which is both a vocation and a task "to struggle in the world of violence to establish His peace not only in their own hearts but in society itself."[55] The first duty of the peacemaker is "to work for the total abolition of war," which is the "great Christian task of our time. Everything else is secondary, for the survival of the human race itself depends on it."[56]

To be a peacemaker is a total commitment, for "peace demands the most heroic labor and the most difficult sacrifice. It demands greater heroism than war. It demands greater fidelity to the truth and a much more perfect purity of conscience."[57] Peace is to be preached at all times and prayer and sacrifice "must be used as the most effective spiritual weapons in the war against war, and like all weapons they must be used with deliberate aim: not just with a vague aspiration for peace and security, but against violence and war."[58]

The Call to Nonviolence

Merton's voice for peace was not only strong in condemning policies and views that he saw as incompatible with the gospel, but he also urged a nonviolent resistance to war, a practical nonviolence. In the most extreme situation of imminent and inevitable nuclear war this would call "all sane and conscientious men everywhere in the world to lay down their weapons and their tools and starve and be shot rather than cooperate in the war effort."[59] Nonviolence is not a pragmatic strategy in the face of escalating nuclear fear but is "defense of and witness to *truth*, not efficacy."[60] Passive acquiescence to evil is not nonviolence.

Rather, a commitment to nonviolence is based on the Christian conviction that "Love and Mercy are the most powerful forces on earth" and therefore "every Christian is bound by his baptismal vocation to see, as far as he can, with God's grace, to make those forces effective in his life, to the point where they dominate all his actions."[61] This may call, after the example of Christ, for the laying down of one's life for one's friends.

Merton enunciated principles for a spirituality of nonviolence, a way of living peace in daily life.[62] The religious basis of Christian nonviolence is faith in Jesus Christ the Redeemer and obedience to his demands of love for all. Following Christ, the Christian is to enflesh the Beatitudes in one's daily life. Most important to Merton were Christ's injunctions to be poor in spirit and to be meek. Christian nonviolence is thus preeminently an experience of faith and not a "tactic" for getting things done. It springs from faith that the reign of God has been established and that the Lord of truth, peace, and justice already rules.

Merton asserted that while we can and must disagree with those who hold policies and positions that are antithetical to the gospel, we cannot judge the adversary to be totally wicked. Principles of nonviolence include openness, communication, and dialogue. He asked whether we are willing to learn something from the "enemy," even some new truth. Nonviolence demands much: humility and restraint, an end to a fanatic self-righteousness of person or cause, not seeking "immediate results" but great trust and hope in Jesus our Peace.

The task for Christians who see the intrinsic evil of war, especially nuclear war, is clear to Merton:

> Every individual Christian has a grave responsibility to protest clearly and forcibly against trends that lead inevitably to crimes which the Church deplores and condemns. Ambiguity, hesitation and compromise are no longer possible. We must find some new and constructive way of settling international disputes. This may be extraordinarily difficult. Obviously war cannot be abolished by mere wishing. Severe sacrifices may be demanded and the results will hardly be visible in our day.[63]

He repeats his conviction that "we still have time to do something about it, but the time is rapidly running out."[64]

At the time of Thomas Merton's sudden and tragic death in 1968 he had come to a personal synthesis of the relationship between faith and responsibility to the world Christ had redeemed. His writings on peace and nonviolence are an eloquent testimony of his passion for peace.[65]

Conclusion

Merton, perhaps the most public monk since Martin Luther, came to the Trappist monastery of Our Lady of Gethsemani after a troubled adolescence and early adulthood, relieved that he was leaving the world forever. But he learned that the world was not so easily left behind and as he came to a greater sense of inner wholeness in his personal journey, he began to experience himself as bound to all of humanity in Christ.

Throughout his monastic life Merton experienced an ever-increasing desire for solitude and the eremitical life. This grew in tandem with his conviction that the social and political problems of his day were rooted in a profound spiritual crisis. Thus he could not but speak from the depths of his solitude. His voice was welcomed, ignored, and rebuked by those who listened.

In this seeming paradox we see again the intrinsic unity between religious experience and commitment to justice and peace. The God who is loved in prayer is the God present in the world, most especially in those who suffer. The suffering can be various: material poverty, political oppression, living a lie rather than one's true self, the effects of national political decisions with regard to war, peace, and justice. Suffering is universal and thus committed compassionate love is never a stranger to the problems of one's time, whether of peace and war in the 1960s or the intricate challenges the world faces today to be a planet of justice, peace, and reconciliation.

Notes

1. The Trappists, members of the Benedictine monastic family, lead a very strict life of prayer, silence, and manual labor in community. When Merton entered the monastery in 1941, practices had hardly changed since the nineteenth century. Following the renewal of religious life after Vatican II, there have been many adaptations and changes in Trappist life but the core values remain the same.

2. Thomas Merton, *The Seven Storey Mountain* (London: Sheldon, 1948), p. 163.

3. E. Glenn Hinson, "*Contemptus Mundi—Amor Mundi*: Merton's Progression from World Denial to World Affirmation," *Cistercian Studies* 26 (1991), pp. 342–43.

4. Thomas Merton, *The Secular Journal of Thomas Merton* (New York: Dell, 1959), p. 155.

5. Thomas Merton, *Contemplation in a World of Action* (Notre Dame, IN: University of Notre Dame Press, 1998), p. 141.

6. Thomas Merton, *Entering the Silence: The Journals of Thomas Merton*, vol. 2, 1941–1952, ed. Jonathan Montaldo (San Francisco: HarperSan Francisco, 1996), p. 223.

7. Ibid., p. 283.

8. Thomas Merton, *The Sign of Jonas* (London: Hollis & Carter, 1953), p. 87.

9. Ibid., p. 314.

10. Thomas Merton, *A Search for Solitude: The Journals of Thomas Merton*, vol. 3, 1952–1960, ed. Lawrence S. Cunningham (San Francisco: HarperSan Francisco, 1996), pp. 132, 136, 150.

11. Ibid., p. 133.

12. Thomas Merton, *Conjectures of a Guilty Bystander* (Garden City, NY: Doubleday Image, 1968), pp. 156–57. The original reflections on this event are in his journal for that year: *A Search for Solitude: The Journals of Thomas Merton*, vol. 3, 1952–1960, ed. Lawrence S. Cunningham (San Francisco: HarperSan Francisco, 1996), pp. 181–82.

13. Ibid., p. 157.

14. Merton, *A Search for Solitude*, p. 200.

15. Thomas Merton, *No Man Is an Island* (New York: Doubleday, 1955), p. 185.

16. Thomas Merton, *New Seeds of Contemplation* (New York: New Directions, 1961), p. 31.

17. Ibid., p. 32.

18. Ibid., pp. 34–36.

19. Quoted in Hinson, "*Contemptus Mundi—Amor Mundi,*" p. 348.

20. Merton, *Conjectures of a Guilty Bystander*, p. 19.

21. Ibid.

22. Thomas Merton, *Thomas Merton in Alaska* (New York: New Directions, 1988), p. 74.

23. J. Norman King, "Thomas Merton (1915–1968)," in *Non-violence—Central to Christian Spirituality: Perspectives from Scripture to the Present*, vol. 8, ed. Joseph T. Culliton, CSB (Toronto: Edwin Mellen, 1982), p. 168.

24. Merton, *Entering the Silence*, p. 463.

25. Ibid.

26. Ibid., p. 146.

27. Thomas Merton, "Gandhi: The Gentle Revolutionary," in *Passion for Peace: The Social Essays*, ed. William H. Shannon (New York: Crossroad, 1995), p. 203.

28. Ibid., p. 205.

29. Ibid.

30. Ibid., p. 206.

31. Merton, *A Search for Solitude*, p. 151.

32. Thomas Merton, *Turning Towards the World: The Journals of Thomas Merton*, vol. 4, 1960–1963, ed. Victor A. Kramer (San Francisco: HarperSan Francisco, 1996), p. 350.

33. Thomas M. King, *Thomas Merton: Mystic at the Heart of America* (Collegeville, MN: Liturgical, 1992), p. 125. See also Thomas Merton, *The New Man* (London: Burns & Oates, 1961), pp. 58–59.

34. Thomas Merton, *The Hidden Ground of Love: Letters on Religious Experience and Social Concerns*, ed. William H. Shannon (New York: Farrar, Straus Giroux, 1985), p. 79.

35. This included even a Trappist monastery, the Abbey of the Genesee, in New York State. Merton comments: "What a grim joke that is! In all their innocence . . . Bl. Sacrament temporarily in the shelter with the monks etc. One shudders a little" (*The Hidden Ground of Love*, ed. William H. Shannon [New York: Farrar, Straus, Giroux, 1985]), pp. 145–46).

36. Thomas Merton, "The Root of War is Fear," in *Passion for Peace: The Social Essays*, ed. William H. Shannon (New York: Crossroad, 1995), p. 222.

37. Merton, *The Seven Storey Mountain*, pp. 310–16.

38. Merton, *Entering the Silence*, p. 293.

39. Thomas Merton, "Nuclear War and Christian Responsibility," in *Passion for Peace: The Social Essays*, ed. William H. Shannon (New York: Crossroad, 1995), p. 40.

40. Ibid., p. 47.

41. King, *Thomas Merton*, p. 130.

42. Thomas Merton, "Religion and the Bomb," in *Passion for Peace: The Social Essays*, ed. William H. Shannon (New York: Crossroad, 1995), p. 76.

43. Merton, "Nuclear War and Christian Responsibility," p. 46.

44. Merton, *Entering the Silence*, p. 203.

45. Merton, *The Hidden Ground of Love*, p. 145.

46. Merton, "Religion and the Bomb," p. 77.

47. Ibid., p. 78.

48. The bishops did condemn total warfare, declaring: "Any act of war aimed indiscriminately at the destruction of entire cities or of extensive areas along with their population is a crime against God and (humanity). It merits unequivocal and unhesitating condemnation" (*GS* 80).

49. Thomas Merton, "Christian Action in World Crisis," in *Passion for Peace: The Social Essays*, ed. William H. Shannon (New York: Crossroad, 1995), p. 89.

50. Ibid., p. 50.

51. Ibid., p. 51.

52. Merton, "The Root of War is Fear," p. 14.

53. Thomas Merton, "The Shelter Ethic," in *Passion for Peace: The Social Essays*, ed. William H. Shannon (New York: Crossroad, 1995), p. 26.

54. Merton, *A Search for Solitude*, p. 149.

55. Merton, "Nuclear War and Christian Responsibility," pp. 39–40.

56. Merton, "The Root of War is Fear," pp. 12–13.

57. Thomas Merton, "Peace: A Religious Responsibility," in *The Nonviolent Alternative*, ed. Gordon C. Zahn (New York: Farrar, Straus, Giroux, 1971, 1980), p. 113.

58. Merton, "The Root of War is Fear," p. 13.

59. Merton, "Nuclear War and Christian Responsibility," p. 46.

60. Thomas Merton, "Notes for *Ave Maria* (Non-Violence . . . Does Not . . . Cannot . . . Mean Passivity)," in *Passion for Peace: The Social Essays*, ed. William H. Shannon (New York: Crossroad, 1995), p. 325.

61. Merton, "The Shelter Ethic," p. 25.

62. Thomas Merton, "Blessed Are the Meek: The Christian Roots of Nonviolence," in *The Nonviolent Alternative*, ed. Gordon C. Zahn (New York: Farrar, Straus, Giroux, 1971), pp. 208–18.

63. Merton, "Peace," pp. 127–28.

64. Ibid., p. 128.

65. Merton's writings on peace, originally intended for publication in 1962, were finally published in 2004 as *Peace in the Post-Christian Era*, ed. Patricia A. Burton (Maryknoll, New York: Orbis Books, 2004).

8

Dorothy Day:
Prophet of Poverty

As Dorothy Day grew older, people would sometimes say to her, "You will be canonized a saint someday." She would retort, "I don't want people to dismiss me that easily." Now that the first steps toward her possible canonization are underway (and not without controversy, including resistance from her family), it is clear that whatever the outcome of the Church's investigations, Dorothy Day cannot be dismissed easily from the history of American Catholic life in the twenty-first century.

A Modern Catherine of Siena

It is not surprising to learn that Day has been compared to Catherine of Siena. Peter Maurin, who co-founded the Catholic Worker movement with Day, had hoped that she would be a modern Catherine of Siena, persuading the bishops of the United States to open houses of hospitality in every diocese.[1]

Rather than reliance on the hierarchy to initiate the works of mercy, Day's faith, love, and courage led her to a lifetime of direct service to the poor while her gifts as a writer made the vision of the movement concrete and challenging in every issue of *The Catholic Worker*.

There are some striking parallels between the lives of Catherine and Dorothy Day. Both were laywomen, not religious, although Catherine was a member of the Mantellates, a Dominican third order. Both were women of profound prayer whose loyalty to the Church led them to call it to account for its lack of gospel values. Both were peacemakers: Catherine tried to make peace among the warring factions of Italy while Dorothy's pacifist commitment led to confrontations with both Church (especially during World War II) and state—a pacifist stance is never congenial in a country with a gigantic defense budget and nuclear arms. Both traveled widely during their lives and attracted many followers.

But there are important differences. Catherine made a vow of virginity as a child, while Dorothy was a single mother of one daughter. She longed for marriage and permanent male companionship, but had to suffer the breakup of a relationship with a man she loved deeply because of her movement toward the Catholic Church. Catherine died at thirty-three and Day at eighty-three.

Eileen Egan, a close friend of Day's, recalled that she often quoted Catherine's words, "I have left myself in the midst of you, so that what you cannot do for me you can do for those around you."[2] She was also fond of Catherine's saying, "All the Way to heaven is Heaven, because He said I am the Way."[3]

Catherine's "two feet of love" are seen in Dorothy Day's commitment to poverty and prayer, all of which is suffused with her love of God and a commitment to love in action.

Born to Write

Dorothy Day was born on November 8, 1897, in Brooklyn, New York, to Grace Satterlee Day and John Day. She was the middle child of five siblings, with two older brothers and a younger sister and a younger brother.

Her father was a sports writer and when Dorothy was six the family moved to Oakland, California, so that he could take a new job. But the newspaper plant was destroyed in the San Francisco earthquake of 1906 (an event that she remembered all her life) and the family moved to Chicago. Dorothy was nine years old.

Like many American families of the time, the Days were nominally Protestant but seldom attended church. She asked her parents "why we did not pray and sing hymns,"[5] but they did not have an answer for her. When Dorothy was ten she began to sing in the choir of the local Episcopal Church of Our Savior and was baptized and confirmed.

Her family valued reading, education, and writing and she inherited her parents' love of literature and her father's writing talent. As a teenager she began to read the accounts of Jack London about the class struggle in the United States and England and Upton Sinclair's novel *The Jungle*, which described the conditions in the stockyards in Chicago, where she was living. Moved by these accounts of poverty and injustice, and the conditions she saw for herself when she took her baby brother in his carriage for walks in the poorest areas of the city, she desired "even then to play my part. I wanted to write such books that thousands upon thousands of readers would be convinced of the injustice of things as they were."[6]

At sixteen she enrolled in the University of Illinois on a scholarship and studied there for two years. As a college student she began to write for a local paper and to observe the social conditions of the times and the gap between the rich and the poor. Her profound social conscience was growing and she joined the Socialist Party at the university.

Her years of formal academic study ended when she was eighteen when her family moved to New York. She began to write for the *New York Call*, a socialist newspaper. Some of her assignments included covering labor meetings and she wrote about the "bread riots," strikes, and unemployment.

In 1917 she was arrested for the first time when she joined a suffragist protest at the White House in Washington, DC. While in jail she participated in a hunger strike, but wondered if the protests were actually doing any good. During this time of incarceration she read the Bible, but when she was released forgot about it.

Haunted by God

The next several years were a time of searching, drifting, and relationships that turned sour. Day had an abortion out of fear that the man she loved would leave her. Friends remembered that she talked of God and seemed "haunted by God."[7] She wrote an autobiographical novel *The Eleventh Virgin* and the five thousand dollars she earned for the screen rights in 1924 enabled her to buy a house in Staten Island, New York. This became a place of solitude for her writing.

Here she lived with her common-law partner Forster Batterham; they had similar political views but he was upset by her growing interest in religion. To her joy, she became pregnant but Forster was upset, since he opposed having children (his own and anyone else's). Day had become increasingly interested in Catholicism, which deepened the conflicts between them, especially since she had decided to have their child baptized. Their daughter Tamar Teresa was born in 1926.

The tensions increased between Dorothy and Forster and he left her in 1927. She was then conditionally baptized and entered the Catholic Church. After a few years of traveling in California and Mexico, she eventually returned to New York and began to write for *Commonweal*, a journal edited by lay Catholics. It was 1932 and the Great Depression had descended upon the United States.

A Prayer Answered

In December Day was sent on assignment by *Commonweal* to cover a hunger march in Washington, DC, organized by the Communists to call for legislation to combat the growing social injustice of American life that the Depression was making clear. As she watched the marchers, she felt the distance that her conversion to the Catholic Church had brought into her life: "I could write, I could protest, to arouse the conscience, but where was the Catholic leadership in the gathering of bands of men and women together, for the actual works of mercy that the comrades had always made part of their technique in reaching the workers?"[8]

After the march ended on December 8 she went into the unfinished Shrine of the Immaculate Conception and prayed a prayer of desperation and entreaty: "There I offered up a special prayer, a prayer which came with tears and anguish, that some way would open up for me to use what talents I possessed for my fellow workers, for the poor."[9] When she returned to New York, Peter Maurin was waiting for her at her apartment. Her true call in life was about to unfold.

The Catholic Worker Movement

Although Dorothy always insisted that Maurin was the real founder of the Catholic Worker movement, it is more correct to say that the two together demonstrated a synergy that led to the movement's beginnings and growth. Maurin, born in France, had been a teacher in a Christian Brothers' school, an itinerant worker in Canada, and a caretaker at a boys' camp in New York. He was convinced that the Church's social teachings had the power to change the social order, to remake society.

Maurin was the thinker while Day was the writer and practical organizer. He introduced her to the riches of the Christian tradition on economic and social issues. These included patristic writings, those of the saints, and papal encyclicals such as *Rerum novarum* by Pope Leo XIII (1891) and the very recent *Quadragesimo anno* written by Pius XI in 1931. Maurin had a vision of revolution, a "personalist, communitarian revolution,"[10] which he intensively began to communicate to her.

Maurin could and did sit for hours and demand people's attention as he philosophized. Day and other Workers produced the issues of *The Catholic Worker* (still only one cent today as in 1933) and fed the poor and clothed them in Houses of Hospitality. Maurin dreamed of "agronomic universities"—communal farms run on the principles of Catholic social teaching. Dorothy and others organized them but they were never a success.

In one sense, everything that Dorothy Day did from the day in December 1932 when she met Peter Maurin to her death on November 29, 1980, was simple and all of a piece: editing and writing for *The Catholic Worker*; founding Houses of Hospitality, where the poor could be fed and housed; running soup and bread lines; writing books and articles, and protesting the social injustices of each decade, from the Depression to the struggles of the farm workers in the 1970s. She lived a pacifist commitment during World War II and throughout her life, protesting nuclear weapons, actions that included some time in jail. She lived an intense life of prayer whose fruits were evident in her life.[11] She read the classics with a special love for Dostoyevsky (whose phrase from *The Brothers Karamazov*, "Love in practice is a harsh and dreadful thing," is symbolic of her life), was an opera lover, and a faithful listener to the Saturday afternoon Metropolitan Opera radio broadcasts in New York.

Her powerful personality led some people to wonder if the Catholic Worker movement would dissolve after her death, but more than twenty years later it continues to grow, with new Houses of Hospitality being opened in many American cities and *The Catholic Worker* being published by a new generation.

The Catholic Worker Vision

Dorothy Day's interpretation of the "two feet of love" is seen concretely in the vision of the Catholic Worker movement, which dates its beginning to May 1, 1933—May Day, an important socialist and labor holiday on which the first issue of *The Catholic Worker* was published.

In 1940, Day wrote of the "aims and purposes" of the movement: "The vision is this. We are working for a 'new heaven and a new *earth*, wherein justice dwelleth.' We are trying to say with action, 'Thy will be done on *earth* as it is in heaven.' We are working for a Christian social order."[12]

The Worker's vision is incarnational, recognizing the presence of Christ in all of reality, most especially the poor. "Love is the reason for our existence," she stressed.[13] She often said that the Sermon on the Mount is the "manifesto of the movement."[14] The "harsh and dreadful love" that she often spoke of meant that Christ is sought and found in every person, in every circumstance. This vision breaks down the traditional dichotomy between the "spiritual" and the "material," between religion and everyday life, and challenges the person of faith to make her or his life one of loving service to Christ present in the reality of life.

The Catholic Worker movement arose out of a sense of call and personal responsibility: "No one asked us to start an agency or institution of any kind. On our responsibility, because we are our brother's keeper, because of a sense of personal responsibility, we began to try to see Christ in each one that came to us."[15]

The vision and central values of the Worker challenged and continue to challenge many American cultural values: community rather than individualism, voluntary poverty in contrast to wealth and affluence, pacifism and opposition to nuclear weapons in a country that first used the atomic bomb on civilian populations and continues to feed a swollen defense budget, religious faith as the heart of one's commitment in contrast to the slogan that "religion has nothing to do with politics." Over the years ". . . the Catholic Worker community came to represent an even greater contrast to the prevailing American culture"[16] as the poverty of the Great Depression era gave way to the post-World War II focus on middle class respectability and a comfortable life in the suburbs.

A Seamless Vision

The values that are at the heart of the Worker's vision: voluntary poverty, community, love for all especially the least, personal responsibility, pacifism, and nonviolence, are woven from the "sincerity and seamlessness of [Day's] life."[17] It is a faith vision: God exists, God loves us and all people, we are called to make that love real in our lives. As faith is deepened, "we will see Christ in each other, and we will not lose faith in those around us."[18]

The power of Dorothy Day's presence was rooted in the integrity of her life. She lived what she believed and if that discomfited and challenged others, so be it. She was clear-headed about the failures of the Worker movement—it was not a paradise, community life was rugged and a struggle, poverty was not "nice" (it was dirty and uncomfortable)—but she would not retreat from nor weaken the force of her convictions of the kind of world Christ wanted people to establish and the way we are to live with each other.

Voluntary Poverty: The Non-Negotiable Commitment

Although Day was raised in a middle-class family, at an early age she began to be conscious of the poverty around her, first in Chicago and later in 1916 when she was eighteen and moved with her family to New York. As she traveled around this huge city, she realized that

> the poverty of New York was appallingly different from that of Chicago. The very odors were different. The sight of homeless and workless men lounging on street corners or sleeping in doorways in broad sunlight appalled me. . . . Above all the smell from the tenements, coming up from basements and areaways, from dank halls, horrified me. It is a smell like no other in the world and one can never become accustomed to it.[19]

When she found a job on the *New York Call*, one of her assignments was to become a "one person diet squad" and to live on five dollars a week. She rented a cheap room and found ways to eat sparingly: roasted sweet potatoes and fruit from pushcarts and meals of soup and bread for ten cents. Transportation was by foot and friendly reporters supplemented her food budget by taking her out for lunch or supper. While Day saw this assignment as a personal challenge, her articles emphasized not her own struggles but the poverty and squalor of the slum tenements around her.

Because the *Call* was a socialist paper, her job brought her in contact with many radical thinkers and writers of the day. Earnest and lengthy conversations and debates went on between anarchists and all variety of socialists about the kind of world they wanted to live in and how to change it. A critique of the poverty around them was central to their arguments. Reflecting back on this time of her life, Day wrote:

> On the one hand, as young people we were attracted to the people, to the poor, and we lived in slums and suffered in order to do the work we chose. Our was the natural virtue of voluntary poverty. We helped others, it is true, but we did not deprive ourselves in order to help others.[20]

Dorothy Day and Peter Maurin did not confuse voluntary poverty with destitution, which is the absence of the essentials of life: food, shelter, medical care, education, beauty, and the joy of life. She wore second-hand clothes from the donations that came to the Worker but she also bought second-hand books and loved to listen to opera and observe the beauties of nature.

The Fundamental Plank

The vision of the Catholic Worker implodes if voluntary poverty is removed from it. Day spoke of voluntary poverty as "the most fundamental and necessary plank" of the movement and stressed that "I do feel strongly that we must put everything we have into the work of embracing voluntary poverty for ourselves."[21]

Poverty is to be the constant experience of the Worker's life: "We need always to be thinking and writing about poverty, for if we are not among its victims its reality fades from us. We must talk about poverty, because people insulated by their own comfort lose sight of it."[22]

She contrasted the voluntary poverty of the Worker with the vow of poverty in religious life. Religious congregations usually begin in poverty but often become wealthy through accumulating property and buildings. The constitutions of religious congregations provide norms for living the vow of poverty, and the effect is "something neat and well-ordered as a nun's cell."[23]

In contrast, voluntary poverty is messy, uncomfortable, without limits, and with the power to take from one not only material possessions but one's time, privacy, a family keepsake—and one's idealism, sense of confidence in life and others, one's experience of God. Poverty is a desert in which everything is lost in order to gain what is essential.

In a society in which "more" is the goal and norm of life, voluntary poverty critiques these values with a daily witness that detachment from material things brings the gift of freedom: "Once we begin not to worry about what kind of house we are living in, what kind of clothes we are wearing, once we give up the stupid recreation of this world—we have time, which is priceless, to remember that we are our brother's keeper and that we must . . . try to build a better world."[24] The freedom that voluntary poverty brings is rooted in the trust that "we will always get what we need" and the reality of Christ's promise to "take no thought for what you shall eat or drink—the Lord knows you have need of these things."[25]

Another dimension of poverty and freedom is linked to the Worker's commitment to pacifism and nonviolence. Day wrote that "our whole modern economy is based on preparation for war, and this is surely one of the great arguments for poverty in our time."[26] The greater one's income and the more one buys, the more taxes one pays (all goods are taxed) and thus one is "helping to support the state's preparations for war exactly to the extent of your attachment to worldly things of whatever kind."[27]

For Day and Maurin, the choice to live in voluntary poverty is a decision of faith. To live an insecure life demonstrates radical trust in Christ, who also lived a poor life, often without a place to lay his head (Luke 9:58). The gospel paradox of receiving more than what we give away is obvious to her: "The more you give away, the more the Lord will give to you. It is a growth in faith. It is the attitude of the man whose life of common sense and faith is integrated."[28]

While the spiritual and psychological fruits of living in voluntary poverty sound wonderful, the reality is a daily challenge. Day described poverty in compelling language:

> Our poverty is not a stark and dreary poverty, because we have the security which living together brings. But it is that living together that is often hard. Beds crowded together, much coming and going, people sleeping on the floor, no bathing facilities, only cold water. These are the hardships. Poverty means lack of paint, it means bed-bugs, cockroaches and rats and the constant war against these. Poverty means body lice. A man fainted on the coffee line some months ago and just holding his head to pour some coffee between his drawn lips meant picking up a few bugs. Poverty means lack of soap and Lysol and cleaning powders.[29]

And these are not the hardest demands of the life of poverty, for "we suffer these things and they fade from memory."[30] Much more difficult is to "give up our own possessions and especially to subordinate our own impulses and wishes to others—these are hard, hard things; and I don't think they ever get any easier."[31]

The inner freedom that is the fruit of voluntary poverty takes a long time to take root:

> You can strip yourself, you can be stripped, but still you will reach out like an octopus to seek your own comfort, your untroubled time, your ease, your refreshment. It may mean books or music—the gratification of the inner senses—or it may mean food and drink, coffee and cigarettes. The one kind of giving up is not easier than the other.[32]

Day's Theology of Poverty

The life of voluntary poverty that was so crucial to Dorothy Day's vision of the Christian life has solid theological foundations. It is first a recognition that God is not only in the midst of the poor but "is on the side even of the unworthy poor."[33] By sharing the life of the poor in a real and radical way one finds God in ways undreamed of in the homes of the middle class and the wealthy.

Second, to be poor with the poor is to experience "a profound, redeeming revelation of God's presence and grace."[34] To believe in faith that God is with the poor is one thing, but to experience (in the midst of dirt, lice, and unpalatable food) the reality of God's presence in the most unlikely of persons is grace. To respond to such a call is to cast oneself on the providence of God in a radical way, trusting that in the midst of the hardships of this freely chosen life God's presence will be real.

Third, living voluntary poverty is an ongoing experience of conversion. The radical call of the gospel becomes flesh and blood in the poor with whom one shares daily life. One's "spiritual and cultural bearings" disappear and

> the warm feelings of self-satisfaction and the spiritual elation quickly vanish. Calling nothing their own, tossed into an unusual mix of human personalities, the Workers survive only by letting go of expectations, previous stereotypes and unchangeable truths about serving others . . . In this spiritual wasteland, people of faith can live only in blind faith and submit themselves to the transforming power of God's mysterious presence in the poor.[35]

Thus the image of the life of voluntary poverty as a desert is particularly appropriate, for the stripping of self and one's physical, psychological, and spiritual possessions in the midst of the poor allows one to become open and vulnerable to the transforming action of the Spirit. As Jesus confronted the central temptations of life, bread, honor, and power (Matt 4:1–11; Luke 4:1–13), so also the life of poverty that Dorothy Day embraced and motivated others to embrace can lead to a profound conversion to radical gospel living. But it can also lead to cynicism and giving up; there is no guarantee what will happen in the desert.

Lastly, poverty and love are inextricably bound together. Poverty as asceticism is not the whole story of Day's vision. Rather, she emphasized that poverty "is the only way we have of showing our love."[36] Sharing the life of the poor, offering hospitality (food and beds), listening to those who demanded unending amounts of one's time, living with people one would never choose to live with—all of this is explainable only in terms of love, a love that continues to give even when one's heart feels empty and one's hands are empty. The love of God and the love of neighbor—

Catherine of Siena's "two feet" of love—thus find concrete expression in Dorothy Day's commitment to voluntary poverty.

Voluntary poverty, the "fundamental plank" of the Catholic Worker vision as enunciated by Day and Maurin, is thus a choice for a radical way of life, one that involves real physical and psychological hardships of deprivation and the precariousness of daily life. Having theorized about voluntary poverty as a young woman before her adult conversion, she knew the difference between the "natural virtue" and the response to God's call in faith. Poverty as a desert of the "long loneliness" of life promised rich fruits, but they may be a long time in coming.

Over twenty years after Day's death, in a society and world in which the gap between rich and poor continues to widen, her vision of the necessity of voluntary poverty remains a powerful challenge to all Christians who wish to live the gospel's radical call to commitment and loving service.

"All My Life I Have Been Haunted by God"

Although Dorothy Day wrote a great deal about her life and the Catholic Worker, chronicling her early years, the relationship with Forster Batterham, her life with Tamar, and the experiences and growth of the Catholic Worker movement, there is a certain reticence in her writings about her relationship in prayer with God. Some things are said, but many more are hinted at.[37]

In her autobiography *The Long Loneliness*, published in 1952, she describes some early experiences of searching for God. Like many American families, Day's was nominally Protestant though they seldom attended church. She recalls that she heard very little of religion as a child and "yet my heart leaped when I heard the name of God."[38]

She recalls that as a child growing up with her brothers and sisters she "did not search for God . . . but took Him for granted."[39] She was taught to say some simple evening prayers but nothing else. Church services were not part of her childhood memories although a Catholic young woman who worked for the family did take her to Mass once. She remembers prayers in school (these were the early 1900s), such as saying the Our Father together.

When the family moved to California she began to spend time reading the Bible, and had a "sense of holiness in holding the book in my hands."[40] A Methodist neighbor began to take Dorothy to church and Sunday school with her and she entered into a pious stage: "I believed, but I did not know in what I believed. I became disgustingly, proudly pious. I sang hymns with the family next door. I prayed on my knees beside my bed . . . No one went to church but me. I was alternately lonely and smug."[41] At the time of the California earthquake in 1906, Dorothy was having dreams that "were linked up with my ideas of God as a tremendous Force, a frightening impersonal God, a Voice, a Hand stretched out to seize me, His child, and not in love."[42]

When the family moved to Chicago after the earthquake, Dorothy recounts meeting a neighbor, Mrs. Barrett, "who gave me my first impulse towards Catholicism."[43] Coming into the Barretts' flat to find her friend Kathryn, she saw Mrs. Barrett down on her knees, praying. She taught Dorothy how to pray and so "for many a night after that, I used to plague my sister with my long prayers. I would kneel until my knees ached and I was cold and stiff."[44] She described it as a game—playing saints with her sister.

Another religious influence was the sermons of John Wesley, which she read when she was thirteen; his evangelical piety was strongly attractive. Two years later, she wrote a rather self-conscious, pious letter to a friend. One of the delights of her life at the time was to take her baby brother for walks in the nearby park: "How I love the park in winter . . . God is there. Of course, He is everywhere but under the trees and looking over the wide expanse of lake He communicates himself to me and fills me with a deep quiet peace."[45]

In contrast, her adolescent sexual feelings were disturbing and seemed to have nothing to do with God:

> It is wrong to think so much about human love. All those feelings and cravings that come to us are sexual desires. We are prone to have them at this age, I suppose, but I think they are impure. It is sensual and God is spiritual. We must harden ourselves to these feelings, for God is love and God is all, so the only love is of God and is spiritual without any taint of earthliness.[46]

Reflecting back on her childhood and adolescence, Day wrote: "All those years I believed. I had faith. The argument of authority, of conscience, of creation—I felt the validity of these . . . I read St Augustine at this time and he spoke also of this love."[47]

All of this seemed to disappear in the next few years as she became absorbed in her work and her friendships with radical and socialist friends. As a university student she felt "that religion would only impede my work. I wanted to have nothing to do with the religion of those whom I saw all about me. I felt that I must turn from it as from a drug."[48] And yet paradoxically she continued to search for God:

> Many a morning after sitting all night in taverns or coming from balls at Webster Hall, I went to an early morning Mass at St Joseph's Church on Sixth Avenue and knelt in the back of the church, not knowing what was going on at the altar, but warmed and comforted by the lights and silence, the kneeling people and the atmosphere of worship.[49]

The Search Deepens

When Day became pregnant with her daughter Tamar, she was surprised to find that she began to pray daily. She did not pray on her knees, but while walking. She wondered, "Do I really believe? Whom am I praying to?"[50] At first she chided herself that she was praying simply because she was happy to be pregnant and so prayer was an opiate—the Marxian phrase "religion is the opiate of the people" played in her consciousness.

But then she realized that she was praying because she was happy, not because she was unhappy. This became a powerful motivation to continue praying: in thanksgiving, saying the *Te Deum* as she walked along the beach, praying to Mary while she did the housework. She began to attend Mass regularly on Sundays.

Her growing religious consciousness brought her into conflict with her partner, Forster, whose great love for creation had no room for the Creator. During her pregnancy she read the *Imitation of Christ* and decided to have their child baptized since she felt "it was the greatest thing I could do for my child. For myself, I prayed for the gift of faith."[51] When Tamar Teresa was born in March 1926, the young woman in the bed next to her offered her a medal of St Thérèse of Lisieux when Dorothy told her daughter's name. Dorothy replied, "I don't believe in these things" but the woman reminded her that "if you love someone you like to have something around which reminds you of them."[52]

Dorothy's journey continued. She had been reading Williams James's *Varieties of Religious Experience*, which led her to read Teresa of Avila's *Autobiography* and she "fell in love with her."[53] Step by step she moved closer to an explicit faith commitment and entering the Catholic Church but she "felt all along that when I took the irrevocable state it would mean that Tamar and I would be alone, and I did not want to be alone. I did not want to give up human love when it was dearest and nearest."[54]

This tension increased and she became ill; the doctors said her condition was caused by "nerves" and no doubt it was. Finally, in December there was an enormous explosion between Dorothy and Forster and he left her once again. This time she decided that she would not let him back into the house, for "my heart was breaking with my own determination to make an end, once and for all, to the torture we were undergoing."[55]

The next day she went to the nearby town of Tottenville and was baptized conditionally since she had been already baptized in the Episcopal Church. Sister Aloysha, who had accompanied Dorothy throughout this difficult time, was her godparent.

She made her first confession that day and received the Eucharist for the first time the next day. These were not consoling experiences: "I had no particular joy in partaking of these three sacraments, Baptism, Penance and Holy Eucharist. I proceeded about my own active participation in them grimly, coldly, making acts of faith, and certainly with no consolation whatever."[56]

In the first few months after she entered the church, she felt very alone, although a priest named Father Zachary in the parish of Our Lady of Guadaloupe in New York, became her confessor and helped her a great deal. He prepared her for confirmation and introduced her to the liturgy through the St. Andrew's missal. She was confirmed on Pentecost in 1928, and took the name Maria Teresa. She was now fully a Catholic.

The Retreat

When Dorothy Day entered the Church, she became a traditional Catholic of her time and throughout the post–Vatican II years. Thus, daily Mass, regular confession, spiritual reading, the Scriptures, especially the psalms, the Rosary, and the Benediction of the Blessed Sacrament were all essential parts of her life.

Two important events in her journey of faith were the retreat of Father John J. Hugo and her time of solitude in 1943. In 1940 her New Year's resolution was to "pay no attention to health of body but only that of soul."[57] This emphasis on the spiritual had been heightened in the preceding years when she was introduced to making retreats and then the retreat of Hugo.

In 1943 her friend Sister Peter Claver introduced her to Father Pacifique Roy, a Canadian Josephite priest stationed in Baltimore. They were all sitting around in the house at Mott Street having coffee "when Father Roy started to talk to us about the love of God and what it should mean in our lives. He began with the Sermon on the Mount, holding us spellbound, so glowing was his talk, so heartfelt."[58]

Day began to travel occasionally to Baltimore to attend days of recollection conducted by Father Roy. Her notes of those days speak of the rigor of Christianity, the call to sanctity, heaven as beginning here on earth. She wrote that "it was as if we were listening to the gospel for the first time."[59] The perspective of Father Roy and Father Hugo was of a sharp distinction between the Christian life and ordinary life and this appealed very strongly to her.

In 1940 a Catholic Worker retreat under the direction of Father Roy was planned for the Labor Day weekend at the Eston farm. Five priests and over one hundred laypeople made the retreat. Dorothy recalled that "Scripture became a love letter and retreat notes we took we kept rereading, going back to them to try to recapture that flow of rapturous assent to Truth."[60]

Roy told her that while he was holding retreats, the person giving this one was Father Hugo. At the time Hugo was a young priest of the Pittsburgh diocese. His retreat was based on that of Onesimus Lacouture, a Canadian Jesuit who had developed this particular pattern of retreat, which was very rigorous. Another retreat was arranged for August 1941 in Oakmont, Pennsylvania.

It was a serious, disciplined time: five days of complete silence, four conferences a day followed by an hour of prayer, and fasting. Hugo began by quoting St. Augustine: "He who says he was done enough has already perished."[61] She wrote that "there was not much talk of sin in our retreat.

Rather there was talk of the good and the better. The talk was of the choice we had to make and not to make between good and evil."[62] Hugo reminded the group about the seed falling into the ground and dying, and "presented the Gospels in the full meaning of their radical and uncompromising spirituality."[63] Day was very much attracted to this kind of spirituality and Hugo became her spiritual adviser for many years.[64]

In 1942 she made another retreat under Hugo that was focused on the "Four Great Truths": the supernatural, the Glory of God, the Supreme Dominion, and the Folly of the Cross.[65] One of the fruits of this retreat was a new sense of the way God was leading her:

> I have always been so sure I was right, that I was being led by God—that is, in the main outlines of my life, that I confidently expected Him to show His will by external events. And I looked for some big happening, some unmistakable sign. I disregarded all of the little signs. I begin now to see them and with such clearness that I have to beg not to be shown too much, for fear I cannot bear it. I need strength to do what I have to do—strength and joy and peace and vision. Lord, that I may see! That prayer is certainly answered most overwhelmingly in this retreat.[66]

The retreat in various forms continued for over a decade and Catholic Worker retreats of diverse forms were held for many years. Day made some changes in her life; she stopped smoking and drinking (though that was usually just a glass of wine with her Italian neighbors) and her speech lost its saltiness. The effects of the retreat in her life were profound: "It was hearing the Gospel anew that gave a new force to her character. It was a reinforced spirituality. And if there had ever been any questions about her course, they were gone now. She was on the track. Nothing could change her."[67]

Later Maryfarm near Newburgh, New York, became a retreat farm, an oasis from the overwhelming demands of the Worker houses in New York City. Retreats were absolutely necessary for Day:

> It is not only for others that I must have these retreats. It is because I too am hungry and thirsty for the bread of the strong. I too must nourish myself to do the work I have undertaken: I too must drink

at these good springs so that I may not be an empty cistern and unable to help others.[68]

A Time of Solitude

Eileen Egan, a close friend of Day's, gives us an insight into her prayer in the midst of World War II. They attended midnight Mass together in 1943 in Farmingdale, New York. Egan remembers that Dorothy

> prayed for all human beings, especially those who were suffering and dying. She prayed for all associated with the Catholic Worker and mentioned by name Joseph Zarrella and Gerry Griffin, then driving ambulances in the "theater" (strange word for war) in the Middle East.[69]

Such intercessory prayer was a continuing thread of her prayer all her life.

This description of her prayer occurred in the midst of a time of extended prayer and solitude. In September 1943 she announced in her *Worker* column that she would leave the Worker movement for a year to read, think, and pray. This was also linked with her increasing concern for her daughter Tamar's future.

This period of Day's life began with a time of prayer at the Grail, a woman's Catholic action movement in Ohio. Then she and Tamar moved to Farmingdale, Long Island, where Tamar attended an agricultural school and Dorothy took a room in an abandoned orphanage close to a Dominican convent. She saw Tamar each afternoon after school, but the rest of the day was her own: early morning Mass, two hours of prayer, and reading after breakfast. She describes her prayer at this time: "Sometimes I prayed with joy and delight. Other times each bead of my rosary was as heavy as lead, my steps dragged, my limbs were numb. I felt a dead weight. I could do nothing but make an act of will and sit or kneel, and sigh in an agony of boredom."[70]

She supported herself by reviewing books and writing articles. The year was actually only six months long since she "came to the conclusion . . . that such a hermit's life for a woman was impossible . . . Community, whether the family, or convent, or boarding house, is absolutely necessary."[71]

Day's Theology of Prayer

The tapestry of Day's lived theology of prayer includes diverse threads. The experience of the retreats gave her a new vision of the interplay of human and divine love. Without them she stressed that "I would never have a glimpse of this mystery, an understanding of it. I could never have endured the sufferings involved, could never have persevered."[72] Prayer gave her strength and courage to live the vision of the Catholic Worker movement: voluntary poverty, community life, a nonviolent pacifist commitment. Over the years, her writings and reflections,[73] seen most clearly in her column "On Pilgrimage" in *The Catholic Worker*, demonstrate the depth and breadth of her strength and vision.

And everything in her life flowed from love and spoke of love.

Love Is the Measure

Some people see the Catholic Worker movement as defined by poverty and others by community. But for Dorothy *love* is the "final word":

> We cannot love God unless we love each other, and to love we must know each other. We know Him in the breaking of bread, and we know each other in the breaking of bread, and we are not alone any more. Heaven is a banquet and life is a banquet, too, even with a crust, where there is companionship. We have all known the long loneliness and we have learned that the only solution is love and that love comes with community.[74]

The interplay of the "two feet of love"—of God and neighbor—is very clear in Day's thought. Hosea's words, "I will now allure her, and bring her into the wilderness, and speak tenderly to her" (2:14), spoke strongly to her and was a key theme of the Hugo retreat. She was strongly attracted to "this love, this foolishness of love."[75] Paraphrasing the retreat conferences, she stresses that love

> is a choice, a preference. If we love God with our whole hearts, how much heart have we left? If we love with our whole mind and soul and strength, how much mind and soul and strength have we left? . . . If we do not learn to enjoy God now we never will.[76]

She was very clear that we must love God totally and completely *now*. Because love is a choice, it is demanding—feelings are helpful but love of God cannot be based on feelings. She was consoled by Pascal's saying that "Thou wouldst not seek Him if thou hadst not already found Him" and stressed that "it is true too that you love God if you want to love Him."[77]

In 1946, at the time of atomic bomb tests, she wrote that in this situation "there is nothing we can do for people except to love them . . . the most important thing is to love . . . dear God, please enlarge our hearts to love each other, to love our neighbor, to love our enemy as well as our friend."[78]

A Harsh and Dreadful Love

The call to love each person—especially the poor—was for Day the challenge of the reality of love, not the fantasy. In her writings she often spoke of the advice of the monk, Father Zossima, in Dostoyevsky's *The Brothers Karamazov*, who tells a woman, "Love in action is a harsh and dreadful thing compared to love in dreams."[79] Day lived the truth of this: caring for the poor, being patient with guests at the Worker houses who were mentally ill, living in community with people she would never have chosen, being misunderstood and attacked during World War II and throughout her life for her pacifism, missing the daily presence of a man who loved her. When she wrote that "we must love to the point of folly,"[80] she knew what this demanded: "We pray for love. We get it, and it comes in strange forms and ways . . . We had better not presume to ask for love. God may take us at our word."[81]

For the Catholic Worker "love in action" is personalism, a communitarian Christianity; they "denounce Marxism, nationalism and capitalism as dehumanizing collective systems, which rob the individual of dignity."[82] Love in action is the works of mercy—feeding the hungry, clothing the naked, visiting the prisoner, caring for each other day in and day out—these are the works of love, the steps of love which, walked over a lifetime, define Day's life as one of concrete, generous, persevering love. When asked what they were trying to do, Day replied, "We are trying to make people happy."[83]

This daily love of others calls persons to a radical self-emptying in the manner of Jesus (Phil 2:5–8). It means "voluntary poverty, stripping one's self, putting off the old man, denying one's self, etc. It also means non-participation in those comforts and luxuries which have been manufactured by the exploitation of others. While our brothers suffer, we must be compassionate with them. While our brothers suffer from lack of necessities, we will refuse to enjoy comforts."[84]

The daily life of the Worker houses, diverse as they are, demands "vulnerability and openness to the other—specifically to the guests."[85] The lack of privacy, sharing working, living, and eating space is difficult enough but "when the Worker vision of an active, compassionate love is thrown into the mixture,"[86] persons are tested to the marrow of their bones and spirit. It is only the power of Christ's death and resurrection that makes these "experiments in truth" (to use Gandhi's phrase) possible and real.

Conclusion

The remarkable life of Dorothy Day—journalist, single mother, co-founder of the Catholic Worker and its "soul" for almost fifty years, pacifist—is a modern incarnation of Catherine of Siena's image of walking on the two feet of love. For Day these feet were poverty, a radical self-emptying in love with and for the poor, and prayer, in which her heart was filled with the love of God who loved her "to the point of folly."

As she walked steadily and with perseverance, Day's life was suffused and penetrated by love, a harsh and dreadful experience: poor food and difficult living situations, insecurity, a life that had nothing of the romantic about it (as new Workers quickly discover). This love is difficult, demanding, harsh, and life-long. Dorothy Day walked faithfully and we are all the richer for it—if we follow on our own two feet of love.

Notes

1. Eileen Egan, *Peace Be with You* (Maryknoll, NY: Orbis, 1999), p. 304.

2. Ibid.

3. Dorothy Day, *Little by Little: Selected Writings of Dorothy Day,* ed. Robert Ellsberg (New York: Knopf, 1983), p. 104.

4. William D. Miller has authored two biographies of Dorothy Day: *A Harsh and Dreadful Love: Dorothy Day and the Catholic Worker* (Garden City, NY: Image, 1974) and *Dorothy Day: A Biography* (San Francisco: Harper & Row, 1962).

5. Quoted in William D. Miller, *A Harsh and Dreadful Love: Dorothy Day and the Catholic Worker Movement* p. 50.

6. Quoted in Egan, *Peace Be with You*, p. 263.

7. James Allaire and Rosemary Broughton, *Praying with Dorothy Day* (Winona, MN: Saint Mary's, Christian Brothers, 1995), p. 17.

8. Dorothy Day, *The Long Loneliness* (San Francisco: Harper & Row, 1952), p. 165.

9. Ibid., p. 166.

10. Egan, *Peace Be with You*, p. 266.

11. In the early 1970s I planned to attend a day of renewal sponsored by the Chicago-area Catholic Charismatic Renewal groups at a retreat center north of the city. A friend who was arranging a ride for me to the retreat center asked me if I "minded" riding in the same car as Dorothy Day. Of course I did not! When we began our trip, I asked her a few questions about the Worker. Then she said, "We are talking too much—we must pray!" And so she led us in the Rosary for the entire duration of the trip, about one and a half hours. I was very disappointed!

12. Day, *Little by Little*, p. 91.

13. Ibid., p. 114.

14. Quoted in Angie O'Gorman and Patrick G. Coy, "Houses of Hospitality: A Pilgrimage into Nonviolence," in *Revolution of the Heart: Essays on the Catholic Worker*, ed. Patrick G. Coy (Philadelphia: Temple University Press, 1988), p. 244.

15. Dorothy Day, *Meditations* (New York: Newman, 1970), p. 54.

16. Daniel DiDomizio, "The Prophetic Spirituality of the Catholic Worker," in *Revolution of the Heart: Essays on the Catholic Worker*, ed. Patrick G. Coy (Philadelphia: Temple University Press, 1988), p. 228.

17. Nancy L. Roberts, *Dorothy Day and the Catholic Worker* (Albany: State University of New York, 1984), p. 5.

18. Day, *Little by Little*, pp. 91–92.

19. Day, *The Long Loneliness*, p. 51.

20. Ibid., pp. 86–87.

21. Quoted in Roberts, *Dorothy Day and the Catholic Worker,* p. 10.

22. Day, *Little by Little*, p. 106.

23. Ibid.

24. Quoted in Roberts, *Dorothy Day and the Catholic Worker,* p. 11.

25. Day, *Meditations*, p. 52.

26. Day, *Loaves and Fishes*, p. 82.

27. Ibid.

28. Day, *Meditations*, p. 49.

29. Ibid., p. 48.

30. Day, *Little by Little*, p. 110.

31. Ibid.

32. Ibid.

33. Day, *Meditations*, p. 50.

34. DiDomizio, "The Prophetic Spirituality of the Catholic Worker," p. 224.

35. Ibid., pp. 222–23.

36. Day, *Little by Little*, p. 109.

37. The Catholic Worker–Dorothy Day papers are held at the archives of Marquette University in Milwaukee, Wisconsin. They include the journals Day kept over the years.

38. Day, *The Long Loneliness*, p. 12.

39. Ibid., p. 17.

40. Ibid., p. 20.

41. Ibid.

42. Ibid., p. 21.

43. Ibid., p. 24.

44. Ibid., p. 25.

45. Ibid., pp. 33–34.

46. Ibid., p. 34.

47. Ibid., p. 36.

48. Ibid., p. 43.

49. Ibid., p. 84.

50. Ibid., p. 132.

51. Ibid., p. 136.

52. Ibid., p. 140.

53. Ibid.

54. Ibid., p. 145.

55. Ibid., p. 148.

56. Ibid.

57. William D. Miller, *Dorothy Day: A Biography* (San Francisco: Harper & Row, 1982), p. 334.

58. Day, *The Long Loneliness*, p. 246.

59. Ibid., p. 250.

60. Miller, *Dorothy Day: A Biography*, p. 338.

61. Day, *The Long Loneliness*, p. 255.

62. Ibid., p. 256.

63. Miller, *Dorothy Day: A Biography*, p. 340.

64. The theology of the "retreat" was seen as controversial because of its Jansenistic tendencies of opposing nature and grace. Hugo was silenced and Lacouture was sent to a very rural area of Canada. Their ideas were discussed in various theological journals and at one point Day was summoned to the New York

chancery and told of this situation (William D. Miller, *Dorothy Day: A Biography* [San Francisco: Harper & Row, 1982] p. 340). Hugo published *Applied Christianity* in 1944, an amplification of Lacouture's ideas.

65. Miller, *Dorothy Day: A Biography*, p. 361.

66. Ibid., p. 362.

67. Ibid., p. 341.

68. Day, The Long Loneliness, p. 263.

69. Egan, *Peace Be with You,* p. 278.

70. Quoted in Miller, *Dorothy Day: A Biography*, p. 368.

71. Ibid., p. 368.

72. Miller, *A Harsh and Dreadful Love*, p. 186.

73. In 1963 she said that she wanted to write a book about her experience of the "spiritual adventure," the courage and perseverance she received from the retreats that sustained her (William D. Miller, *A Harsh and Dreadful Love: Dorothy Day and the Catholic Worker Movement* [Garden City, NY: Doubleday Image, 1974], p. 186), but she never did.

74. Day, *The Long Loneliness*, pp. 285–86.

75. Ibid., p. 255.

76. Ibid., pp. 256–57.

77. Ibid., p. 139.

78. Day, *Little by Little*, pp. 97–98.

79. Quoted in Egan, *Peace Be with You,* p. 290.

80. Day, *Little by Little*, p. 99.

81. Quoted in Miller, *Dorothy Day: A Biography*, p. 363.

82. Roberts, *Dorothy Day and the Catholic Worker*, p. 9.

83. Day, *Little by Little*, p. 102.

84. Day, *Meditations*, p. 48.

85. O'Gorman and Coy, "House of Hospitality," pp. 244–45.

86. Ibid., p. 245.

9

"Be Reconciled": Four South African Voices

The gospel call to reconciliation flows from the recognition that those who live in Christ are new creations, for the bondage of sin is gone and radical new life has been given. The work of transformation is being lived out today in the South African context, where for many decades it appeared that unity and reconciliation were utopian dreams. And yet, since 1994 people speak of a "new South Africa," not without problems and challenges, but one that has been swept clean of the social structures of apartheid and is trying to make this call to reconciliation real.

A brief glance at the history of South Africa in the twentieth century brings back images of both great suffering and great hope:

the victory of the National Party in 1948 and the imposition of apartheid—separateness in Afrikaans—in every dimension of life
20,000 women protesting the pass laws in 1956
the agonies of the Sharpeville massacre in 1960
the defiance of the Soweto uprising in 1976

Nelson Mandela walking free in February 1990

the ecstasies of the first democratic elections and Mandela's inauguration
    as president in 1994

the revelations of sufferings beyond imagination in the hearings of the
    Truth and Reconciliation Commission (TRC)

the HIV/AIDS pandemic that threatens to unravel the social fabric of
    the country

Desmond Tutu, the retired Anglican archbishop of Cape Town, describes the reborn South Africa as the "rainbow people of God." His optimism about what is happening in this country has given hope to others around the world that if peaceful change can happen in South Africa with its tortured history, then this is not impossible in other troubled areas of the world. South Africa has demonstrated that the freedom so longed for by the black majority can be achieved without a bloody civil war and that steps toward reconciliation are happening.

The lived praxis of a "new creation" in South Africa is the fruit of the sufferings and deaths of thousands who gave of themselves in order to make their vision of a country founded on human dignity and the respect of each person come true. In the lives and writings of four South Africans—Denis Hurley, Nelson Mandela, Beyers Naudé, and Desmond Tutu—we find the foundations of this new South African reality. Three are church leaders and one is the renowned former president of the new South Africa who now likes to describe himself as "an unemployed pensioner."

Four Lives, Four Radical Commitments

Naude, Hurley, and Mandela were born in the second decade of the twentieth century while Tutu is in his seventies. The lives of these four men, two black and two white, have been interwoven in various ways as their vision for unity, reconciliation, justice, and peace describe the basis of a new way of living in South Africa.

Beyers Naudé

The oldest of the four, Beyers Naudé, was born on May 10, 1915. He was the son of a Dutch Reformed Church minister who had fought in the

South African War (1899–1902). He followed his father into the ministry and rose rapidly in the church's hierarchy. It seemed likely that he would eventually lead the church as its senior moderator.

However, by the late 1950s he began to question his church and its theological positions, which supported apartheid. He was troubled by the interpretation of Scripture that justified "separateness" and his growing awareness of the sufferings of black, Indian, and "colored" (mixed race) people who had been forcibly removed from their homes by the policy of "separate development" and dumped miles away in areas with little or no possibilities of a humane life.

A decisive turning point came when he visited the hostels where men working in the gold mines in Johannesburg lived. He saw the starkness of the hostels, the rows of bunk beds, the crowded conditions, lack of sanitation facilities and privacy, the separation from their wives and families who lived in rural areas far from the city. "I will never forget that experience as long as I live. I said to myself, 'If this is what apartheid is all about, it is evil, it is inhuman, it is something which can never be supported.'"[1]

This powerful awakening to the evil of apartheid led him to life-changing decisions. On March 21, 1960, at Sharpeville, a township near Johannesburg, sixty-nine black people were killed by police fire as they protested the pass laws. Later that year he participated in the Cottesloe Conference, an ecumenical gathering to discuss the role of the church in seeking racial justice in South Africa. Two years later he became the editor of a new ecumenical periodical, *Pro Veritate*, and in August 1963 left his position as pastor of a congregation to begin work with the new Christian Institute.

In his final sermon to the congregation in August 1963 he declared that the choice before him was "a choice between obedience in faith and subjection to the authority of the church. And by unconditional obedience to the latter, I would save face but lose my soul."[2]

He and his wife Ilse, who supported her husband's decision, now left behind the security of white privilege under the mantel of the church to walk into an unknown future on the side of oppressed peoples of South Africa. Naudé became the first director of the Christian Institute, a multiracial organization of Christians. Their interracial gatherings violated the apartheid laws and scandalized many whites.

In October 1977, a year after the Soweto uprisings, the Christian Institute and *Pro Veritate* were both shut down by the Nationalist government and the leaders of the institute, including Naudé, were placed under a banning order for five years. This was a particularly odious punishment, as the banned person was, with few exceptions, restricted to his or her home and allowed to meet with only one person at a time. Phone lines were tapped, one's house was under constant police surveillance, and letters were opened. Banning was intended to eliminate the person's influence and presence in ordinary society, not just in the antiapartheid movement.

Naudé found that the years of his banning (which extended to 1984) were, paradoxically, very important ones because he did an enormous amount of personal counseling with the persons who came, one by one, into his office. Reflecting on the hardships of these years he said that the most severe was "the lack of social intercourse, the prohibition of meaningful political and theological discussion, and the opportunity to relax in the company of a small circle of friends."[3]

After the banning order was lifted, he served as general secretary of the South African Council of Churches from 1985 to 1987. He participated in the writing of the *Kairos Document* in 1985, a statement of church leaders that condemned the "state theology" of the government and called for prophetic action by the church against apartheid.

Naudé stands as a symbol of those white South Africans who awakened to the evil of apartheid and put their lives on the line to resist this evil system. His contribution to the struggle against apartheid has been a very significant one, as Peter Moatshe, a black minister of the Dutch Reformed Church, stresses:

> It is probably true to say that until the emergence of Desmond Tutu and Allan Boesak as national and international church leaders, Beyers Naudé could justly be described as the single most important church person this country has so far produced.[4]

Denis Hurley

Denis Hurley was born a few months after Naudé, on November 9, 1915, in Cape Town, and over the years they frequently worked and marched together against apartheid.[5] The first son and second child of Irish Catholic parents who had settled in South Africa, he decided early to become a priest: "All I know is that I was certain of it since I was about six years old. It was a kind of instinctive compulsion."[6] He entered the

Missionary Oblates of Mary Immaculate in 1932; he did his novitiate in Ireland and his theological studies in Rome.

While he was growing up racial inequality was accepted without question; "I would have been surprised if anyone had pointed out its injustice to me while I was still at school."[7] Life in an international community in Rome gave him his first experience of living with people of other races. After his ordination in 1939 he returned to South Africa and realized the centrality of the racial question: "I saw that the South African treatment of the African was an offense against human dignity and freedom and from then on this conviction was working subconsciously on me."[8]

His interest in social problems developed from involvement in Catholic Action activities while a theology student in the 1930s. Catholic Action was an attempt to involve the laity in the work of the Church but only under the guidance and direction of the hierarchy—no initiatives by the laity were welcomed or anticipated. Hurley's thesis topic for his licentiate was based on the recent social encyclical of Pope Pius XI, *Quadragesimo anno*, issued in 1931.

He was briefly engaged in parish work and then began to teach at the newly established OMI Scholasticate in Pietermaritzburg. In 1947 he was consecrated vicar apostolic of Natal, and at thirty-one, was the youngest bishop in the world; in 1951 he was made archbishop of Durban.

Hurley's strong convictions on racial equality shaped his leadership as bishop in his own diocese and in the South African hierarchy, though not all bishops agreed with him[9] and clergy and white laity were also often opposed to him. He recognized early "that there would have to be a black government."[10]

A turning point in Hurley's life came when Pope John XXIII called Vatican II, which met in four sessions from 1962 to 1965. While he ruefully remembers that he saw no need for a council initially, his work as a member of the Central Preparatory Commission transformed his attitudes and he worked diligently to shape the conciliar vision, making important contributions to the documents on the Church, seminary education, the laity, religious liberty, and the Church in the modern world.

Hurley's vision of the Church has also been shaped by his ecumenical involvements, which have been pivotal in his work against apartheid. As the apartheid government became ever more repressive, it became necessary for Christians in South Africa who were committed to human dignity and equality to work together to end this evil. In 1976, together with other Christian leaders, he founded Diakonia in Durban as a concrete way to express Christian witness. Diakonia focused on issues such as wages and service of domestic workers (who worked in white homes), industrial conditions, youth problems, and much more.

In 1984 he helped lead a campaign to gather a million signatures on a petition rejecting apartheid, "seeking the creation of a non-racial, democratic South Africa, free of oppression, economic exploitation and opposing the Tri-cameral constitution."[11]

Hurley's most public act of witness occurred in 1984 and 1985 when he exposed police atrocities in South-West Africa (now Namibia), which was under the control of South Africa. Hurley was accused of violating the Police Act by speaking out. He was called to court in February 1985, the first archbishop in thirty-one years to appear in a court anywhere in the world.[12] But the case was anticlimactic, for the prosecutor withdrew the charges, citing that the evidence was not sufficient. Hurley regretted that the trial did not take place since it would have been an opportunity to expose the government's atrocities, a full disclosure of which had to wait until the TRC's work from 1996 to 1998.

Hurley officially retired on his seventy-fifth birthday in 1991 and left office as the archbishop of Durban the following year. His retirement years included ten years as pastor of Emmanuel Cathedral in Durban, ecumenical and social justice ministry, and writing his memoirs. He died suddenly of a massive heart attack on February 13, 2004.

Nelson Mandela

The name *Nelson Mandela* was alternately revered and reviled during his twenty-seven years in prison; now he is internationally recognized as a prophetic leader of peace and reconciliation.[13]

Nelson Rolihlahla Mandela was born on July 18, 1918, in the village of Mvezo in the Transkei region of the eastern Cape of South Africa. He later spoke of the significance of this year: the end of World War I, the Bolshevik revolution in Russia, and the efforts of a delegation of the newly formed African National Congress who went to London to plead for the rights of black South Africans.[14] Mandela was a royal member of the Tembu clan of the Xhosa tribe and thus a prince among his people. As a young boy his father sent him to live with the regent of his clan to be educated. He watched the regent preside at tribal meetings and observed how he tried to draw consensus from often conflicting views. This was a lesson that he applied much later as president of South Africa.

At sixteen he participated in the traditional Xhosa manhood rites and was circumcised. Soon after the regent sent him to Clarkebury, a Methodist educational institution. Since his great-grandfather had founded the school and Mandela was of the royal family, he expected the other pupils to treat him with respect, but he had a rude awakening—he was just another pupil from a rural village. But Mandela soon settled in, and completed his initial studies there and at another Methodist school, Healdtown. In 1939 he enrolled at the University of Fort Hare, the only university open to blacks in South Africa and the focus of intellectually elite black South Africans. A year later he was expelled for his role in a student government protest over the poor food served to the students.

He learned that the regent had arranged a marriage for him to which he did not agree and so he left for Johannesburg. Here he met Walter Sisulu, his lifelong friend and mentor, studied law, and joined the African National Congress Youth League in 1944. He married Evelyn Mase in 1944 and they began a family.[15]

From this point on the activities of what was later to be termed "the Struggle" became the focus of Mandela's life: the Defiance Campaign of 1952, the signing of the Freedom Charter in 1955, the Treason Trial of 1958 in which he and 155 people of all races were accused of high treason and acquitted, the formation of the military wing of the African National Congress, *Umkhonto we Sizwe* ("the sword of the nation"), and the Rivonia trial of 1964 in which he and seven others were sentenced to life imprisonment. They had expected the death penalty and were relieved at the sentence. In 1961 he had declared that "the struggle is my life. I will continue fighting for freedom until the end of my days."[16] The struggle now continued from his prison cell on Robben Island off the shore of Cape Town, in which he and his companions would experience the full extent of apartheid "justice."

During the twenty-seven years Mandela spent in prison his reputation varied from the "freedom fighter" who held the hopes of black South Africa to the "communist terrorist" of white fears. During the late 1980s he and state presidents P. W. Botha and later F. W. de Klerk began a series of talks that were the preliminary events leading to the unbanning of the African National Congress on February 2, 1990, and Mandela's release from prison a few days later on the 11th.

In 1993, during the intricate and delicate negotiations for a new government, he and de Klerk were awarded the Nobel Peace Prize. The prayers and hopes of the world and South Africa were fulfilled in April 1994 during the three days of voting for a new democratic South African government. Mandela was inaugurated as president of a free South Africa on May 10. He served until 1999. Now in retirement he is a roving ambassador for peace throughout the world and a vocal advocate for children and education.

Desmond Mpilo Tutu

The future Anglican priest and archbishop was born on October 7, 1931, in the town of Klerksdorp in the then Transvaal province. His father was a school teacher and his son followed in his footsteps. After finishing high school at the Johannesburg Bantu High School he obtained a teacher's diploma at the Pretoria Normal College in 1953 and in 1954 received his B.A. through the University of South Africa, a distance learning institution that provided education for black and white students.

After a few years of teaching, he followed a call to priestly ministry in the Anglican Church by studying theology at St. Peter's College in Rosettenville and was ordained in 1961. The next years were filled with varied ministries: parish ministry, further theological studies in London, theology lecturer in South Africa and Lesotho, and ecumenical work in England as associate director of the Theological Education Fund of the World Council of Churches.

When he and his wife Leah and their children (they have three daughters and one son) returned to South Africa in 1975, tension was building in the country as the apartheid government became ever more repressive. He was appointed dean of St. Mary's Cathedral in Johannesburg, the first black priest to hold this position. Housing was provided for the dean in a white suburb but Tutu refused to apply for permission to live in this "whites only" area; instead, he and his family moved to Soweto, the huge black township on the edge of Johannesburg.

His ministry at the cathedral lasted only a short time because in 1976 he was made the bishop of Lesotho and in 1978 returned to Johannesburg as the General Secretary of the South African Council of Churches.

In those very turbulent years of the Struggle, Tutu's leadership became striking and fearless. Nelson Mandela recalls that Tutu was "public enemy number one to the powers-that-be."[17] He was arrested a number of times during protest meetings and gatherings, visited those most affected by the poverty and suffering of apartheid, and became their voice in his speeches and writings. He supported economic sanctions against South Africa and consistently advocated nonviolence.

Describing his call to preach and promote justice he said:

> Speaking for myself, I want to say that there is nothing the government can do to me that will stop me from being involved in what I believe is what God wants me to do. I do not do it because I like to do it. I do it because I am what I believe to be the influence of God's hand . . . I cannot help it when I see injustice . . . I cannot keep quiet.[18]

In 1984 Tutu received the Nobel Peace Prize for his efforts toward justice in South Africa. A year later he was named the bishop of Johannesburg and in 1986 the archbishop of Cape Town, the primatial see of the Church of the Province of Southern Africa. The archbishop's residence was in the white suburb of Bishopscourt and although the Group Areas Act, which mandated residential segregation, was still enforced, Tutu declared he would not seek a government permit to reside there. An activist archbishop, he traveled widely throughout the world, calling attention to the situation in South Africa. At home he continued to speak and act for justice.

It was in his home that Nelson Mandela and his wife Winnie spent the first night after Mandela's release from prison on February 2, 1990. When he voted for the first time on April 27, 1994, Tutu said, "It was giddy stuff, like falling in love. The sky looked more blue and beautiful. I saw the people in a new light. They were beautiful, they were transfigured. I too was transfigured."[19]

He had set three goals for himself when he became archbishop of Cape Town: the ordination of women to the priesthood (passed in 1992), division of the large archdiocese into smaller dioceses (not accomplished), and "the liberation of all our people, black and white,"[20] which was achieved in 1994.

After the first democratic government began to function, Tutu said that the church now could move away from the political stage. This was interpreted and criticized as a "back to the sanctuary" approach, a focus on church issues and not on justice issues. Tutu did not mean that the church was now to be preoccupied with its internal life but that since the government was one for which they had fought for such a long time, the church no longer needed to speak as it had spoken. But it did need to continue to speak.

When he turned sixty-five in 1996, Tutu retired as archbishop of Cape Town, but his plans for retirement leisure were put on hold when he was appointed chair of the TRC. Under his leadership, the TRC hearings were a "mixture of trial, confessional and morality play, with an African dimension."[21] One of the more famous moments of the TRC occurred when Tutu tried to coax a partial apology from Winnie Madikizela-Mandela for her involvement with the murder of the teenager Stompie Seipei in 1988. He said to her, "You are a great person and you don't know how your greatness would be enhanced if you were to say: 'Sorry. Things went wrong. Forgive me.'"[22] She managed to say, "It is true that things went horribly wrong," but went no further.

After the work of the Commission was finished and its report given to the government in October 1998 (not without great controversy, since it included some serious accusations against the African National Congress for human rights violations in its camps in Zambia and elsewhere) Tutu could now retire. A diagnosis of prostate cancer and treatment for it in South Africa and the United States slowed him down a bit, but in his seventies he remains a strong and lively presence in South African life.

The Faith That Does Justice

The lives of these four leaders have been shaped by their religious faith to various degrees. Of the four, Mandela is the most circumspect about his experience. During his youth, when he lived with the regent and his wife, "religion was a part of the fabric of life"[23] and he attended church each week. He was baptized as a Methodist in his home village of Qunu on the only day he ever attended church there. In his early religious socialization he experienced that "Christianity was not so much of beliefs as it was the powerful creed of a single man, Reverent Matyolo,"[24] the local Methodist minister. Mandela experienced the fire-and-brimstone variety, "seasoned with a bit of African animism."[25] God was wise and all-powerful, but was also a vengeful God who did not ignore sin and made sure it was punished.

Since Mandela attended schools run under Methodist auspices, it was this religious ethos that influenced his faith development. However, his biographer Anthony Sampson states that "the Methodism of Healdtown and Clarkebury did not make a deep religious impact on Mandela" and that "he would never be a true believer."[26] However, the strict moral practice of Methodism did influence him: the discipline, the emphasis on simplicity, shaped his character and all his life he has disapproved of heavy drinking and swearing.

When he began to study law in Johannesburg, he met Nat Bregman, who was working in the same firm. According to Mandela, Nat "seemed entirely color-blind and became my first white friend."[27] Nat was a member of the Communist Party and introduced Mandela to the views of the Party. But at the time Mandela considered himself "quite religious and the party's antipathy to religion put me off."[28] In the 1950s he described himself as a member of the Wesleyan Church.

During the years of his long imprisonment on Robben Island, Mandela attended any and all church services that were held, supposedly only missing one. While religious practice in and of itself can be ambiguous, his respect for religion and religious leaders who have been on the side of freedom and human dignity can be said to indicate a deep well-spring of moral conviction that was especially evident when he emerged from prison. He was not embittered but was ready to work together with any and all persons of good will, even former enemies, in order, first, to move South Africa into the ranks of world democracies and, second, to make this new South Africa a place of justice, peace, and reconciliation. His charismatic presence as a person whose hands are open in friendship and reconciliation demonstrates the highest ideals of all world religions.

Tutu: A Public Faith

Hurley, Naudé, and Tutu are all church leaders and thus faith is central to their life and work. Their writings demonstrate this in various ways. Of the three, Desmond Tutu has given the most public expression of his life of faith and prayer. He has stated clearly that "for me the most important—the most cardinal fact about our life is the spiritual—that encounter with God in prayer, in worship, in meditation."[29] He asserts strongly that his faith is the well-spring of his commitment to justice and liberation:

I want to say that there is nothing the government can do that will stop me from being involved in what I believe God wants me to do . . . I cannot help it when I see injustice, I cannot keep quiet. I will not keep quiet, for as Jeremiah says, when I try to keep quiet, God's word burns like a fire in my breast.[30]

While Tutu was general secretary of the South African Council of Churches (SACC), he emphasized the importance of prayer in his life and that of the SACC. He described Jesus both as a man for others and as a man of prayer, and thus an example for Christians in both dimensions. For Jesus "prayer and communion with the Father were like breathing for him"[31] and thus this twofold movement of prayer and action must mark the life of disciples as well.

When he described the prayer life of the staff of the SACC at Diakonia House in Johannesburg, he was also hinting at his own rhythm of prayer: daily staff prayer, celebration of the Eucharist, "substantial Bible study" once a month, and a yearly retreat for the senior staff are paralleled in his own life with daily prayer, the Offices, Eucharist, Scripture reading, other reading, days of prayer, and a yearly longer retreat.[32]

In 1992, during the negotiations for a democratic government, Tutu spoke about the need for contemplation. It had been suggested to him that he now needed to spend much more time in prayer and while he rejected any dichotomy between action and contemplation, he did respond by saying that perhaps the "balance being weighted more and more in favour of the hidden, the inner life, for the sake of all that we hold dear and for which we have prayed and striven and continue to do so."[33] This emphasis on the inner life in a time of immense tension and uncertainty was "not being pietistic. It is to cultivate an authentic spirituality in the transition of much flux, bewilderment, violence and turbulence."[34]

As chair of the TRC he brought this same concern for prayer to the sessions of the Commission and so there was prayer at the beginning and end of each day and a pause at mid-day. As people told of their heart-wrenching experiences of suffering, prayer surrounded them, together with some hymn singing and the symbol of a candle of hope burning. Tutu relied on the intercessory prayer of the Anglican monks and nuns around the world during the TRC.

Though he was sometimes criticized for this overtly religious atmosphere, he told his critics that "I was a religious leader and had been chosen as who I was. I could not pretend I was someone else."[35] Just as the Commission used experts in many fields (e.g. psychology, medicine, etc.), he was also convinced that "theological and religious insights and perspectives would inform much of what we did and how we did it."[36]

Denis Hurley

Hurley's life has been a unity of faith and justice. Reflecting on his long life of social engagement, he described his social commitment as "a natural conviction about justice—it was instinctive"[37] and based on the spirituality of gospel. This is well illustrated in his episcopal motto, "where the Spirit of the Lord is, there is freedom" (2 Cor 3:17–18).

The life of an archbishop is filled with many occasions of public prayer: celebrating the Eucharist, preaching, presiding at funerals, ordaining priests and deacons, officiating at religious professions, and leading prayer at various official civic occasions.

Hurley's public liturgical presence is grounded in his conviction that "faith and liturgy are inseparable. Faith is the inspiration of the liturgy. Liturgy is the expression of faith."[38] During Vatican II he was a champion of the efforts directed to renew the liturgy and in one of his council speeches stated that "if we wish to renew the apostolic spirit in the church (and this, I think, is the aim of this ecumenical Council), it will be necessary to reform the liturgical life."[39]

As a bishop he emphasized that a significant dimension of his episcopal ministry was to lead his people in prayer. The prayer life of the bishop shapes the prayer of all those whom he leads and guides: priests, religious, and laity.

As Hurley speaks of the convictions that guide the prayer of a bishop, the themes of his own prayer begin to come to light. Prayer is meeting God in mystery, and especially in the "risen humanity of the crucified Christ communicating himself to us."[40]

The presence of God is a sacramental presence—experienced most especially in the Eucharist. Thus the bishop is "one with the community in the body of Christ" and he himself is a "sacrament of Christ's presence for that community."[41] He must be this to both the clergy and the whole Christian community, emphasizing that while private and liturgical prayer are distinct, there is no real separation, for it is through prayer that one comes to a profound conviction of Christ's presence.

This unity of prayer flows from Hurley's conviction that the love of God and neighbor cannot be separated. The vision of Vatican II that he strove so long and so hard to make real in his diocese was the same synthesis—Christian insertion in daily life and prayer are inseparable.

Beyers Naudé

Beyers Naudé's faith was shaped in the Reformed tradition of trust and commitment to God in Christ and steeped in the word of God. His father Jozua completed his theological studies for the ministry in 1909 and served a number of congregations. His parents had a "deep unshakeable faith in God"[42] and this was communicated to their children through daily Bible reading and prayer and Sunday worship. Sunday was kept strictly as a day of rest and prayer and the children could not join their friends at dances and the movies.

When Beyers was sixteen, he experienced a conversion to the Christian faith. Though he had been raised in a devout Christian family, it was at Pentecost in 1930, as a result of his father's sermons, that he decided to "give his life to Christ."[43] As he planned his future, he resolved to study for the ministry since as a minister's son he qualified for a scholarship at the University of Stellenbosch. He entered into these studies with some hesitation, and determined that if during his years at the university he decided not to become a minister, he could become a teacher.

One of his professors was B. B. (Bennie) Keet, who taught ethics and dogmatics. Keet did not agree with the emerging hardline Reformed theology; later when the Dutch Reformed Church began to shape its theological underpinning for apartheid, Keet spoke out against it.

Naudé finished his theological studies in 1939 and was called to his first pastorate. When he was banned in October 1977 and the Christian Institute closed down, he prayed as he left the offices of the Institute for last time: "Thank you, God, for your goodness in allowing me nearly forty years of ministry in Your service."[44]

His life and ministry have been based on "the rocklike Christian faith which he shares with [his wife] Ilse. It was this faith which led him to question apartheid and has sustained him on a lifelong political and spiritual journey."[45]

The faith that does justice and works toward reconciliation and peace in South Africa with its tortured history is clearly the core of the personal commitments of these four prominent leaders. Public statements about prayer and commitment point to deep rivers of a living spirituality in their lives.

Reconciliation: Challenge and Opportunity

The South Africa that was born in April 1994 went through a long and difficult labor. When this new player on the world stage began to walk and talk the language of newness, of ending the injustices of apartheid in order to build a society of justice, peace, and reconciliation, the world held its collective breath. Was this really possible?

A central word in the South African vocabulary is *reconciliation,* or *ukubuyisana*, a Zulu word that means "to return to each other," "to come back to each other."[46] The word has been used by all sorts of groups before and after 1994, including the apartheid government. Its opponents declared "no reconciliation without justice."[47] The preamble of the Constitution of South Africa, ratified in 1996, states that a primary purpose of this "supreme law of the Republic" is to "heal the divisions of the past and establish a society based on democratic values, social justice and fundamental human rights."[48] The commission set up by the new government mandated not only a Truth Commission, but a Truth *and* Reconciliation Commission.

Reconciliation is about creating new relationships, not merely going back to the past and setting wrongs right, and "this restored relationship . . . is essentially a new or renewed reality."[49] These relationships can be interpersonal when the wrongs have hurt individuals, but in the South African context social reconciliation is key. Here a society, a people, become new as it "recovers its dignity and honour."[50]

For Christians the fullness of reconciliation is anticipated in the reign of God, when God will be all things to all people, and all people will be one in the unity and love of God. But until that time we live in an "already but not yet" experience of reconciliation.

Human Dignity as Non-Negotiable

On September 22, 1963, Beyers Naudé preached his farewell sermon to this congregation and announced that he was leaving the ministry in order to work for the Christian Institute. It was a decision that cost him and his wife and family a great deal of suffering and church leaders pleaded with him to reconsider, but he would and could not.

He exhorted the stunned congregation: "O my church, I call today with all the earnestness that is in me: awake before it is too late, stand up and stretch out the hand of Christian brotherhood to all who reach out to you in sincerity. There is still time, but time is becoming short, very short."[51]

Christian community and solidarity in common humanity was the vision that animated Naudé's decision. Human dignity and equality are the bedrock of reconciliation. If we cannot understand, accept, and act together as equal daughters and sons, then reconciliation is impossible.

The theme of the absolute human dignity of each person is found throughout the writings and speeches of these four leaders. In 1966, ten years before the Soweto uprising and twenty-eight years before the first democratic elections, Denis Hurley asserted that "we are in desperate need of a moral value to create our South African cultural consensus and that that moral value must be respect for human dignity."[52]

The evil of apartheid took root because of the lack of respect for each person as created in the image of God; instead, the social sin of racism grew and flourished as the government decided that some people were more human than others. Every person became "less whole than we would have been without apartheid."[53]

The lack of human dignity in South Africa was the prime motive for Mandela's decision to devote his life to the struggle for freedom:

> It was this desire for the freedom of my people to live their lives with dignity and self-respect that animated my life, that trans- formed a frightened young man into a bold one, that drove a law- abiding attorney to become a criminal, that turned a family-loving husband into a man without a home, that forced a life-loving man to live like a monk.[54]

We share one common humanity, equal in dignity. Apartheid was in total contradiction to the core African value of *ubuntu*, which Tutu describes as "what it means to be truly human, it refers to gentleness, to compassion, to hospitality, to openness to others, to vulnerability, to be available for others and to know that you are bound up with them in the bundle of life, for a person is only a person through others."[55] If we could recognize this, then transformation would take place.

The first step toward living *ubuntu* is to come to know others, especially the people that we have decided are so different from us. This is a constant theme in Hurley's writings when he ponders how change is possible. He stressed that the first step must be "a significant number of white South Africans endeavouring to see in their nonwhite neighbours not a menace to whiteness but the warm and precious value of human dignity."[56]

The strangers that we meet can become friends and neighbors when we are open to seeing them not as threats, but as persons like ourselves. Hurley realized that not only would such person-to-person contacts be difficult under the restrictive apartheid laws, but that in meeting real people, the contacts are not always easy since one enters a new cultural world. Yet he insists that only through these contacts will doors open to create real relationships, which are not created in books and lectures but in real human encounters. It is in this way that the abstract principle of human dignity becomes the living experience of Christian love.

"A Crisis of Love"

This is the phrase that Hurley used to describe the South African situation.[57] Quoting one of his favorite theologians, Pierre Teilhard de Chardin, he wrote: "Love alone is capable of uniting living beings in such a way as to complete and fulfil them, for it alone takes them and joins them by what is deepest in themselves."[58] It is love that "is the supreme test of the Christian spirit."[59]

In every possible way apartheid was the opposite of loving and caring relationships. It separated and divided people, kept them apart by both laws and fear, and systematically destroyed human dignity—the dignity of the black majority through injustice of every kind and the dignity of the white minority through incessant propaganda of white supremacy.

Even before he left the ministry, Naudé felt compelled to state clearly where he stood since there was so much controversy surrounding his activities. In a sermon in 1962 he declared that "all people are called to love one another . . . the outcome of this love is that I should allow other people to have the same rights and opportunities as my group demands."[60] This appears to be an ordinary Christian principle but it was a radical and disconcerting statement for his congregation to hear.

In the late 1960s Naudé and the Christian Institute were engaged in a joint project with the South African Council of Churches to explore the churches' role in ending racial injustice. Its final statement, *A Message to the People of South Africa*, issued in September 1968, asserted that "the Gospel of Jesus Christ declares that God is love; separation is the opposite force of love . . . apartheid is a view of life and of man which insists that we find our identity in dissociation and distinction from each other."[61]

The path of Christian love to racial peace would be "a way of the Cross," an ascent in pain for the human heart, which "inflicts its share of hurts and bruises—anxieties, disillusionments and renunciations."[62] This recalls Dorothy Day's refrain that "love in practice is a harsh and dreadful thing." But the end of the cross is not death, but life.

Hurley challenged white South Africans to

expand the areas of love, to push their frontiers ever outwards in an adventure, agonising to old prejudices, but more than amply rewarding through the response to be found in that treasure of warm humanity waiting on the other side of the barrier White South Africans have so feared to cross.[63]

It is love that casts out fear, while fear intensifies if it is not confronted.

Love is not a good feeling of wishing the other well from a distance but a commitment to one's sisters and brothers. Love of God and love of neighbor form an indivisible unity. In the sermon that Desmond Tutu preached when he was enthroned archbishop of Cape Town on September 7, 1986, he insisted that Christian love looks for the God hidden in human flesh:

And if we take the incarnation seriously we must be concerned about where people live, how they live, whether they have justice, whether they are uprooted and dumped as rubbish in resettlement camps, whether they are detained without trial, whether they receive an inferior education, whether they have a say in the decisions that affect their lives most deeply.[64]

"Made for Togetherness"

Asserting human dignity and loving one another slowly brings the human family into the unity that is God's intent. Tutu describes this unity as essential to our humanity:

> We are human because we belong. We are made for community, for togetherness, for family, to exist in a delicate network of interdependence . . . We are sisters and brothers of one another whether we like it or not, and each one of us is a precious individual.[65]

We are caught up in God's "centripetal process, a moving towards the Centre, towards unity, harmony, goodness, peace and justice; one that removes barriers . . . none is an outsider, all are insiders, all belong."[66] He, too, quoted Teilhard de Chardin's vision of the unity of all persons and all creation in the dynamic love of Christ.[67]

In the 1980s, when tensions were enormous and violence filled the townships of the country, Tutu described an incident in which he saw two young women who were attending a funeral for victims of the violence; they were sitting on the grass and holding each other. He remarked to a companion, "This is the South Africa we are working for,"[68] for one was black and one was white.

In the midst of all his years of struggle and imprisonment, Mandela "never lost hope that this great transformation would occur,"[69] a miracle of courage, of learning to love and to work for the unity and reconciliation of all South Africans.

A practical way to this unity throughout the years of the Struggle was the growth of ecumenical cooperation. Hurley, Tutu, and Naudé were no strangers to each other, working and marching together in protest throughout the years of apartheid. Though the Catholic Church in South Africa did not join the SACC until 1995, it had observer status for many years.

In the late 1950s Naudé, working with other ministers, began to establish Bible study groups, which became ecumenical. This experience was extremely significant in his theological and spiritual development:

> Through my private theological study I developed a totally new concept about the nature of the church. I realised that the church in

the New Testament sense was the one body of Christ and that all
the historical divisions which had grown up since the Reformation,
between the different confessional groups, and the divisions which
had grown in South Africa, were no longer valid, they could not be
maintained and that therefore one of the major tasks would be to
help Christian people realize what the concept of church and Christian unity was.[70]

He now realized that Christian unity was mandated by the Bible.
This profoundly influenced the formation of the Christian Institute,
which was consciously ecumenical from its beginnings. Naudé scandalized some by reaching out a welcoming hand to invite Catholics into the
work of the Institute.

Hurley, too, saw the ecumenical movement as essential to the social
transformation of the country, which he described as "a collaboration in
love, a fraternal rivalry of love, to see what powerful social forces, what
impulses of the Christian conscience can be concentrated on the sore
spots of humanity."[71]

Human dignity, love, desire for unity—all are essential to the process
of reconciliation.

Reconciliation: Doing the Work of Jesus

Apartheid was based on a systematic denial of the "chief work that Jesus
came to perform on earth [which] can be summed up in the word 'Reconciliation.'"[72] The divine intent that human beings are made "for fellowship, for *koinonia*, for togetherness, without destroying our
distinctiveness, our cultural otherness"[73] was rejected by apartheid's
insistence that human beings are to be separate, alienated, and disunited.

Reconciliation is both the goal and the process of the transformation
of the South African people. Abolishing the apartheid laws and changing
the political order to one of democracy and freedom is not sufficient to
build a new South African community. Reconciliation is a multilayered
experience of emerging unity and dynamic hope.

The structures of apartheid were social structures; every aspect of
life was affected by law: place of residence, freedom of movement,
employment, the quality of education, health care, the types of trans-

portation. The aim of apartheid was to keep people apart and it did its work well.

Reconciliation between persons who have harmed each other personally is not sufficient to heal the wounds and suffering of this apartness. Social reconciliation is necessary and this begins with social conversion, in which persons as members of social groups begin to recognize that they have sinned and have damaged the unity of the human family.

Such conversion is painful, for it demands that what was hidden and twisted in the social soul is now brought out into the open for healing. Hurley has described this suffering as a "dark night of the soul."[74] Social conversion and reconciliation are the great task of the church and if the church cannot effect it, then he felt that church would be shown to be irrelevant.

Reconciliation is found at the foot of the cross, where divisions are healed, for Christ "is our peace; in his flesh he has made both groups into one and has broken down the dividing wall, that is, the hostility between us" (Eph 2:14). Tutu declared that "through the Cross God has said 'No' to racism and its injustice and oppression."[75] The "Yes" of the Christian community to the gift of peace and unity in Christ must include the work of reconciliation.

South Africans danced in the streets on Nelson Mandela's inauguration day, May 10, 1994, but they were a wounded people. Every person had been traumatized and broken by the evils of apartheid, even if they did not feel this, for they lived in a country whose whole ethos had been in opposition to Christ's call for unity and love.

A few days later when he opened Parliament, Mandela called for a far-ranging program of social reconciliation and transformation that would affect every aspect of South African life: health (especially that of children), education, ending poverty, working against the abuse of women and children, provision of good housing for the poor, job creation. All of these goals were aimed at creating "a people-centred society" in which the freedom and dignity of the individual in community would be the driving force of public policy.

In 1964, in his speech at the dock before he was sentenced to life imprisonment, Mandela had declared that "we believe that South Africa belongs to all the people who live in it, and not to one group, be it black or white."[76] This was the conviction that shaped his term as president. His experience throughout his life of living and working with people different than himself—from Indian and white colleagues in the Struggle whom he trusted completely to the Afrikaners he met in prison who "could be changed, as he put it, by 180 degrees—and how the same people who could not bear to touch black flesh could be reassured by a handshake"[77] convinced him that reconciliation on a national scale was possible.

The Truth and Reconciliation Commission

In order to ensure that the process of transformation moved forward in South Africa, Parliament passed the Promotion of National Unity and Reconciliation Act in 1995 which established the Commission. The TRC's mandate was to "uncover the truth about our apartheid past in order to facilitate the process of national reconciliation."[78] While telling the truth in and of itself does not cause reconciliation, it is indispensable to the process. The "truth (that) will make you free" (John 8:32) is the foundation of a society that respects human dignity, is just, and cares for its weakest and most vulnerable members. President Nelson Mandela nominated Archbishop Desmond Tutu as the chair of the TRC; Dr. Alex Boraine, a Methodist, was the deputy chair. The first meeting of the Commission in December 1995 with sixteen of the seventeen members represented a cross-section of South Africa: ten blacks, six whites, including two Afrikaners. The TRC included the full spectrum of left to right political beliefs, together with Christians, a Muslim, a Hindu, and "some lapsed believers and possibly an agnostic or two."[79] Seven commissioners were lawyers and three were active ordained ministers.

Under Tutu's leadership, the commissioners were challenged to begin their work with a retreat under the direction of his spiritual counselor, Dr. Francis Cull. During this retreat they "kept silence for a day, seeking to open ourselves to the movement and guidance of the transcendent Spirit, however conceived or named."[80] There was another retreat day at the close of the Commission's work on Robben Island, where Mandela and so many others had been imprisoned.

The Commission tried to engage all South Africans in the work so that everyone who wished would be given the opportunity to tell their stories. Since it was not actually physically possible for every South

African who had suffered under apartheid to come before a Commission hearing, some churches and religious bodies around the country organized opportunities for their members to tell their stories in a local, supportive community. During 1996, 1997, and part of 1998, the national TV evening news program usually included an update on the work of the Commission that day and a longer program was aired on Sundays that focused on a major theme of the Commission's work.

The Commission has been criticized for the requirements that led to amnesty for the perpetrators of apartheid crimes and now that the payment of reparations has been delayed, some have cynically said that the criminals have walked free while the victims still suffer.[81] The TRC originated as part of the bargain of the "negotiated revolution." President F. W. de Klerk had insisted on a general amnesty and so the amnesty process of the TRC was a compromise: individuals would be granted amnesty by the Commission "on the condition that the perpetrators revealed the truth, and could prove that their actions had been politically motivated."[82]

Tutu's evaluation of the work of the TRC is very instructive. The Commission was charged with providing as complete a picture as possible of the "crimes against humanity" of apartheid. Its mandate was to "promote national unity and reconciliation," not to "achieve" it,[83] since reconciliation is a process, a national project in which each South African is challenged to make a contribution. Without reconciliation and forgiveness, there is no future.

Hurley distinguishes between the public process of the TRC and the individual experience of reconciliation, which is not organized. Reflecting on the years of the TRC, he said that "the churches didn't do anything methodical but here and there were experiences, eg the retreats on healing led by Fr. Michael Lapsley."[84] Lapsley is an Anglican priest who lost his hands and part of his hearing in a letter bomb blast in Zimbabwe in the early 1990s.

But he stressed that reconciliation is going on because the Constitution of South Africa describes a multiracial ethos and so "people of all races have to meet and will find out that all are human beings, people like themselves."[85] This is happening in sport, as previously "all-white" sports like rugby and cricket become multiracial. But, he observed, "we still have a long, long way to go."[86]

Forgiveness: The Soul of Reconciliation

Sometimes it is ruefully observed that in the new South Africa no white person now admits to voting for the apartheid government, so how can reconciliation go forward when there is lack of personal and social responsibility for the evils of apartheid? And what is the dynamic of forgiveness within the process of reconciliation?

Forgiveness is first based on truth, on admitting that evil has been done. Thus the South African body was a Truth *and* Reconciliation Commission. But forgiveness is not cheap; it is not a shaking of hands after the confession of wrong and a desire to let bygones be bygones.

John de Gruchy, a leading South African theologian, stresses that "forgiveness properly understood can never replace justice."[87] Those who have done evil must confess their offenses and take responsibility for their actions. Forgiveness and moral accountability are intertwined: "Perpetrators of crimes are accountable both to their victims and to the rule of law, and no one has the right to demand forgiveness; this prerogative rests with the victims alone."[88] But forgiveness goes beyond the strict limits of justice since "the only way to redeem the past, to break the cycle of violence, is not to take revenge, but to have the moral courage to forgive."[89]

In his reflections on the work of the TRC, Archbishop Tutu describes the dynamic of forgiveness.[90] First, horror of what has been done must be brought into the light—not excused, not denied, but fully acknowledged. Second, if the perpetrator of evil has been able to acknowledge that she or he did wrong, then hopefully there will be remorse, confession, and sorrow, including asking for forgiveness from the victim(s) of the evil. Third, it is hoped that the victim will respond with forgiveness, as was seen so many times in the TRC hearings. But forgiveness cannot be forced and the televised hearings of the TRC provided scenes of both victims and perpetrators hugging each other in forgiveness and reconciliation and also of perpetrators being scorned by those they had injured, or in many cases, the families of those who had been tortured and murdered.

Forgiveness is not amnesia, nor is it condoning the evil that has been done. Tutu stresses that is crucial *not* to forget, so that the memory of the atrocities will help to prevent further evil in the future. Forgiveness eliminates the possibility of revenge, but "it is a loss that liberates the victim,"[91] as many who participated in the TRC hearings demonstrated.

While the confession of the evil done is important for forgiveness, it does not depend on it. Jesus forgave those who crucified him even as he was dying. But if the perpetrator can acknowledge the wrong he or she has done, then the relationship can go forward in a new way, one that will not have the same dynamic of evil and hatred.

Forgiveness and faith are also woven together, for "it is an act of faith that the wrongdoer can change."[92] This is also a social act of faith: can those who made apartheid the rule of law and implemented it in obscenely evil ways be trusted to change?

Lastly, Tutu reminds us that the process of forgiveness is not complete until the victim receives reparation for the evil committed. In South Africa apartheid mandated a society of immense economic, social, and political disparity in every aspect of civic life. Hospitals that served the black population had far fewer resources than those in the white community which, for example, led to the first human heart transplant in 1967. Spending on education was similarly skewed; during the apartheid years twenty times as much money was spent on a white pupil as on a black pupil.

The restitution that is part of forgiveness has two dimensions. The TRC process included the provision of reparations to those who had suffered because of the actions of the apartheid government. They have requested money for education of the children left behind when their parents were murdered, medical assistance, money for tombstones, and memorials. To its shame the South African government has moved very slowly to release these funds.

The second aspect of restitution is the transformation of South African society into one of justice; thus the initiatives toward equality in education, health care, providing clean water, electricity, the plans for millions of units of housing, and so on are so crucial.

How will we know that reconciliation is being achieved? We return to the basic principles on which it is based: when people respect each one's dignity as a human being, when love and compassion are part of the social ethos, when people recognize and celebrate their interdependence, then the process of reconciliation is well underway.

Nelson Mandela is the most striking example of the power of forgiveness in South African national life. Some people who emerged from years in prison for their actions against apartheid were bitter and angry that so many years of their lives had been wasted.

In Mandela's own life there had been a transformation from the person who had taken pleasure in confronting his enemies. His African National Congress comrade and colleague Oliver Tambo recalled of those days that "when I want a confrontation, I ask for Nelson."[93] Mandela's experiences with a few Afrikaners in prison convinced him that the South Africa he hoped to lead had to be based on forgiveness, not on revenge and a bloody civil war.[94]

When he was released from prison on February 1990, he confounded many by the concrete acts of forgiveness and reconciliation that he initiated. At the press conference on his first day of freedom, he said that he "knew that people expected me to harbor anger towards whites. But I had none. In prison, my anger toward whites decreased, but my hatred for the system grew."[95]

He gave a retirement party for Niël Barnard, the former head of intelligence. One Sunday he visited a Dutch Reformed church in Pretoria where the congregation was so effusive in their welcome that he needed guards "to protect me from being killed out of love."[96] He met the widows and wives of both black and white leaders so that all would feel they had a place in the new South Africa. He gave a lunch for Percy Yutar, the prosecutor in the Rivonia trial, now in his eighties. Yutar was deeply impressed by Mandela's initiative: "It shows the great humility of this saintly man."[97] He visited ex-president P. W. Botha in November 1995, who in typical fashion wagged his finger and warned Mandela that disaster was ahead if Afrikaner generals were prosecuted. Mandela "watched with amused tolerance."[98]

His wife Graca Machel has described Mandela's forgiveness and tolerance as very African: "It is there in our culture. When we are faced with such a challenge we draw from that culture which is very deep inside ourselves."[99] At the same time she emphasizes that Mandela's ability to forgive has saved South Africa from disaster:

> He symbolises a much broader forgiveness and understanding and reaching out. If he had come out of prison and sent a different message, I can tell you this country could be in flames . . . Some people criticise that he went too far. There is no such thing as going too far if you are trying to save this country from this kind of tragedy.[100]

The fear that Msimangu in Alan Paton's novel *Cry the Beloved Country* raised—"I have one great fear in my heart, that one day when they turn to loving they will find we are turned to hating"[101]—has been answered by Mandela with a forceful "No."

Conclusion

South Africa regained its place in the family of nations in 1994 as its representatives sat in their chairs at the United Nations, the Commonwealth of Nations, and other international bodies, and as its athletes competed in international events. The world looked to its peaceful, democratic revolution as a sign of hope to all.

The lives and writings of the leaders we have considered—Denis Hurley, Nelson Mandela, Beyers Naudé, and Desmond Tutu—show in a striking manner the power of faith to focus the vision for justice, peace, and reconciliation in a context that had dehumanized both white and black. This faith now calls all South Africans to be ministers of reconciliation to each other in the power of the Spirit of Christ in which there is a "new creation; everything old has passed away: see, everything has become new!" (2 Cor 5:17–18).

Notes

1. Colleen Ryan, *Beyers Naudé: Pilgrimage of Faith* (Cape Town: David Philip, 1990), p. 48.

2. Ibid., p. 81.

3. Ibid., p. 200.

4. Ibid., p. 191.

5. See Hurley's tribute to Naudé, "Beyers Naudé—Calvinist and Catholic," in *Facing the Crisis: Selected Texts of Archbishop D. E. Hurley*, ed. Philippe Denis (Pietermaritzburg: Cluster Publications, 1997), pp. 144–61.

6. Desmond Fisher, *Archbishop Denis Eugene Hurley* (Notre Dame, IN: University of Notre Dame Press, 1965), p. 14.

7. Ibid., p. 25.

8. Ibid.

9. In 1964, responding to Hurley's speech, "Apartheid: A Crisis of the Christian Conscience," Archbishop William Patrick Whelan of Bloemfontein stated that "the

theory of apartheid was not immoral but that it would be immoral to level ethnic groups into an amorphous cosmopolitan mass" (Desmond Fisher, *Archbishop Denis Eugene Hurley* [Notre Dame, IN: University of Notre Dame Press, 1965], p. 30).

10. Phone interview with Archbishop Denis E. Hurley, October 15, 2001.

11. Frederick Amoore, "Denis Hurley: His Witness to Love of Neighbor," in *Facing the Crisis: Selected Texts of D. E. Hurley*, ed. Philippe Denis (Pietermaritzburg: Cluster, 1997), p. 214. The Tri-cameral Constitution was an effort by the apartheid government to co-opt Indians and colored people (those of mixed racial background) into the government by creating a three-house Parliament, but blacks continued to be excluded.

12. Ibid., p. 215.

13. Two important studies of Mandela's life are his autobiography *Long Walk to Freedom* (New York: Little, Brown, 1994), and Anthony Sampson, *Mandela: The Authorised Biography* (London: HarperCollins; Johannesburg: Jonathan Ball, 1999).

14. Sampson, *Mandela,* pp. 3–4.

15. Their marriage broke up in 1955 because of their conflicts over his involvement in the Struggle and her religious convictions as a Jehovah's Witness. He married Winnie Nomzamo Madikizela, a social worker who was sixteen years younger than him, in 1958. She suffered much during his years in prison but the marriage did not survive his release from prison and they were divorced in 1995. In 1998 he married Graca Machel, the widow of Samora Machel, president of Mozambique.

16. Nelson Mandela, *The Struggle is My Life* (London: International Defence and Aid Fund for Southern Africa, 1978), p. 155.

17. Nelson Mandela, *Long Walk to Freedom* (Boston: Little, Brown, 1994), p. xiii.

18. Desmond Mpilo Tutu, *Hope and Suffering: Sermons and Speeches* (Johannesburg: Skotaville, 1983), p. xiii.

19. Desmond Mpilo Tutu, *No Future Without Forgiveness* (London and Johannesburg: Rider, 1999), p. 3.

20. Ibid., p. 9.

21. Sampson, *Mandela,* p. 529.

22. Quoted in ibid., p. 540.

23. Mandela, *Long Walk to Freedom*, p. 17.

24. Ibid.

25. Ibid.

26. Sampson, *Mandela,* p. 19.

27. Mandela, *Long Walk to Freedom*, p. 65.

28. Ibid.

29. Tutu, *Hope and Suffering*, p. 147.

30. Ibid., p. 148.

31. Desmond Mpilo Tutu, "We Drink Water to Fill our Stomachs (1979)," in *The Rainbow People of God: South Africa's Victory over Apartheid*, ed. John Allen (London and New York: Doubleday, 1994), p. 30.

32. An Anglican priest who ministered in the diocese of Johannesburg when Tutu was bishop there recalled that he would visit each member of the clergy regularly and had very pointed questions to ask about one's spiritual discipline and rhythm of prayer. As archbishop he did the same, visiting the other bishops to offer support and encouragement to a deeper life of prayer.

33. Desmond Mpilo Tutu, "Nurturing Our People (1992)," in *The Rainbow People of God: South Africa's Victory over Apartheid*, ed. John Allen (London and New York: Doubleday, 1994), p. 231.

34. Ibid.

35. Tutu, *No Future Without Forgiveness*, p. 72.

36. Ibid., p. 73.

37. Phone interview with Archbishop Denis E. Hurley, October 15, 2001.

38. Denis E. Hurley, "Liturgy and Catechetics (1963)," in *Facing the Crisis: Selected Texts of Archbishop D. E. Hurley*, ed. Philippe Denis (Pietermaritzburg: Cluster Publications, 1997), p. 39.

39. Denis E. Hurley, "Excerpts from Archbishop Hurley's Speeches During the Second Vatican Council (1962–1965)," in *Facing the Crisis: Selected Texts of Archbishop D. E. Hurley*, ed. Philippe Denis (Pietermaritzburg: Cluster Publications, 1997), p. 30.

40. Denis E. Hurley, "The Bishop at Prayer in His Church (1970)," in *Facing the Crisis: Selected Texts of Archbishop D. E. Hurley*, ed. Philippe Denis (Pietermaritzburg: Cluster Publications, 1997), p. 102.

41. Ibid.

42. Ryan, *Beyers Naudé,* p. 13.

43. Ibid., p. 18.

44. Ibid., p. 2.

45. Ibid., p. 207.

46. Mark Hay, *Ukubuyisana: Reconciliation in South Africa* (Pietermaritzburg: Cluster Publications, 1998), p. 13.

47. Ibid.

48. *The Constitution of the Republic of South Africa* (Pretoria, 1996), p. 1.

49. Hay, *Ukubuyisana,* p. 14.

50. Ibid., p. 15.

51. Ryan, *Beyers Naudé,* p. 81.

52. Denis E. Hurley, *Human Dignity and Race Relations* (Johannesburg: South African Institute of Race Relations, 1966), p. 1.

53. Tutu, *No Future Without Forgiveness*, p. 154.

54. Mandela, *Long Walk to Freedom*, pp. 543–44.

55. Desmond Mpilo Tutu, "Agents of Transformation (1986)," in *The Rainbow People of God: South Africa's Victory over Apartheid*, ed. John Allen (London and New York: Doubleday, 1994), p. 122.

56. Hurley, *Human Dignity and Race Relations*, p. 10.

57. Denis E. Hurley, *A Time for Faith* (Johannesburg: South African Institute of Race Relations, 1965), p. 15.

58. Ibid. See Pierre Teilhard de Chardin, *The Phenomenon of Man*, trans. Bernard Wall (London: Collins, 1959), p. 265.

59. Denis E. Hurley, "Apartheid: A Crisis of the Christian Conscience (1970)," in *Facing the Crisis: Selected Texts of Archbishop D. E. Hurley*, ed. Philippe Denis (Pietermaritzburg: Cluster Publications, 1997), p. 61.

60. Quoted in Ryan, *Beyers Naudé*, p. 70.

61. Ibid., p. 121.

62. Hurley, "Apartheid: A Crisis of the Christian Conscience," p. 75.

63. Ibid.

64. Tutu, "Agents of Transformation," p. 113.

65. Tutu, *No Future Without Forgiveness*, p. 154.

66. Ibid., p. 213.

67. Ibid., p. 214.

68. Desmon Mpilo Tutu, "You Don't Reform a Frankenstein (1985)," in *The Rainbow People of God: South Africa's Victory over Apartheid*, ed. John Allen (London and New York: Doubleday, 1994), p. 100.

69. Mandela, *Long Walk to Freedom*, p. 542.

70. Ryan, *Beyers Naudé*, pp. 50–51.

71. Hurley, *A Time for Faith*, p. 6.

72. Tutu, *Hope and Suffering*, p. 133.

73. Ibid., p. 73.

74. Denis E. Hurley, "Our Need for Reconciliation" (Durban: Archdiocese of Durban, 1975), p. 3.

75. Desmond Mpilo Tutu, "A Miracle Unfolding (1994)," in *The Rainbow People of God: South Africa's Victory over Apartheid*, ed. John Allen (London and New York: Doubleday, 1994), p. 256.

76. Mandela, *The Struggle is My Life*, pp. 156–57.

77. Sampson, *Mandela,* pp. 584–85.

78. John de Gruchy, "The TRC and the Building of a Moral Culture," in *After the TRC: Reflections on Truth and Reconciliation in South Africa*, ed. Wilmot James and Linda Van De Vijver (Athens: Ohio University Press; Cape Town: David Philip, 2000), p. 169.

79. Tutu, *No Future Without Forgiveness*, p. 65.

80. Ibid., pp. 71–72.

81. See *After the TRC: Reflections on Truth and Reconciliation in South Africa*, ed. Wilmot James and Linda Van De Vijver (Athens: Ohio University Press; Cape Town: David Philip, 2000), whose writers present a wide variety of perspectives on

the TRC. Antjie Krog, who coordinated the South African Broadcasting Corporation radio team during the TRC, describes her experiences in *Country of My Skull* (Johannesburg: Random House, 1998).

82. Sampson, *Mandela,* p. 529.

83. Tutu, *No Future Without Forgiveness*, p. 126.

84. Phone interview with Archbishop Denis E. Hurley, October 15, 2001.

85. Ibid.

86. Ibid.

87. de Gruchy, "The TRC and the Building of a Moral Culture," p. 170.

88. Ibid.

89. Ibid., p. 171.

90. Tutu, *No Future Without Forgiveness*, pp. 218–19.

91. Ibid., p. 219.

92. Ibid, p. 220.

93. Sampson, *Mandela,* p. 520.

94. Mandela described the actions of the warder James Gregory who treated his wife Winnie with kindness when she visited him in prison, of Kobie Coetsee, the minister of justice, Colonel Gawie Marx, Warrant Officer Swart, who cooked for him when he was in a type of halfway house in Victor Verster prison beginning in December 1988. See *Long Walk to Freedom*, pp. 449–50, 456–57, 463–64, 472–75.

95. Ibid., p. 495.

96. Sampson, *Mandela,* p. 522.

97. Ibid., p. 523.

98. Ibid., p. 522.

99. Ibid., p. 533.

100. Ibid.

101. Alan Paton, *Cry the Beloved Country* (London: Penguin, 1958), p. 235.

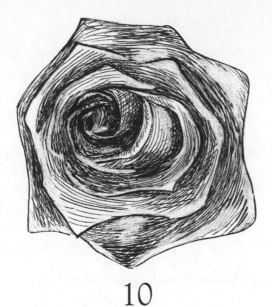

10

Mysticism, Suffering,
and Political Love

In our world suffering is a permanent part of the landscape of human life. Wars, terrorist attacks, poverty, HIV/AIDS and other diseases, oppression and injustice of multiple kinds, and degradation of the environment all contend for space on the front pages of newspapers and the lead items in the TV news. The forms of suffering are different in our age—AIDS instead of bubonic plague, nuclear weapons rather than the longbow of medieval times—but no one escapes the pervasiveness of suffering.

Albert Nolan has identified suffering as "the new starting point for modern theology and spirituality in most of the Christian world today,"[1] as a fundamental sign of our times. Johann Baptist Metz strengthens this perspective by stating that "there is no suffering in the world that does not concern us."[2] He asks if this is a religious or a political statement. Is there a dividing line between the religious and the political? Can a believer demarcate life into these two compartments and feel a sense of security that the political will not interfere with one's religious journey?

As the chapters of this book have shown, this is not only an idle fantasy, but a type of heresy, since the Christian believer is bound inextricably to others in our common humanity and our corporateness as the body of Christ.

A tour of any bookstore today reveals that the "spirituality industry" is alive and well. Witness the plethora of introductions to the lives of the saints and mystics, books on prayer, meditation, and psychological and spiritual health. Many are neatly packaged in "small bytes" for busy Christians rushing from one task to another. Seldom do they address the intersection of spirituality and injustice and oppression. A privatized spirituality is a cocoon spirituality, incapable of assisting persons to be involved in the challenges of political and social life. Indeed, it may well be not only a distorted spirituality but a heretical one, if it fails to locate itself in the midst of the suffering of the world.

The Social Radiation of the Mystic

Mystics are persons in their society, even if hermits or cloistered monks or nuns. They speak the language of their society, eat the common foods, are immersed in the day-to-day cultural mores of their time and place. However, they are not merely persons in society as everyone else of their time and age is, but persons with a particular "social radiation."[3]

The mystic journey is an inward experience to the depth of reality, known in God, a desire for union with Holy Mystery. But during the journey, which is never complete on earth, the mystic may attempt to communicate her or his experience to others—in prose or poetry, gesture, music, art, oral instructions, or sermons. The energy of the mystic experience radiates out to others, not only encouraging them to embark more intensely on their own journey, but also to learn that one's relationship with God has social implications.

As we survey the mystics whose lives and thought have been studied in this book, we see many evidences of this "social radiation."

Catherine of Siena, content for three years in the prayerful solitude of the closet in her family's home, moved out at the command to Christ—first to care for the sick and poor, and later to denounce the evils of Church and society and to call for radical reform. The "two feet" of love of God and love of neighbor were inextricably one in Catherine's experience and her reflections in her *Dialogue*.

The insight of Ignatius of Loyola that one is to seek and find God in *all things* is a very clear example of social radiation. Not only is God affirmed to be in the midst of life, but equally important is his conviction that God can be found in the midst of ordinary experience, the quotidian rhythm of life that everyone experiences. God is not remote but accessible; it is Ignatius's mystical genius that identified ways to seek and find God in all things, thus adding a new dimension to the implications of the depth of the mystic journey.

The tension between the Martha and Mary images in Christian spirituality, with their dichotomy between prayer and action, describes how difficult the Christian spiritual tradition has found it to understand and express this dialectic. The weight of the tradition has been to exalt prayer over service, but there are also strong voices such as Teresa of Avila and Evelyn Underhill who had experienced their unity and who asserted this unity as the goal of Christian life.

Evelyn Underhill, a mystic closer to our own times, demonstrated in her life and writings an evolution of thought on this crucial question. Her earlier writings, including the seminal *Mysticism*, paid scant attention to the social world of the mystic and the social implications of mystical experience. But beginning in the 1920s and continuing to her death in 1941, she began to affirm the intrinsic unity of prayer and action. One's prayer life, she maintained, had everything to do with one's politics, voting patterns, and interpretation of social issues. Moving to a pacifist stance by the early 1930s, she confounded those who had seen her writings as a soothing prayer balm for early-twentieth-century Christians.

Thomas Merton shows the same dynamic in his life and writings. Entering the Trappist Order in 1941, he saw himself as rejecting the world and its problems, everything that was harmful and pleasurable. His journey to consciousness that he is one of humanity, not separate and distinct in his monastic commitment, is clearly outlined in his prolific writings. From the mid-1950s until his death in 1968, he, like Underhill, dismayed and confounded some of his supporters with his writings on racism, the nuclear arms race, war and peace, and the social implications of Christian commitment. Others cheered at hearing his new voice and urged him to leave the monastery and join the revolution. But Merton was always clear that his was a monastic call, and one that led him to progressively deeper solitude.

Dorothy Day's life proclaimed the unity of love of God and neighbor lived in voluntary poverty and nonviolent witness. Her radical witness, flowing from her profound faith, has had a lasting impact on the ethos of American Catholicism, challenging it to be countercultural whatever the era and its social problems.

The South African experience of passing from the night of the injustice and oppression of apartheid to the light of freedom, human dignity, and justice since 1994 has brought hope to a world often starved for good news. The lives and writings of Denis Hurley, Nelson Mandela, Beyers Naudé, and Desmond Tutu present the vision of reconciliation and unity in the new South Africa from the viewpoint of committed Christian faith.

Other Voices

Other mystics who have not been the focus of this book also contribute important insights about the relationship of prayer and social commitment. Julian of Norwich (1373–1416? 1423?), an English anchoress whose *Revelations* (based on her visions of Christ in his passion) is a key text of the Christian mystical tradition, pondered and prayed about the mystery of suffering and God's goodness. Known for her saying that "all will be well and all manner of things will be well," Julian offers insights on sin and sufferings that are strong and challenging. Writing in an England already experiencing the first of many episodes of the pandemic of bubonic plague, Julian's parable of the "Lord and the Servant" (chap. 51) stresses that God's love is stronger than sin, that sin is no-thing, that God has the last word of love in the face of suffering. This is not a concession to an easy optimism but an assertion that God is loving and gracious. Julian speaks of the unity of Christ's suffering and human suffering: "for when he was in pain we were in pain, and all creatures able to suffer pain suffered with him."[4] If this is true, must not Christians mirror that love and solidarity with those who suffer in their particular social reality?

Another woman mystic, Hadewijch of Antwerp, who lived in the thirteenth century, also adds weight to the evidence that mysticism and the practice of love are one. As a beguine, a member of a movement of women who lived singly or in small communities without formal vows, devoting themselves to prayer and works of charity, this emphasis flowed from her experience.

But you must still labor at the works of Love, as I long did and his friends did and still do. For my part I am devoted to these works at

any hour and still perform them at all times: to seek after nothing but Love, work nothing but Love, protect nothing but Love, and advance nothing but Love.[5]

Hadewijch's word for Love is *Minne*—the all-consuming passion of her life—experienced in prayer and served in deeds of love. These were "the works of love as demonstrated in the humanity of Jesus, which the Beguines, like other medieval religious women (and some men, notably the Franciscans), tried to take as their pattern."[6] *Minne* demands that "one must adorn himself with all the virtues that God clothed himself when he lived as Man."[7]

Hadewijch is a mystic of integration who emphasizes that one's mind, affectivity, and will are to be drawn together in loving action. Thus one becomes "full grown," imitating the Beloved in every way: "to work with his hands; to walk with his feet; to hear with his ears where the voice of the Godhead never ceases to speak through the mouth of the Beloved."[8] As we begin to be one with God, we see the world with God's eyes, including its suffering.

Meister Eckhart (1260–1328), German Dominican theologian and mystic, who describes the mystic journey in apophatic images of darkness and negation, also affirms the intrinsic union of the search for God and the serving of those in need: "I have said before: If a man were in an ecstasy, as Saint Paul was, and knew that some sick man needed him to give him a bit of soup, I should think it far better if you would abandon your ecstasy out of love and show greater love in caring for the other in his need."[9] Eckhart, whose Dominican charism is rooted in sharing with others the fruit of one's contemplation, extends that to include practical charity.

Suffering: The Desert and Dark Night

The sheer amount of suffering in the world can numb us with its endless repetition, but when we stop to think that all of this happens to real people like ourselves, not just impersonal numbers—refugees fleeing for their lives, mothers cradling their newborn children infected with HIV/AIDS, victims of crime, people imprisoned for their stands for justice—our minds and hearts cry: "Why all this suffering? What can we do? Is there anything we can do?"

The suffering is not only writ large throughout the globe; it touches each of us in our own experiences of pain and suffering, of limit and failure: the death of someone we love, loss of a job, the effects of aging, a life-threatening illness, failure of a project to which we have devoted our best efforts. Our own personal suffering burns in the depth of our hearts as we shout or moan, "Why me? Why now? What can I do?"

Indeed, what can we do in the face of such incredible suffering and injustice in our world and our own lives? We feel that we are up against a solid brick wall of suffering and there is no way out. We have reached an impasse, a situation in which "every normal manner of acting is brought to a standstill . . . and is experienced not only in the problem itself but also in any situation rationally attempted."[10]

The collective darkness of humanity in its suffering reveals the shadow side of humanity.[11] The darkness of the world, the power of social sin writ large, bears down on us with the might of a freight train let loose from the tracks.

In a real impasse, the more we try to act as if rational solutions will solve our collective problems and help us to find meaning in our personal suffering, the more the suffering intensifies. Another way must be found: not to think our way out of the suffering but to enter into the fullness of the power of the suffering, trusting that there is a way to life in the midst of utter darkness. Constance FitzGerald writes:

> impasse can be the condition for creative growth and transformation *if* the experience of impasse is fully appropriated within one's heart and flesh with consciousness and consent; *if* the limitations of one's humanity and human condition are squarely faced and the sorrow of finitude allowed to invade the human spirit with real, existential powerlessness; *if* the ego does not demand understanding in the name of control and predictability but is willing to admit the mystery of its own being and surrender itself to this mystery; *if* the path into the unknown, into the uncontrolled and unpredictable margins of life, is freely taken when the path of deadly clarity fades.[12]

How can this be done? How can we face impasse and persevere in the journey toward personal wholeness and social justice? How can we make friends with the darkness in a way that leads to life?

Two powerful images in the history of Christian spirituality speak to these heart-wrenching questions: the desert and the dark night. Both demand appropriation of the power of suffering, personal and communal; both contain within their dynamic the paradox of negation that is affirmation, of darkness that leads to light.

Desert Suffering

Our images of the physical deserts of our planet include emptiness, starkness, hunger and thirst, lack of comfort, austerity, vulnerability. To travel any of the great deserts such as the Kalahari or the Sahara is to expose oneself to suffering and possible death if the resources one takes along prove totally inadequate. As photos of the deserts make clear, a desert is not only immense stretches of shifting sands, but also includes rocky places and the occasional oasis.

The desert of the heart and spirit is also not one kind of experience, but diverse kinds of limit experiences. The desert is a place of revelation: of our own weakness and sinfulness and of God's presence in that weakness. It is place of testing and trial, of repentance and conversion, of emptiness with the promise of fullness.

What can desert experience mean today as we struggle to make our world a place of justice, peace, and reconciliation? The desert as symbolized by dryness, austerity, with few resources for food and drink, is an arena of purification. In the desert these questions rise up in our hearts: What am I really doing? What do I truly seek? Where is this leading me? For some it has led to prison, often for many years, in order to witness to the justice and rightness of a cause.

The heat of the desert strips away the mummy-like wrappings in which our motivations have been encased and lays them bare. In the desert one cannot go back, for the way back is as fraught with dangers as is the way forward. One seeks God and the things of God, or one perishes, for the desert does not provide fine wine and rich food.

The desert of seemingly endless plodding along the path to justice and peace, thirsty and hungry, demands that we discern the movements of our hearts to find the voice and presence of the Spirit of God. False voices tell us to turn back, to find an easier way, to rest on our accomplishments, to settle for mediocrity. The voice of the Spirit echoes the

Gospel texts of total commitment (Luke 9:23–36), of service, not power over others (John 13:1–13), of death to life (John 12:24–26).

Discernment is essential in the desert: is this a desert of testing? or judgment? of purification? of intimacy with God and others in the midst of austerity? of paradoxical nourishment in the midst of barrenness? of a new strength in the Spirit that is unmistakably not of our own efforts?

Because the desert demands total commitment, it challenges those who have come on the journey expecting the applause of the crowd for their "heroism." The sacrifices are many but in the desert all are trying to survive—there are no spectators. The extremes of physical suffering are intensified by the psychological and spiritual anguish of those who travel the desert of the Spirit. The way ahead is God's road alone—all other paths lead to illusions of oases that prove to be deceptive mirages.

Yet the desert experience, while solitary—each person's desert is unique—is not without support. We travel the desert as a Christian community seeking justice, peace, and reconciliation for our world. Indeed, if someone decides to take a by-path alone, the chances of becoming lost and dying are very high.

Thus the questions raised by an individual about her or his desert experience apply equally to the Christian community—whether a base community, parish, religious congregation, diocese, or the church in a country or region. The community asks itself: is this a desert of testing? or judgment? of purification? of intimacy with God and others in the midst of austerity? of paradoxical nourishment in the midst of barrenness? of a new strength in the Spirit that is unmistakably not of our own efforts?

In addition, it asks: what are we learning about God, ourselves, the gospel's call to total commitment? How is the desert transforming us? How can we support each other in the desert? What do we need from each other in order to travel safely together?

The Dark Night

Sometimes even the desert image is not adequate to the pain and suffering of the journey of *shalom*. The "dark night" as described by John of the Cross (1542–91)[13] depicts different dimensions of the purification of the person (and by extension, the Christian community) that radical faith demands.

John of the Cross collaborated with Teresa of Avila in the reform of the Carmelite Order. A gifted spiritual director and a person of profound contemplative prayer, John realized from his ministry that many people were being given very harmful advice on how to grow in prayer. His books were written as guides to the dimensions of purification and suffering that are integral to the journey to God. The image of *night* is a powerful symbol that describes the process of transformation.

John stresses that we are created for love and union with God. The nights of trials and sufferings are the path to this union. They are a liberation from our false self, from our selfishness and self-centeredness. God and the false self cannot both be at home in the human heart.

John describes the individual person's journey to union with God as a movement from twilight to midnight to dawn, as the night begins, deepens, and then gives way to the morning of God's enduring presence. But the symbol of the "dark night" also contains within its dynamic dimensions that can assist the Christian community in its journey to make the world a place of justice and peace. What is said of the person is true also of the faith community: the strongest in the community gives courage to the weakest as all travel together.

Entering the Nights

The nights can begin with the experience of "limit" in our lives: illness, failure, loss. We ask, "Why is this happening to *me,* to *us*? Where is God?" What gave us confidence in the beginning—road maps with clearly defined goals, idealism, buoyant enthusiasm—have served their usefulness. The road now runs off the edge of the paper. Where to now? Ideals have been shattered by suffering; enthusiasm slacks. All of this is much harder than we ever dreamed.

John of the Cross answers: truly said. The path is much longer, harder, with more pain and suffering than we ever imagined. But, he says, it is the *only way* to God who is our Justice, Truth, and Peace.

John distinguishes between various kinds of "nights" in this time of suffering. They alternate between "active nights" in which the emphasis is on our own efforts towards liberation, and "passive nights," in which the hidden action of God is dominant. The "passive nights" are more important since it is in the quiet, hidden, and profound suffering of these nights that God's transforming action occurs.

Letting Go of God

The dark night is a crisis of limits: of our humanity, of our experience and images of God. It "reveals the pathology of our psyche, both personal and collective."[14]

In the life of faith, the temptation is to become comfortable with images of God that fit our experience and desires. God is a faithful parent (mother or father or both), a friend, lover, consoler; perhaps a shepherd, a teacher, a revolutionary, or a rebel. God has become part of our household, an object among other prized possessions.

But the dark night shatters this cozy faith experience and "challenges our understandings, attitudes, relationship, and actions"[15] in relation to God. The force and power of these images fall away and there is "nothing" left. No wonder the person feels that God has abandoned him or her and is filled with terror at the possibility that perhaps there is "no God" after all.

The purification of the night gradually discloses the One who is beyond all images and ideas of the Divine Reality. Nothing that we can understand is God. John of the Cross insists that "since the intellect cannot understand the nature of God, it must journey in submission to Him rather than by understanding, so it advances by not understanding."[16]

If this purification of our concepts and images of God does not happen, then we are in great danger of mistaking our images of God for the reality of God, of worshiping our own projections of God. This teaching of John of the Cross follows that of Freud and demonstrates that "he is acutely aware that the religious movement towards God can emerge either from the desire for satisfaction or from the drive to be morally assured."[17] John is not a psychotherapist, but is speaking in theological terms of the transformation of the person in and through grace, the very life of God.

In the work of God's *shalom* it is extraordinarily important to know who we are serving: God who is Holy Mystery, or a God who seems to encourage comfort and mediocrity. The work of the Spirit in the passive night of the spirit is focused on ensuring that we never again mistake our ideas of God, however true and consoling, for God who is beyond anything we can imagine or speak about.

Becoming Our True Self in God

In the dark night we meet the limits of our desires, of what we can accomplish by ourselves. Things do not "work" as they once did; satisfaction and consolation now belong to the past. The night of the spirit is "a process of self-transcendence in which the person is challenged to surrender to the mystery of God and to allow the entire psychic structure to be transformed by God's love."[18]

The whole person, on both the conscious and unconscious levels, meets the light of God's presence and love—a light so bright it is total darkness to the spirit. The night is a time of profound healing of the personality. *Nothing else and no one else* but God now suffices. All created reality is now seen in relation to God, who is Ultimate. Our reason for existence is known in God alone. And, still, everything is dark.

The passage from darkness to true light in God is also an experience of communities of faith, especially those who suffer injustice and oppression. Gustavo Gutiérrez describes this as part of the spiritual journey of the people of Latin America:

> On this journey of an entire people towards its liberation through the desert of structural and organized injustice that surrounds us . . . it is very important to persevere in prayer, even if we hardly do more than stammer groans and cries, while in this struggle the image of God in us is purified in an extraordinary "dark night."[19]

In the dark night of injustice many fears and temptations arise: not only the fear of death (often a very real fear), but also of weakening in the struggle, finding an easier way, a more comfortable life. The call in the dark night is to trust the darkness, to continue to desire to make God's *shalom* real.

In the testing of the dark night the truth of the person and the community is revealed. Paradoxically, there is no place to hide. The light is so dark that it blinds. It penetrates into the innermost depths of a community, showing forth both mud and gold, weakness and strength. We meet our true self in God, not separate but united in Love.

New Birth

Two children are born in the dark night of the spirit: the new self, united to God in love, and God's *shalom* made present in creation. The dark night is a process of labor in which the person is reborn in the Spirit (John 3:5–8); the pain and suffering that are analogous to the process of physical birth strip away the illusions one has about one's abilities, gifts, and talents. And just as the mother must cooperate in the process of giving birth to her child, so must the person intentionally allow the darkness to be dark, to become darker, to walk securely in the darkness that leads to light, to new life.

In the night when all is dark, the seeds of the kingdom begin to grow (Mark 4:26–28). The gardener or farmer must not pull up the plant each day to inspect the roots and to hurry growth; likewise, the growth of compassion, love, peace, justice, and reconciliation is slow but deep and thorough. Anchored and rooted in God, good fruit appears.

Walking in darkness that is both personal and communal, the person and community realize that nothing human is alien, for all is in God: "The joys and the hopes, the griefs and the anxieties of the [people] of this age, especially those who are poor or in any way afflicted, these too are joys and hopes, the griefs and anxieties of the followers of Christ" (GS 1).

Living in the Night

In order to walk securely in the night of the spirit, no matter how dark and painful it may become, four things are needed on the journey. The first is trust in the God of love who accompanies us in the darkness. We are called to surrender ourselves in faith and trust to God who is loving Mystery. The anguish of the night must not be fought or rationalized as a cloud of depression that will soon lift[20] but must be accepted in dark faith, for "it is precisely as broken, poor and powerless that one opens oneself to the dark mystery of God in loving, peaceful waiting."[21]

Second, one is called to bear the suffering, not just for oneself but for the world, and to echo the words of Paul: "in my flesh I am completing what is lacking in Christ's afflictions for the sake of his body, that is the church" (Col 1:24). The dark night is not only about one's transformation in love, but also the redemption and liberation of the world. The paradox of grace is that when we accept the suffering and enter into the mystery of the cross, then we are no longer held captive by evil, injustice and oppression. Martyrs such as Archbishop Oscar Romero of El Salvador who was assassinated in 1980 experienced this truth. He was fearless in denouncing the violence of the government of El Salvador because in living the dynamic of the cross—"whenever I am weak, then I am strong" (2 Cor 12:10)—strength and courage are given.

Third, perseverance is essential when walking in the darkness. We cannot return to where we had been secure and happy in our Christian commitment, but are called to go forward, no matter the pain and suffering. The temptation is to stop, say "enough," and find a comfortable place that demands much less than this journey that demands everything.

Lastly, dark faith is also dark love. Perseverance is possible because we love, not because we simply endure the suffering. St. Thérèse of Lisieux (1873–97), who experienced eighteen months of intense darkness when her faith was so tested that she wrote out the Creed in her own blood and carried it on her heart, died exclaiming, "Oh, I love Him! My God, I love you!"[22] The whole dynamic of the teaching of John of the Cross moves toward union in love; the dark night is not the end.

When does dark love move into the light, when is pain transformed into the joy of God's loving presence? Again, there are no time-tables but only the unique experience of each person, each community, on the journey.

Political Love

In a world of suffering, bandages and soothing medicines are not sufficient. The causes of injustice and oppression must be identified and the transformation of social, political, and economic structures is imperative. Thus personal charity and "political love"[23] must be the "two feet" of our century's journey toward social wholeness.

The biblical call to intensive love of God and neighbor is the foundation of the unity of prayer and social commitment. The text from 1John provides the biblical basis of this unity: God is love (4:16) and in knowing the love of God for us we are to love one another (4:7, 11). God whom we cannot see is truly known in the experience of loving others.

This unity is given more theological flesh by Karl Rahner, who articulated the unity of the love of neighbor and the love of God. Rahner inquired whether the love of neighbor was a secondary act of the love of God. His conclusion was that "explicit love of neighbor is the primary act of the love of God."[24] This is true on the level of being, not merely morally or psychologically. One can only love God by loving one's visible brothers and sisters.

This unity is in tension and never fully realized. It appears easier to love God in private prayer and meditation than in the concrete situations of life—family, community, society, nation. But Rahner reminded us that the end of all seeking of God is found in the neighbor.

This unity is seen also in mysticism and political love, a love that is attentive to the social context, to the multiple forms of suffering of one's society and culture, indeed of the world. Such a love is specific and concrete as it responds to the signs of the times.

The inner dynamic of the mystic journey is present in the self-giving of political love. Schillebeeckx parallels the experience as knowing "the same repentance and *metanoia*, the same asceticism and self-emptying, the same suffering and the same dark nights and the losing itself in the other."[25] Political love is as demanding as the severest physical ascetic practices of the mystics; it is loyal to truth even to martyrdom, as the Church in Latin America especially has demonstrated.

Mysticism and political love are thus constitutive dimensions of Christian faith. Neither is complete by itself and in fact is dangerous: "Without prayer or mysticism politics soon becomes cruel and barbaric; without political love, prayer or mysticism soon becomes sentimental or uncommitted interiority."[26]

Segundo Galilea expresses this unity in terms of the experience of Jesus: "The mystic and the politician are united in the one call to contemplation, since the source of their Christian vision is the same—the experience of Jesus encountered in prayer and in our brothers (sisters), particularly the 'least' (Matt 25:40)."[27]

Growing in Political Love

It may be safe to assume that most Christians are hopping along on the one foot of prayer while the second foot of political love is securely tied to the first leg. No wonder the praxis of Christian life is distorted.

What are the ways to grow in political love so that one's life is a journey of both feet? The *kairos* of suffering in the world presents multiple entry points for the enfleshment of political love. Global suffering is hydra-like in its forms—from international injustice, economic oppression, wars, the sale of arms, environmental degradation, racism, sexism, the HIV/AIDS pandemic, the oppression of women, sexual violence, slavery, child prostitution, and forced military service—to its local incarnations in each continent, city, neighborhood, and village.

Thus the first step of political love is involvement and immersion in and with an experience of suffering that is nearby. The phrase "think globally but act locally" assumes greater urgency here since the temptation in the face of global suffering is to back away from its enormity. But suffering is not only 10,000 miles away as the TV news graphically portrays, but very near to each of us.

Response to suffering demands conversion and asceticism: conversion from an individual spirituality of comfort to an asceticism of self-emptying and service. The unity of love of God and neighbor, of mysticism and political love, is concrete not abstract. As Dorothy Day often commented, "Love in practice is a harsh and dreadful thing."

Thus responding to suffering will entail suffering, for sideline sympathy is never sufficient when the gospel call is to empathetic compassion and self-giving. Learning to walk on the "two feet" will lead one onto paths of darkness, of disillusionment, of purification of motives, of the fullness of the nights of the Christian mystical tradition. The journey of love is not to be "word or speech" (1 John 3:18) but deeds of transforming love and justice, a spirituality of praxis, as the liberation theologians remind us.

And the Foot of Prayer?

But perhaps a person is hopping along only on the foot of political love, a one-legged journey that is as difficult as only traveling on the foot of prayer. Since the journey must be made on two feet, the challenge is equally demanding: to seek God and one's neighbor in political love and service.

Here the call is to dare the fullness of the journey to find one's true self in God, as Merton reminded us so often. Action without contemplation is rootless. What is the depth and richness of the soil in which grows the desire to transform the world of injustice? The unity between the love of God and love of neighbor is precisely that, for one does not exist independently of the other.

And while the service of the neighbor is a true act of love of God, it is not an explicit act without a living faith. Thus the activist is called also to the same dynamic: conversion, self-emptying, suffering, surrender, purification, the nights of seeking/losing/finding oneself in God—in the midst of the praxis of transforming love.

Mystic Love

It is the energy of love that drives the world; it is God's love as the heart of all reality that courses through our veins and the smallest subatomic particle of creation. To seek and find God is the heart of the mystic journey; in our own day it is a call that can never be separated from political love and the quest for a just and peaceful world.

Pierre Teilhard de Chardin, a mystic in love with created reality, spoke often of love as the driving force in all of creation, as it moves toward the Omega Point—Christ—when God will be all in all. Every act of love moves all of us closer to that point of union; every act of selfishness and injustice is a step backward.

Christian life in this new century must be lived as a quest for transformation in God, transformation that is personal, communal, ecclesial, and social. The mystics of all ages have known this. We can do no less.

Notes

1. Albert Nolan, *God in South Africa* (Cape Town and Johannesburg: David Philip, 1988), p. 49.

2. Johann Baptist Metz, *A Passion for God: The Mystical-Political Dimension of Christianity*, trans. J. Matthew Ashley (New York: Paulist, 1998), p. 145.

3. Gershom Scholem, "Mysticism and Society," *Diogenes* 58 (1967), pp. 5–6.

4. Julian of Norwich, *Showings*, trans. Edmund Colledge, OSA, and James Walsh, SJ (New York: Paulist, 1978), chap. 18, p. 210.

5. Hadewijch, "Letter 17," in *The Complete Works*, trans. Mother Columba Hart, OSB (New York: Paulist, 1980), p. 84.

6. Grace M. Jantzen, *Power, Gender and Christian Mysticism* (Cambridge: Cambridge University Press, 1995), p. 142.

7. Hadewijch, "Letter 30," in *The Complete Works*, trans. Mother Columba Hart, OSB (New York: Paulist, 1980), p. 117.

8. Ibid., p. 118.

9. Meister Eckhart, "Counsels of Discernment," in *Meister Eckhart: The Essential Sermons, Commentaries, Treatises and Defense*, trans. Edmund Colledge, OSA, and Bernard McGinn (New York: Paulist, 1981), no. 10, p. 258.

10. Constance FitzGerald, "Impasse and Dark Night," in *Women's Spirituality: Resources for Christian Development*, 2d ed., ed. Joann Wolski Conn (New York: Paulist, 1996), p. 411.

11. Constance FitzGerald, "The Transformative Influence of Wisdom in John of the Cross," in *Women's Spirituality: Resources for Christian Development*, 2d ed., ed. Joann Wolski Conn (New York: Paulist, 1996), p. 442.

12. FitzGerald, "Impasse and Dark Night," pp. 413–14.

13. The writings of John of the Cross are commentaries on his poems, considered to be among the very finest Spanish poetry. His teachings on prayer are found in *The Ascent of Mount Carmel, The Dark Night of the Soul, The Spiritual Canticle,* and *The Living Flame of Love.*

14. John Welch, *When Gods Die* (New York: Paulist, 1990), p. 157.

15. Ibid., p. 158.

16. John of the Cross, "The Living Flame of Love," in *The Collected Works of St. John of the Cross*, trans. Kieran Kavanaugh, OCD, and Otilio Rodriguez, OCD (Washington, DC: Institute of Carmelite Studies, 1979), 3.48, p. 629.

17. Michael Buckley, "Atheism and Contemplation," *Theological Studies* 40 (1979), p. 694. Two important studies that explore images of God from the psychoanalytic perspective are Ana-Maria Rizzuto, *The Birth of the Living God: A Psychoanalytic Study* (London and Chicago: University of Chicago Press, 1979), and Ann Belford Ulanov, *Finding Space: Winnicott, God and Psychic Reality* (Louisville, KY: Westminster John Knox, 2001).

18. Welch, *When Gods Die,* p. 160.

19. Gustavo Gutiérrez, *We Drink From Our Own Wells*, trans. Matthew J. O'Connell (Maryknoll, NY: Orbis, 1984), p. 129.

20. Gerald G. May describes some of the significant differences between the dark night and depression: dark night experiences are not usually associated with loss of effectiveness in life or work, as occurs in primary depressions; compassion for others is usually enhanced while in clinical depression the person is self-absorbed; in the dark night the person would not really have things otherwise; while the depressed person hopes for a radical change; one is more apt to feel graced and consoled in the presence of a person experiencing the dark night in contrast to feelings of frustration, resentment, and annoyance in dealing with a depressed person. See *Care of Mind, Care of Spirit* (San Francisco: Harper & Row, 1982, 1992), pp. 102–12. The list of differences is given on pp. 109–10. See also Keith Reeves Barron, "The Dark Night of God," *Studies in Formative Spirituality* 13 (1992), pp. 49–72; Kevin Culligan, "Saint John of the Cross and Modern Psychology," *Studies in Formative Spirituality* 13 (1992), pp. 29–48; Maria Edwards, RSM, "Depression or Dark Night?" *Contemplative Review* 18/4 (1985), pp. 34–37; Gerald G. May, *The Dark Night of the Soul* (San Francisco: HarperSanFrancisco, 2004).

21. FitzGerald, "Impasse and Dark Night," p. 420.

22. Thérèse of Lisieux, Saint, *Story of a Soul: The Autobiography of St. Thérèse of Lisieux*, trans. John Clark, OCD (Washington, DC: ICS, 1996), p. 271.

23. The term is Edward Schillebeeckx's. See his *Jesus in Our Western Culture*, trans. John Bowden (London: SCM, 1987), p. 75.

24. Karl Rahner, "Reflections on the Unity of the Love of Neighbour and the Love of God," in *Theological Investigations*, vol. 6, trans. Karl-H. and Boniface Kruger (London: Darton, Longman & Todd, 1969), p. 247.

25. Schillebeeckx, *Jesus in Our Western Culture*, p. 74.

26. Ibid., p. 75.

27. Segundo Galilea, "Liberation as an Encounter with Politics and Contemplation," in *Theology of Liberation, Concilium*, vol. 6, no. 10, ed. Claude Geffré and Gustavo Gutiérrez (London: McGraw-Hill and Stichting Concilium, 1974), p. 33.

BIBLIOGRAPHY

Abbott, Walter M., ed. *The Documents of Vatican II*. New York: Guild Press, American Press, 1966.

Aelred of Rivaulx. *Sermon 17 on the Assumption*. PL 195, 303–16.

Allaire, James, and Rosemary Broughton. *Praying with Dorothy Day*. Winona, MN: Saint Mary's, Christian Brothers, 1995.

Amoore, Frederick. "Denis Hurley: His Witness to Love of Neighbour." In *Facing the Crisis: Selected Texts of Archbishop D. E. Hurley*, pp. 209–25. Edited by Philippe Denis. Pietermaritzburg: Cluster Publications, 1997.

Augustine, Saint. *Sermons III/Vol. III (51–94) on the New Testament*. Translated by Edmund Hill, OP. Edited by John E. Rotelle, OSA. New Rochelle, NY: New City, 1991.

Augustine, Saint. *Sermons III/Vol. 4 (94A–147A) on the New Testament*. Translated by Edmund Hill, OP. Edited by John E. Rotelle, OSA New Rochelle, NY: New City, 1992.

Augustine, Saint. *Sermons III/ Vol. 5 (148–83) on the New Testament*. Translated by Edmund Hill, OP. Edited by John E. Rotelle, OSA New Rochelle, NY: New City, 1992.

Augustine, Saint. *Sermons III/ Vol. 7 (230–72B) on the New Testament*. Translated by Edmund Hill, OP. Edited by John E. Rotelle, OSA. New Rochelle, NY: New City, 1993.

Backhouse, Halcyon, ed. *The Best of Meister Eckhart*. New York: Crossroad, 1995.

Bernard of Clairvaux, Saint. *Sermon II on the Assumption*. PL 2143.

———. *Sermon III on the Assumption*. PL 2144–46.

———. *Sermon 57 on the Song of Songs*. PL 1463.

Brame, Grace A. "Evelyn Underhill: The Integrity of Personal Intellect and Individual Religious Experience as Related to Ecclesiastical Authority." *Worship* 68 (1994), pp. 23–45.

Buckley, Michael. "The Contemplation to Attain Love." *The Way Supplement* 25 (1975), pp. 92–104.

———. "Atheism and Contemplation." *Theological Studies* 40 (1979), pp. 680–99.

Butler, Cuthbert. *Christian Mysticism*. London: Armstrong, 1922, 1967.

Caputo, John D. "Fundamental Themes in Meister Eckhart's Mysticism." *The Thomist* 42 (1978), pp. 197–225.

Catherine of Siena, Saint. *The Dialogue*. Translated by Suzanne Noffke. New York: Paulist, 1980.

Clément, Olivier. *The Roots of Christian Mysticism*. Translated by Theodore Berkeley, OCSO. London: New City, 1993.

The Cloud of Unknowing. Edited by William Johnston. Garden City, NY: Doubleday Image, 1973.

Conn, Walter. "Merton's 'True Self': Moral Autonomy and Religious Conversion." *Journal of Religion* 65 (1985), pp. 513–29.

The Constitution of the Republic of South Africa. Pretoria, 1996.

Cropper, Margaret. *Evelyn Underhill*. London: Longmans, Green, 1958.

Curtayne, Alice. *Saint Catherine of Siena*. London: Sheed & Ward, 1934.

Day, Dorothy. *On Pilgrimage*. New York: Catholic Worker Books, 1948.

———. *The Long Loneliness*. San Francisco: Harper & Row, 1952.

———. *Loaves and Fishes*. San Francisco: Harper & Row, 1963.

———. *Meditations*. New York: Newman, 1970.

———. *Little by Little: The Selected Writings of Dorothy Day*. Edited by Robert Ellsberg. New York: Knopf, 1983.

D'Costa, Gregory. *The Practice of Love*. Gujarat, India: Gujarat Sahitya Prakash, 1991.

de Gruchy, John. "The TRC and the Building of a Moral Culture." In *After the TRC: Reflections on Truth and Reconciliation in South Africa*, pp. 167–71. Edited by Wilmot James and Linda Van De Vijver. Athens: Ohio University Press and Cape Town: David Philip, 2000.

DiDomizio, Daniel. "The Prophetic Spirituality of the Catholic Worker." In *Revolution of the Heart: Essays on the Catholic Worker*, pp. 217–38. Edited by Patrick G. Coy. Philadelphia: Temple University Press, 1988.

Dupré, Louis. "The Christian Experience of Mystical Union." *Journal of Religion* 69 (1989), pp. 1–13.

Dyckman, Katherine, Mary Garvin, and Elizabeth Liebert. *The Spiritual Exercises Reclaimed*. New York: Paulist, 2001.

Egan, Eileen. *Peace Be with You*. Maryknoll, NY: Orbis, 1999.

Fatula, Mary Ann. *Catherine of Siena's Way*. London: Darton, Longman & Todd, 1987.

Finnegan, Mary Jeremy. "Catherine of Siena: The Two Hungers." *Mystics Quarterly* 17 (1991), pp. 173–80.

Fiorenza, Elisabeth Schüssler. *Bread Not Stone: The Challenge of Feminist Biblical Interpretation*. Boston: Beacon, 1984.

————. *But She Said: Feminist Practices of Biblical Interpretation*. Boston: Beacon, 1992.

Fisher, Desmond. *Archbishop Denis Eugene Hurley*. Notre Dame, IN: University of Notre Dame Press, 1965.

FitzGerald, Constance. "Impasse and Dark Night." In *Women's Spirituality: Resources for Christian Development*, 2d ed., pp. 410–35. Edited by Joann Wolski Conn. New York: Paulist, 1996.

————. "The Transformative Influence of Wisdom in John of the Cross." In *Women's Spirituality: Resources for Christian Development*, 2d ed., pp. 436–51. Edited by Joann Wolski Conn. New York: Paulist, 1996.

Francis and Clare: The Complete Works. Translated by Regis J. Armstrong and Ignatius C. Brady. New York: Paulist, 1982.

Frohlich, Mary. *The Intersubjectivity of the Mystic: A Study of Teresa of Avila's "Interior Castle."* Atlanta, GA: Scholars, 1993.

Galilea, Segundo. "Liberation as an Encounter with Politics and Contemplation." In *Theology of Liberation*. Concilium. Vol. 6, no. 10, pp. 19–33. Edited by Claude Geffré and Gustavo Gutiérrez. London: McGraw-Hill and Stichting Concilium, 1974.

Greene, Dana. *Evelyn Underhill: Artist of the Infinite Life*. London: Darton, Longman & Todd, 1991.

Gutiérrez, Gustavo. *We Drink From Our Own Wells*. Translated by Matthew J. O'Connell. Maryknoll, NY: Orbis, 1984.

Haas, Adolf. "The Mysticism of St. Ignatius According to His *Spiritual Diary*." In *Ignatius of Loyola: His Personality and Spiritual Heritage (1556–1956)*, pp. 164–99. Edited by Friedrich Wulf. St. Louis, MO: Institute of Jesuit Sources, 1977.

Hadewijch. *The Complete Works*. Translated by Mother Columba Hart, OSB. New York: Paulist, 1980.

Haight, Roger. "Foundational Issues in Jesuit Spirituality." *Studies in the Spirituality of Jesuits* 19/4 (1987), pp. 1–61.

Happold, F. C. *Mysticism: A Study and an Anthology*. Harmondsworth, UK: Penguin, 1963.

Hay, Mark. *Ukubuyisana: Reconciliation in South Africa*. Pietermaritzburg: Cluster Publications, 1998.

Heffner, Blake R. "Meister Eckhart and a Millennium with Mary and Martha." In *Biblical Hermeneutics in Historical Perspective*, pp. 117–30. Edited by Mark S. Burrows and Paul Rorem. Grand Rapids, MI: Eerdmans, 1991.

Hinson, E. Glenn. "*Contemptus Mundi—Amor Mundi*: Merton's Progression from World Denial to World Affirmation." *Cistercian Studies* 26 (1991), pp. 339–49.

Hurley, Denis E. *A Time for Faith*. Johannesburg: South African Institute of Race Relations, 1965.

————. *Human Dignity and Race Relations*. Johannesburg: South African Institute of Race Relations, 1966.

————. "Our Need for Reconciliation." Durban: Archdiocese of Durban Archives, 1975 (typewritten).

————. "Excerpts from Archbishop Hurley's Speeches During the Second Vatican Council (1962–65)." In *Facing the Crisis: Selected Texts of Archbishop D. E. Hurley*, pp. 25–38. Edited by Philippe Denis. Pietermaritzburg: Cluster Publications, 1997.

————. "Liturgy and Catechetics (1963)." In *Facing the Crisis: Selected Texts of Archbishop D. E. Hurley*, pp. 39–47. Edited by Philippe Denis. Pietermaritzburg: Cluster Publications, 1997.

————. "Apartheid: A Crisis of the Christian Conscience (1964)." In *Facing the Crisis: Selected Texts of Archbishop D. E. Hurley*, pp. 58–76. Edited by Philippe Denis. Pietermaritzburg: Cluster Publications, 1997.

————. "The Bishop at Prayer in his Church (1970)." In *Facing the Crisis: Selected Texts of Archbishop D. E. Hurley*, pp. 101–3. Edited by Philippe Denis. Pietermaritzburg: Cluster Publications, 1997.

————. Phone interview, October 15, 2001.

Ignatius of Loyola, Saint. *The Spiritual Exercises of St. Ignatius*. Translated and edited by Louis J. Puhl, SJ. Chicago: Loyola University Press, 1951.

————. *The Spiritual Exercises of St. Ignatius Loyola*. Translated by Elisabeth Meier Tetlow. Lanham, MD: University Press of America, 1987.

————. *The Spiritual Exercises and Selected Works*. Edited by George E. Ganss. New York: Paulist, 1991.

James, William. *The Varieties of Religious Experience*. New York: Collier-Macmillan, 1961.

Jantzen, Grace M. *Power, Gender and Christian Mysticism*. Cambridge: Cambridge University Press, 1995.

John of the Cross, Saint. *The Collected Works of St. John of the Cross*. Translated by Kieran Kavanaugh, OCD, and Otilio Rodriguez, OCD. Washington, DC: Institute of Carmelite Studies, 1979.

Johnston, William. *The Inner Eye of Love: Mysticism and Religion*. San Francisco: Harper & Row, 1978.

————. *Mystical Theology: The Science of Love*. Maryknoll, NY: Orbis, 1995.

Julian of Norwich. *Showings*. Translated by Edmund Colledge, OSA, and James Walsh, SJ. New York: Paulist, 1978.

Kinerk, Edward E. "Eliciting Great Desires: Their Place in the Spirituality of the Society of Jesus." *Studies in the Spirituality of Jesuits* 16 (November 1984), pp. 1–29.

King, J. Norman. "Thomas Merton (1915–1968)." In *Non-violence—Central to*

Christian Spirituality: Perspectives from Scripture to the Present. Toronto Studies in Theology, Vol. 8, pp. 163–96. Edited by Joseph T. Culliton, CSB. Toronto: Edwin Mellen, 1982.

King, Thomas M. *Thomas Merton: Mystic at the Heart of America*. Collegeville, MN: Liturgical/Michael Glazier, 1992.

La Bonnardière, Anne-Marie. "Les Deux Vies, Martha et Marie (Luc 10:38–42)." In *Saint Augustin et la Bible*, pp. 411–25. Edited by Anne-Marie La Bonnardiere. Paris: Beauchesne Editions, 1986.

Lonergan, Bernard J. F. *Method in Theology*. New York: Herder & Herder, 1972.

Luther, Martin, "Commentary on 1 Corinthians 7." In *Luther's Works*, vol. 28, pp. 1–56. Translated by Edward Sittler. Edited by Hilton C. Oswald. St. Louis, MO: Concordia, 1973.

Mandela, Nelson. *The Struggle is My Life*. London: International Defence and Aid Fund for Southern Africa, 1978.

———. Foreword to *Desmond Tutu: The Rainbow People of God*, pp. xiii–iv. Edited by John Allen. London and New York: Doubleday, 1994.

———. *Long Walk to Freedom*. Boston: Little, Brown, 1994.

McGinn, Bernard. *The Foundations of Mysticism*. New York: Crossroad, 1991.

———. *The Growth of Mysticism*. New York: Crossroad, 1994.

McIntosh, Mark A. *Mystical Theology: The Integrity of Spirituality and Theology*. Malden, MA: Blackwell, 1998.

McVoy, Heather Jo. "Those Whom Jesus Loved: The Development of the Paradigmatic Story of Lazarus, Mary and Martha Through the Medieval Period." PhD dissertation, Florida State University, 1992.

Meister Eckhart. *Meister Eckhart: A Modern Translation*. Translated by Raymond Blakney. New York: Harper Torchbooks, 1941.

———. *Meister Eckhart: The Essential Sermons, Commentaries, Treatises and Defense*. Translated by Edmund Colledge, OSA, and Bernard McGinn. New York: Paulist, 1981.

———. *Meister Eckhart: Teacher and Preacher*. Edited by Bernard McGinn. New York: Paulist, 1986.

Merton, Thomas. *The Seven Storey Mountain*. London: Sheldon, 1948.

———. *The Sign of Jonas*. London: Hollis & Carter, 1953.

———. *No Man Is an Island*. New York: Doubleday, 1955.

———. *The Secular Journal of Thomas Merton*. New York: Dell, 1959.

———. *New Seeds of Contemplation*. New York: New Directions, 1961.

———. *The New Man*. London: Burns & Oates, 1961.

———. *Conjectures of a Guilty Bystander*. Garden City, NY: Doubleday Images, 1968.

———. *Faith and Violence*. Notre Dame, IN: University of Notre Press, 1968.

————. *Contemplative Prayer.* Garden City, NY: Doubleday Image, 1971.

————. "Peace and Protest." In *The Nonviolent Alternative,* pp. 67–69. Edited by Gordon C. Zahn. New York: Farrar, Straus, Giroux, 1971, 1980.

————. "Peace: A Religious Responsibility." In *The Nonviolent Alternative*, pp. 107–28. Edited by Gordon C. Zahn. New York: Farrar, Straus, Giroux, 1971, 1980.

————. "Blessed are the Meek: The Christian Roots of Nonviolence." In *The Nonviolent Alternative*, pp. 208–18. Edited by Gordon C. Zahn. New York: Farrar, Straus, Giroux, 1971, 1980.

————. *The Hidden Ground of Love: Letters on Religious Experience and Social Concerns.* Edited by William H. Shannon. New York: Farrar, Straus, Giroux, 1985.

————. *Thomas Merton in Alaska.* New York: New Directions, 1988.

————. "The Root of War is Fear." In *Passion for Peace: The Social Essays,* pp. 11–19. Edited by William H. Shannon. New York: Crossroad, 1995.

————. "The Shelter Ethic." In *Passion for Peace: The Social Essays,* pp. 20–26. Edited by William H. Shannon. New York: Crossroad, 1995.

————. "Nuclear War and Christian Responsibility." In *Passion for Peace: The Social Essays,* pp. 37–47. Edited by William H. Shannon. New York: Crossroad, 1995.

————. "Religion and the Bomb." In *Passion for Peace: The Social Essays,* pp. 65–79. Edited by William H. Shannon. New York: Crossroad, 1995.

————. "Christian Action in World Crisis." In *Passion for Peace: The Social Essays,* pp. 80–91. Edited by William H. Shannon. New York: Crossroad, 1995.

————. "Gandhi: The Gentle Revolutionary." In *Passion for Peace: The Social Essays,* pp. 202–9. Edited by William H. Shannon. New York: Crossroad, 1995.

————. "Religion and Race in the United States." In *Passion for Peace: The Social Essays,* pp. 217–27. Edited by William H. Shannon. New York: Crossroad, 1995.

————. "Notes for *Ave Maria* (Non-Violence . . . Does Not . . . Cannot . . . Mean Passivity)." In *Passion for Peace: The Social Essays,* pp. 322–25. Edited by William H. Shannon. New York: Crossroad, 1995.

————. *Entering the Silence: The Journals of Thomas Merton.* Vol. 2, 1941–52. Edited by Jonathan Montaldo. San Francisco: HarperSan Francisco, 1996.

————. *A Search for Solitude: The Journals of Thomas Merton.* Vol. 3, 1952–60. Edited by Lawrence S. Cunningham. San Francisco: HarperSan Francisco, 1996.

————. *Turning Toward the World: The Journals of Thomas Merton.* Vol. 4, 1960–63. Edited by Victor A. Kramer. San Francisco: HarperSan Francisco, 1996.

————. *Contemplation in a World of Action.* Notre Dame, IN: University of Notre Dame Press, 1998.

Metz, Johann Baptist. *A Passion for God: The Mystical-Political Dimension of Christianity*. Translated by J. Matthew Ashley. New York: Paulist, 1998.

Miller, William D. *A Harsh and Dreadful Love: Dorothy Day and the Catholic Worker Movement*. Garden City, NY: Image, 1974.

———. *Dorothy Day: A Biography*. San Francisco: Harper & Row, 1982.

Noffke, Suzanne. "Introduction." In *Catherine of Siena: The Dialogue*, pp. 1–22. Translated by Suzanne Noffke. New York: Paulist, 1980.

Nolan, Albert. 1988. *God in South Africa*. Cape Town and Johannesburg: David Philip, 1988.

O'Donnell, John. "The Trinitarian Vision of Ignatius Loyola in Contemporary Theological Perspective." In *Some Theological Aspects of Ignatian Spirituality*, pp. 25–76. Rome: Centrum Ignatianum Spiritualitatis, 1985.

O'Driscoll, Mary, ed. *Catherine of Siena: Passion for the Truth, Compassion for Humanity*. New Rochelle, NY: New City, 1993.

O'Gorman, Angie and Patrick G. Coy. "Houses of Hospitality: A Pilgrimage into Nonviolence." In *Revolution of the Heart: Essays on the Catholic Worker*, pp. 239–71. Edited by Patrick G. Coy. Philadelphia: Temple University Press, 1988.

Origen. *The Commentary on St. John's Gospel*. Vol. 1. Edited by A. E. Brooke. Cambridge: Cambridge University Press, 1896.

———. *Origen: An Exhortation to Martyrdom, Prayer, First Principles: Book IV, Prologue to the Commentary on the Song of Songs, Homily XXVII on Numbers*. Translated by Rowan A. Greer. London: SPCK, 1979.

Parks, Carola. "Social and Political Consciousness in the Letters of Catherine of Siena." In *Western Spirituality: Historical Roots, Ecumenical Routes*, pp. 249–60. Edited by Matthew Fox. Santa Fe, NM: Bear, 1981.

Paton, Alan. *Cry the Beloved Country*. London: Penguin, 1958.

Pawlikowski, John T. "Spirituality and the Quest for Justice." In *Liturgical Foundations of Social Policy in the Catholic and Jewish Traditions*, pp. 79–97. Edited by Daniel F. Polish and Eugene J. Fisher. Notre Dame, IN: University of Notre Dame Press, 1983.

Price, James R., III. "Lonergan and the Foundation of a Contemporary Mystical Theology." In *Lonergan Workshop*. Vol. 5, pp. 163–95. Edited by Fred Lawrence. Chico, CA: Scholars, 1985.

Rahner, Karl. "Reflections on the Unity of the Love of Neighbour and the Love of God." In *Theological Investigations*. Vol. 6, pp. 231–49. Translated by Karl-H. and Boniface Kruger. London: Darton, Longman & Todd, 1969.

———. "Experience of Self and Experience of God." In *Theological Investigations*. Vol. 13, pp. 122–32. Translated by David Bourke. London: Darton, Longman & Todd, 1975.

————. "Mysticism: Theological Interpretation." In *The Encyclopedia of Theology*, pp. 1010–11. Edited by Karl Rahner. London: Burns & Oates, 1975.

————. "The Spirituality of the Future." *Theological Investigations*. Vol. 20, pp. 143–53. Translated by Edward Quinn. London: Darton, Longman & Todd, 1981.

————. *The Practice of Faith*. Edited by Karl Lehmann and Albert Raffelt. New York: Crossroad, 1986.

Raymond of Capua. *The Life of St. Catherine of Siena*. Translated by George Lamb. London: Harvill, 1960.

Rizzuto, Ana-Maria. *The Birth of the Living God: A Psychoanalytic Study*. Chicago and London: University of Chicago Press, 1979.

Roberts, Nancy L. *Dorothy Day and the Catholic Worker*. Albany: State University of New York Press, 1984.

Ryan, Colleen. *Beyers Naudé: Pilgrimage of Faith*. Cape Town: David Philip, 1990.

Sampson, Anthony. *Mandela: The Authorised Biography*. London: HarperCollins; Johannesburg: Jonathan Ball, 1999.

Schillebeeckx, Edward. *Jesus in Our Western Culture*. Translated by John Bowden. London: SCM, 1987.

Scholem, Gershom. "Mysticism and Society." *Diogenes* 58 (1967), pp. 1–24.

Stierli, Josef. "Ignatian Prayer: Seeking God in All Things." In *Ignatius of Loyola: His Personality and Spiritual Heritage (1556–1956)*, pp. 135–63. Edited by Friedrich Wulf. St. Louis, MO: Institute of Jesuit Sources, 1977.

Teresa of Avila, Saint. *The Collected Works of St. Teresa of Avila*. Vol. 2. Translated by Kieran Kavanaugh, OCD, and Otilio Rodriguez, OCD. Washington, DC: Institute of Carmelite Studies, 1980.

Thérèse of Lisieux, Saint. *Story of a Soul: The Autobiography of St. Thérèse of Lisieux*. 3d ed. Translated by John Clarke, OCD. Washington, DC: ICS, 1996.

Thomas Aquinas, Saint. *Summa Theologica*. Translated by Fathers of the English Province. London: Burns Oates & Washbourne, 1934.

Tutu, Desmond Mpilo. *Hope and Suffering: Sermons and Speeches*. Johannesburg: Skotaville, 1983.

————. "We Drink Water to Fill our Stomachs (1979)." In *The Rainbow People of God: South Africa's Victory over Apartheid*, pp. 25–41. Edited by John Allen. London and New York: Doubleday, 1994.

————. "You Don't Reform a Frankenstein (1985)." In *The Rainbow People of God: South Africa's Victory over Apartheid*, pp. 95–101. Edited by John Allen. London and New York: Doubleday, 1994.

————. "Agents of Transformation (1986)." In *The Rainbow People of God: South Africa's Victory over Apartheid*, pp. 109–24. Edited by John Allen. London and New York: Doubleday, 1994.

———. "Nurturing our People (1992)." In *The Rainbow People of God: South Africa's Victory over Apartheid*, pp. 227–32. Edited by John Allen. London and New York: Doubleday, 1994.

———. "A Miracle Unfolding (1994)." In *The Rainbow People of God: South Africa's Victory over Apartheid*, pp. 252–63. Edited by John Allen. London and New York: Doubleday, 1994.

———. *No Future Without Forgiveness*. London and Johannesburg: Rider, 1999.

Ulanov, Ann Belford. *Finding Space: Winnicott, God and Psychic Reality*. Louisville, KY: Westminster John Knox, 2001.

Underhill, Evelyn. *Mysticism*. New York: E. P. Dutton, 1911, 1961.

———. *The Mystic Way*. Atlanta, GA: Ariel, 1913, 1992.

———. *Practical Mysticism*. Columbus, OH: Ariel, 1914, 1986.

———. *The Life of the Spirit and the Life of Today*. Edited by Susan Howatch. Harrisburg, PA: Morehouse, 1922, 1994.

———. *Concerning the Inner Life*. London: Metheun, 1926.

———. *The Spiritual Life*. London: Hodder & Stoughton; Harrisburg, PA: Morehouse, 1937, 1955.

———. *The Church and War*. London: Anglican Pacifist Fellowship, 1940.

———. *The Letters of Evelyn Underhill*. Edited by Charles Williams. Westminster, MD: Christian Classics, 1943, 1989.

———. *The Collected Papers of Evelyn Underhill*. Edited by Lucy Menzies. London: Longmans, Green, 1946.

———. *Evelyn Underhill: Modern Guide to the Ancient Quest for the Holy*. Edited by Dana Greene. Albany: State University of New York Press, 1988.

———. *The Ways of the Spirit*. Edited by Grace A. Brame. New York: Crossroad, 1990.

Welch, John. *When Gods Die*. New York: Paulist, 1990.

Zahn, Gordon C. "Thomas Merton as Prophet and the Spirituality of Peace." *Cistercian Studies* 20 (1985), pp. 142–53.